Praise for Michael Newton's previo
Hunting Humans: An Encyclopedia of Mc

"Michael Newton has put together the definitive work on an important subject. Unlike a lot of sensationalists, he is aware that the childhoods of these pathetic human beings shed important light on what they become. *Hunting Humans* is must reading for anyone interested in crime, sociology or human behavior."
    — Jack Olsen, author of *Predator*

"*Hunting Humans* is a book which should be hunted down by anyone and everyone who is aware of the menace of murder in our midst — it's a veritable *Who's Who* of who-dunnits in serial slayings."
    — Robert Bloch, author of *Psycho*

"[*Hunting Humans*] offers a treasure trove of valuable data for the serious researcher. I highly recommend it."
    — Maury Terry, author of *The Ultimate Evil*

"A grim but good popular reference work."
    — *Booklist*

"When Newton talks, people had better listen. The 38-year-old 'true crime' buff spent the last eight or 10 years researching multiple murders through police records, newspaper clippings, court records and correspondence with psychiatrists. His haunting homework was then transformed into *Hunting Humans*."
    — *The Republic*

"A must-have book... Highly recommended."
    — *AFRAID*

"[*Hunting Humans*] will be used by law enforcement officials, journalists and screenwriters looking to get no-nonsense information about serial killers."
    — *The Sacramento Bee*

"Entry after entry, *Hunting Humans* shows evil ingenuity that defies imagination."
    — *The Village Voice*

"This is a really important book, one that deserves major attention and media coverage."
    — *The Coast Book Review Service*

"*Hunting Humans* is an unforgettable 347 pages of abominable acts that will stay clenched in your fists from beginning to end."
    — *High Times*

Serial Slaughter

What's Behind America's Murder Epidemic?

Michael Newton
Author of Hunting Humans

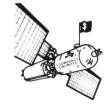

Loompanics Unlimited
Port Townsend, Washington

For Jamie, in a saner, safer world.

mn

This book is sold for informational purposes only. The publisher will not be held accountable for the use or misuse of the information contained in this book.

SERIAL SLAUGHTER: What's Behind America's Murder Epidemic?

© 1992 by Michael Newton
Printed in USA

Published by:
Loompanics Unlimited
PO Box 1197
Port Townsend, WA 98368

Loompanics Unlimited is a division of Loompanics Enterprises, Inc.

COVER: The body of a woman is removed from a Gainesville, Florida apartment. She is believed to be one of five student victims of a serial killer operating near the University of Florida in 1990. Photo by Stephen Morton/Gainesville Sun/Silver Image. Cover design by Daniel Wend/MEDIA Graphics.

ISBN 1-55950-078-6
Library of Congress Catalog Card Number 91-76992

Acknowledgements

In addition to those who helped with the original research for *Hunting Humans*, forerunner of this volume, I wish to thank the following for their contributions to the present work:

Nancy Best, administrative assistant, STF Productions, Inc.

Mary Colurso, Green Bay, WI

Blaine Combs, Bakersfield, CA

Carl Crothers, asst. managing editor, *The Tampa Tribune*

Steve Daniels, State of Wisconsin Department of Corrections

Dave Frasier, reference department, Lilly Library, Indiana University

Capt. Harold Hladky, Los Angeles County Sheriff's Department

Norma Harris, librarian, *The Columbian*, Vancouver, WA

Prof. David Heise, Indiana University

Mike Hoy, publisher, Loompanics Unlimited

Col. Robert Jent, director, Alaska State Troopers

Cathy Johnson, Public Relations Dept., *The Toronto Star*

Steven Keeney, Louisville, KY

Misti Lange, Texas Department of Corrections

Sondra London, Atlanta, GA

Robert Macmaster, Florida Department of Corrections

E.J. McCarthy, editor, Dell Books

Sgt. B.L. Meyer, Quincy (IL) Police Department

Dianne Moggy, Toronto, Canada

Steve O'Keefe, editorial director, Loompanics Unlimited

Rod Poteete, Las Vegas, NV

Eddie Quimby, reference department, Santa Barbara Public Library

Edna Ramirez, librarian, *Standard Times*, San Angelo, TX

Reference Department, *St. Louis Post-Dispatch*

G.J. Schaefer, Starke, FL

Maj. Jerry Shoemaker, Alabama Dept. of Public Safety

James Vandiver, assistant chief of police, Little Rock, AR

Sgt. John Yarbrough, Los Angeles County Sheriff's Department

Nancy Young, White Plains (NY) Public Library

There exists among the intolerably degraded the perverse and powerful desire to force into the arena of the actual those fantastic crimes of which they have been accused, achieving their vengeance and their own destruction through making the nightmare real.

James Baldwin
Notes of a Native Son

Contents

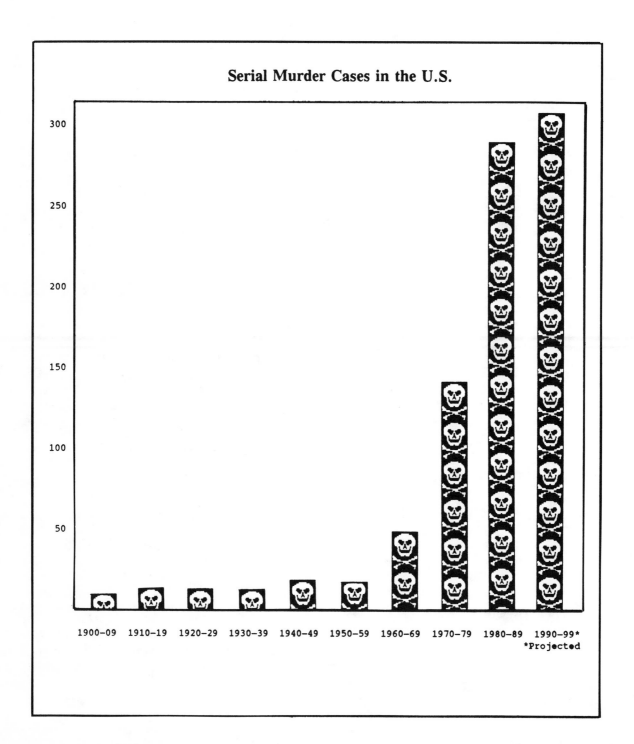

Serial Murder Cases in the U.S.

Introduction

Making the Nightmare Real

America is caught up in the midst of what one expert calls "an epidemic of homicidal mania," plagued by ruthless predators — lately dubbed serial murderers or "recreational killers" — who stalk their human prey at random, often for the sheer joy of killing. Before the year 2000, federal agents estimate some 40,000 men, women, and children will be slaughtered without apparent motive — an average of 11 victims each and every day, year-round.

Grim headlines tell the story, coast-to-coast:

● Seattle, Washington: Authorities continue their search for the Green River Killer, still at large after claiming the lives of 49 female victims between July 1982 and March 1984.

● San Diego, California: Police suspect Seattle's stalker, or a skillful copycat, in the murders of 42 women since June 1985.

● Lake Elsinore, California: Authorities blame one killer for the deaths of 12 women between mid-1990 and the spring of 1991. All the victims are identified as prostitutes or drug abusers.

● Los Angeles, California: Detectives seek new evidence in their hunt for the brutal Southside Slayer, linked to the murders of at least 12 black women since January 1984.

● Sacramento, California: Citizens remain alert to the menace of an unidentified "thrill killer," responsible for six murders during February 1991.

● San Francisco, California: A killer nicknamed the Black Doodler remains at large nearly two decades after the murders of 14 gay men. Authorities profess to know the slayer's name, but surviving witnesses refuse to testify for fear of personal embarrassment, thereby ruling out prosecution.

● St. Louis, Missouri: Authorities announce creation of a special task force to investigate the deaths of 10 known prostitutes since August 1989. A second serial killer, still at large, is blamed for the deaths of three St. Louis women between March 1990 and June 1991.

● Indianapolis, Indiana: A similar task force is organized in response to the murders of 11 gay victims, strangled by an unknown stalker since June 1980.

● Philadelphia, Pennsylvania: Nine female residents are beaten and stabbed to death by the elusive "Frankford Stalker" between 1985 and 1990. Conviction of an unrelated serial killer in other homicides brings police no closer to their man.

● Woonsocket, Rhode Island: Police link one killer with the deaths of three known prostitutes killed between December 1990 and March 1991.

● New Bedford, Massachusetts: Nine women are murdered in the community between July 1988 and April 1989. Murder charges filed against a local attorney are dismissed in July 1991, leaving the case unsolved.

• New York City: An unidentified ".22-caliber gunman" is blamed for the murders of seven taxi drivers in 1990. Meanwhile, in the borough of Queens, a different gunman stalks the "Son of Sam's" old hunting ground, killing two persons and wounding several others between October 1990 and July 1991.

• Washington, D.C.: Police in the nation's capital have at least two serial killers on their hands. One has beaten and strangled 10 prostitutes since 1988, while the other has gunned down five similarly-dressed hookers since April 1989.

• Prince George's County, Maryland: The unsolved murders of five black women recall ugly memories of the elusive Freeway Phantom, still unidentified after a similar series of homicides in the early 1970s.

• Gainesville, Florida: Detectives remain baffled in their search for the man whose mutilation-slaying of five young victims terrorized the college community in September 1990. Physical evidence links the unknown slasher with a similar triple murder in Shreveport, Louisiana, committed in November 1989.

• Miami, Florida: Initially reluctant to admit the presence of a serial killer in their city, detectives now report common links in the deaths of 31 black prostitutes since December 1986.

In any discussion of serial murder, we immediately run afoul of semantics. Self-styled "experts" argue endlessly about the mandatory body count or length of interval between successive crimes required to qualify a "genuine" serial killer, while some — like best-selling author Ann Rule — judge cases by the killer's sex or state of mind. Some clinical psychologists devote their whole careers to analyzing and labeling murderers: depressives, passive-aggressives, paranoid schizophrenics, hysterical personalities, sexual sadists... the roster seems endless.

Striving to bring order out of chaos, the FBI's Behavioral Science Unit has created a system for classifying homicides which, unfortunately, raises more questions than it answers. The first three types of murder — single, double, and triple — are self-explanatory, based on the number of victims slain at one time and place. A fourth category, mass murder, applies where four or more victims are slaughtered at one location, as in October 1984, when gunman James Huberty killed 21 persons and wounded 19 others at a California fast-food restaurant. "Spree" killings are described by the FBI as multiple slayings "at two or more locations with

no emotional cooling-off period between murders."[1] Finally, the Bureau defines serial murder as "three or more separate events with an emotional cooling-off period between homicides," each murder taking place at a different location.[2]

Concise as it may seem, the FBI's taxonomy of murder comes complete with built-in problems, chief among them a persistent failure to define the elusive "cooling-off period" between homicides. According to the Bureau line, spree murders "are all the result of a single event, which can be of long or short duration," depending on the killer's mental state.[3] Thus, sex-slayer Christopher Wilder was considered a serial killer prior to March 1984, when police suspicion of his activities touched off an hysterical "long-term killing spree."[4] Aside from the impossibility of quantifying human moods in any given case, the Bureau's system also fails to make allowance for serial killers like John Gacy, who murder successive victims at one location, or those like Rhode Island's William Sarmento, who are jailed before claiming the mandatory third victim.

In an effort to restore some common sense to the debate, I have adopted the definition of serial murder published in 1988, by the federally-funded National Institute of Justice. In simple terms, the NIJ defines serial murder as "a series of two or more murders, committed as separate events, usually, but not always, by one offender acting alone. The crimes may occur over a period of time ranging from hours to years. Quite often the motive is psychological, and the offender's behavior and the physical evidence observed at the crime scenes will reflect sadistic, sexual overtones."[5]

Using the above criteria, I have identified 835 cases of serial murder since 1900, involving some 1,008 individual killers and an estimated 7,195 to 9,401 victims. The precise number of killers remains uncertain due to unsolved cases, including several incidents of homicide by cults or other groups of unknown size. Likewise, the variance in body counts is based upon the difference between homicides proven in court and murders confessed or suspected without subsequent prosecution.

Geographically, serial killers are found on every continent except the frozen wasteland of Antarctica, with North America claiming 79% of the world total and Europe running a distant second with 17%. Easily leading the pack, the United States claims 76% of the global gross in serial murders. Europe's leaders are England (with 28% of the continental total), Germany (with 27%), and France (trailing with 13%). Third World nations contribute a mere 3% of the total, a fact explained in equal parts by cultural disparity, poor communication, and news censorship imposed by totalitarian regimes.[6]

Numerous sources describe serial murder as a recent phenomenon — and author Eric Van Hoffman dates the appearance of recreational killers, with rather suspicious precision, from the year 1972[7] — but is the problem really new? The terminology is certainly of recent vintage, dating from the early 1970s, but new jargon does not signify a new phenomenon. Criminologist James Reinhardt discussed the subject of "chain killers" as early as 1962, and the problem was already ancient.[8] Serial murder may, in fact, be as old as human history.

The earliest recorded case involves Zu Shenatir, a wealthy resident of 5th-century Aden, who lured young boys to his home with offers of food and money, sodomizing them before he tossed them out an upstairs window, to their deaths. Zu Shenatir's final body count is unknown, but history records that he was ultimately stabbed to death by an intended victim, at his home.

Our next report dates from 13th-century India, where the Sultan of Delhi recorded his clash with homicidal worshippers of the Hindu goddess Kali. Calling themselves "deceivers" or *thags* — corrupted in English as "thugs" — the cultists made a ritual of strangling, robbing, and dismembering their fellow countrymen at random, claiming countless lives before the sect was finally suppressed in 1848. No reliable figures are available on membership or body counts, but British colonial authorities acknowledged 40,000 cult-related murders in the year 1812 alone. Assuming this to be a record year, perhaps ten times the normal rate of homicides, the final victim tally still must total millions over 600 years of cult activity.

Meanwhile, in Europe, serial killers emerged from the ranks of nobles and peasants alike. Gilles de Rais, the richest man in France and confidante to Joan of Arc, was executed in 1440 for slaying upwards of 100 children in perverted sex-and-magic rituals. Margaret Davey, an English cook, was boiled alive in 1542 for poisoning a series of employers without apparent motive. At least five cannibal-slayers were prosecuted as "werewolves" in France and Germany, by clerical authorities, between the years 1573 and 1590. In 1611, Hungarian countess Elisabeth Bathory was convicted of killing some 650 young women, for the purpose of

bathing herself in their blood. Marie de Brinvilliers, the French poisoner, practiced her art on invalids before moving on to friends and relatives, facing execution for her crimes in 1676. Four years later, the court of Louis XIV was rocked by the scandalous "Black Chamber affair," implicating the king's mistress, a self-styled witch, and a defrocked Catholic priest in the ritual sacrifice of several hundred infants. In 1719, Italian authorities executed another female killer, La Tofania, on conviction of poisoning 600 victims.

The European tradition of serial murder continued into the 19th century, with German defendant Gessina Gottfried beheaded in 1828, convicted of poisoning 20-plus victims since 1815. In England, "resurrectionists" Burke and Hare soon tired of robbing graves for medical specimens, strangling 11 persons before they went to the gallows in 1828. An Austrian beggar named Swiatek fed at least six murdered children to his hungry family in 1850, and French cook Helene Jegado was executed a year later, on charges of poisoning 60 persons over two decades. Joseph Phillipe butchered French prostitutes in the 1860s, and Jack the Ripper carried the game to London 20 years later, inspiring a rash of imitators in Moscow, Vienna, Nicaragua — even Texas—by the end of the decade. Amelia Dyer, the British "baby farmer," was convicted in 1896 of killing at least 15 infants. The following year, French necrophile Joseph Vacher was put to death for butchering 14 victims over three years time.

In the United States, the bloodthirsty Harpe brothers terrorized the Wilderness Trail in the 1790s, gutting their victims and dumping the rock-laden corpses in rivers and lakes to avoid discovery. John Dahmen, condemned for two Indiana murders in 1820, confessed several others in Europe and America before he was hanged. New England slayer Samuel Green was credited with "numerous" murders when he went to the gallows in 1822. Four decades later, the Espinoza brothers sought vengeance for the Mexican War by slaughtering 26 Anglos across the Southwest. The murderous Bender clan dispatched a dozen Kansas travelers in 1872 and '73, fleeing the state one jump ahead of vigilante justice. The years 1875 and '76 brought grim news to Boston, with church sexton Thomas Piper convicted of killing three women, and teenager Jesse Pomeroy sentenced to life for the torture-slayings of neighborhood children. Stephen Richards, the "Nebraska Fiend," murdered at least nine victims before his arrest in 1879. In Chicago, sadist Herman Mudgett built a custom-tailored "murder castle" to dispose of female visitors to the 1893 World's Fair; convicted of one murder, he confessed to 26 others before he was hanged. New England nurse Jane Toppan started poisoning her patients back in 1880; at her trial, two decades later, she recited names of 31 remembered victims, while her prosecutors placed the total closer to 100.

In this century, serial killers have provided the media with some of its gorier headlines. Earle Nelson, the Bible-quoting strangler, raped and murdered landladies from coast to coast in the 1920s, before a Canadian hangman's rope cut short his career. Cleveland's "Mad Butcher" was a 1930s sensation, outwitting Eliot Ness and dissecting his 16 victims so expertly that ten of the skulls were never found. National Guard units were mobilized to track Nebraska's Charles Starkweather, random slayer of 11 victims during 1957, and "Sex Beast" Melvin Rees appalled the nation with his grisly murders of eight victims in Maryland and Virginia, two years later. By the time Albert DeSalvo confessed to a series of 13 murders in Boston, escaping prosecution with a crafty plea-bargain in 1967, authorities were noting subtle, scary changes in the ways we kill each other.

Murder in America has always been a "family affair," with the majority of victims known — if not related — to their killers. The connection serves police by making motives obvious and pointing homicide detectives toward a likely suspect, who most often readily confesses in the throes of guilt and grief. When strangers enter the equation, though, predictability goes out the window, and police are left to cast their nets at large, without a firm clue to the murderer's identity.

As late as 1966, some 88% of murders in America were solved by the authorities. Of the remaining 12%, a mere 640 murders fell within the "random, senseless" category typical of serial homicide. By 1981, police were stymied on 22% of domestic murders — 6,304 unsolved killings — and a full 17.8% — 4,007 murders — fell into the "random, senseless" bag. In 1989, the latest year with comprehensive data available at this writing, 32% of American murders went unsolved, with 23.7% — or some 5,096 slayings — apparently devoid of rational motives.[9]

Urban areas with more than 250,000 residents bear the brunt of our new murder epidemic, with New York City's rate of unsolved homicides more than doubling in a decade, from 21% in 1968 to 43% in 1979. Atlanta's unsolved murder rate soared from 13% in 1976 to 38%

four years later, and other cities are keeping pace.[10] Statistics for the first six months of 1990 show a dramatic increase in urban murders over 1989, despite a national declining trend in crime. The numbers reveal a 53% increase in Louisville, Kentucky; 40% in Boston; 24% in Sacramento; 22% in New York City; 18% in Dallas and Philadelphia; 14% in San Diego; and 13% in San Francisco.[11]

In terms of documented serial murders, the recent explosion is even more startling. Between 1900 and 1959, American police recorded an average of 1.7 serial murder cases per year, nationwide. By 1969, authorities were logging five new cases per year, a figure that nearly tripled in the 1970s. The 1980s produced new serial killers at a rate of two per month, and the epidemic continues to escalate. In 1990, the media reported three new cases monthly, for a three-decade increase of some 940% over the "good old days."

How many serial killers are at large in America on any given day? In October 1983, one Robert Heck, a spokesman for the U.S. Department of Justice in Washington, D.C., estimated their number at 35, including five killers active in one unspecified city.[12] A year later, Ann Rule sat down with a friend from the FBI and compiled a list of 57 "open" cases, nationwide.[13] Psychologist Joel Norris was less conservative, in an August 1984 article for *Life* magazine, referring vaguely to "hundreds" of serial killers abroad in the land[14]; four years later, when his book on the subject was finally published, Norris had rounded the figure off to an estimated 500.[15] Not to be outdone, Eric Van Hoffman raised the ante to *5,000* killers at large in 1990, citing — but never directly quoting — a three-year-old FBI report as his source of information.[16]

Ironically, the published "experts" can't even agree on the number of serial killers detained by police. In March 1987, Professor George Hickey, of Indiana's Ball State University, compiled a "comprehensive" list of 143 serial killers identified since 1800.[17] FBI spokesmen are more generous, admitting a total of 120 American serial killers and 40 foreign practitioners in the two decades prior to 1984.[18] My own research, conducted without the FBI's access to confidential law enforcement files, has identified 301 domestic and 56 foreign cases from the same 20-year period, with others undoubtedly missed in the process.

The sad fact is that no one really knows how many random killers stalk our streets. The FBI's best estimates, admittedly conservative, are based on unsolved cases where a killer's victims are discovered and the mode of death or disposition indicates some common link between the several crimes. A killer who successfully conceals the evidence or varies his technique from one crime to the next may theoretically remain at large forever, killing dozens — even hundreds — while police are stymied by a rash of "unrelated" homicides.

The recognized authorities have been no more successful in determining how many victims random slayers claim in any given year. With 5,000 murders unsolved in 1987, Justice sources estimate between 1,000 and 2,500 victims of serial killers included in the crop.[19] Joel Norris blames all 5,000 deaths on serial killers — a yearly average of ten victims for each of his 500 slayers at large[20] — but, again, the plain fact is that *no one knows*.

It took Dean Corll and his accomplices three years to murder 27 boys in Houston, Texas, but the crimes were not revealed until Corll's death, in August 1973. John Gacy spent the best part of seven years planting bodies in the crawlspace underneath his home, in a Chicago suburb, before simple negligence led police to his doorstep. California's Juan Corona was more energetic, claiming 26 lives in three months, but none of his transient victims were even reported missing until a Yuba City farmer stumbled on the first of many shallow graves.

It is alarming to discover that we often don't know who is dead or missing in America today. In 1984, the U.S. Department of Health and Human Resources estimated that 1.8 million children vanish from home every year.[21] Ninety-five percent are listed as runaways, and 90 percent of those return home within two weeks, leaving a "mere" 171,000 children at large on the streets. Five percent of the missing — some 90,000 children — are tagged as abductees, with 72,000 reportedly kidnapped by parents involved in bitter custody disputes. The other 18,000 children are simply gone.

Casting doubt on those statistics, FBI spokesmen report that the Bureau investigated only 150 "stranger abductions" of children between 1984 and 1986, but what does this disclaimer really prove? Federal agents normally remain aloof from kidnap cases in the absence of ransom demands or concrete evidence of interstate flight, and they take no notice whatsoever of runaways. In practice, this means that no one is looking for potential victims of killers like Corll, Gacy, and unknown others still at large.

The case of vanishing adults is even more obscure, with no statistics readily available from any source. A published estimate from 1970, no doubt conservative, suggested that at least 100,000 adults disappear in the United States each year.[22] Again, the vast majority are tagged as runaways — from debt or broken marriages, increasing numbers of the homeless traveling in search of jobs and warmer climates — but the fact remains that some undoubtedly fall prey to human predators. Five victims of Juan Corona's 1971 murder rampage remain unidentified to this day. In North Dakota, Eugene Butler was dead for two years before authorities got around to leveling his rural shack, unearthing six male skeletons in the process. Outside Chillicothe, Missouri, Ray and Faye Copeland paid their transient farm hands off with bullets in the head, and no one gave the missing men a second thought.

The list goes on.

Perhaps the most alarming aspect of the lethal numbers game is a recent suggestion, advanced by certain criminologists, that America's annual murder rate — an average 20,000 yearly victims over the past decade — may itself be the product of faulty record-keeping. Author Carl Sifakis places the yearly murder toll closer to 40,000 victims,[23] and a growing number of analysts share his gloomy outlook, basing their conclusions on new surveys of missing persons, suspicious accidents and suicides, curious "natural" deaths, and the number of unidentified corpses recovered each year.

Medical killers pose another serious problem for homicide detectives and crime statisticians. Physicians like Philadelphia's Morris Bolber, convicted of two murders and suspected of 40 others, are ideally positioned to write death certificates for their chosen victims, speeding the process of disposal without troublesome autopsies. Even major hospitals are not safe, as demonstrated by Donald Harvey, a lethal nurse's aide responsible for the deaths of 80-odd helpless patients between 1970 and his eventual arrest in 1987. Prior to Harvey's stunning confession, all but the last of his victims were listed as dying of "natural causes," dismissed by police and pathologists as unworthy of further investigation. At one Ohio hospital where Harvey plied his trade, an administrator has pled guilty to falsifying records of the victims, seeking to avoid bad publicity.

Having recognized the problem, pressing questions still remain. Who are the murderers among us, and where do they come from? Why does the United States, with barely six percent of the world's population, produce more than three-fourths of all known serial killers? Why has the number of recreational slayers increased nearly tenfold since the mid-1960s? How can authorities best run these monsters to earth, once they begin to kill? And, most important, how can we reverse the deadly trend?

This volume does not presume to offer the last word on serial murder, much less an ultimate solution to the modern "homicidal epidemic." Nonetheless, by studying the most complete and comprehensive roster of serial killers to date, we may be able to detect some patterns... and, perhaps, arrive at some prescriptions for the future.

It is not too late.

The lives we save may be our own.

Part I

Murderers Among Us

"I'm not one of a kind. There's lots of others out there just like me."

— Henry Lee Lucas

"There are other 'Sons' out there — God help the world."

— David ("Son of Sam") Berkowitz

"We serial killers are your sons, we are your husbands, we are everywhere. And there will be more of your children dead tomorrow."

— Ted Bundy

Chapter 1

Making Monsters

Before physicians can eradicate a plague, the sources of contagion must be recognized and understood. The same is true of aberrant behavior on the part of human beings. There can be no cure without a recognition of the cause.

What prompts a given man or woman to adopt a predatory life style, stalking human prey for motives that may seem incomprehensible to others? Are such monsters born complete with killer instincts, an insatiable genetic taste for blood, or are they shaped and educated over time? If we determine how such predators are made, can we disrupt the process soon enough to save their lives and those they will eventually destroy?

It is unusual for psychiatric "experts" to agree on anything beyond vague generalities, but a review of current literature suggests resounding unanimity on the significance of early childhood to the physical and mental health of an adult. The crucial element is variously labeled "bonding" or "attachment," and refers to the emotional connection formed between an infant and its parents, starting virtually from the moment of its birth.

Pediatrician Vera Fahlberg, director of a Michigan treatment center for emotionally disturbed children, explains that "the bond that a child develops to the person who cares for him in his early years is the foundation for his future relationships with others."[1] Successful bonding, according to Dr. Fahlberg, is critical to intellectual development and future self-reliance, management of fear and other negative emotions, and development of what we call a conscience.

Bonding is achieved by stages. In the early weeks of life, an infant signals to its mother with a cry, a smile, a gesture. When its efforts are rewarded with a touch, the baby tries to grasp and feed, regardless of the older individual's identity or sex. With passing time, the infant learns to differentiate between familiar persons and strangers, then between one familiar person and another. As bonding progresses, the child identifies and actively seeks contact with its parents or caretakers.[2]

Predictably, the experts disagree on how much time is needed to complete the bonding process. Published estimates range from one or two weeks to a year or more, and individual differences probably render such estimates fruitless, in any case. According to prevailing theory, human beings learn along a logarithmic curve, with fully half an individual's life knowledge filed away during the first year. Another 25% is acquired in the child's second year, leaving a mere one-quarter of the individual's life knowledge to be logged between age three and death.[3]

In other words, assuming that the experts are correct, the average person's attitude toward life and other human beings is established, for the most part, by the age of two years old. Disruption of the crucial bonding process, in the meantime, may produce a child — or an adult — incapable of feeling sympathy, affection, or remorse. As pediatrician Selma Fraiberg writes, "If we take the evidence seriously we must look upon a baby deprived of human partners as a baby in deadly peril. These are babies being robbed of their humanity."[4]

Based upon her own studies of "detached" children, Dr. Fraiberg notes measurable damage in three areas. First, children deprived of critical bonding form relationships strictly on the basis of personal need, without significant emotional attachment to others. Second, such children often suffer from retardation in the development of conceptual thinking and language skills, even when favorable home environments are provided in the second or third year of life. Finally, follow-up testing of detached children revealed disorders of impulse control, especially in the area of aggressive or violent behavior.[5]

It is difficult, if not impossible, to say precisely when attachment bonds are broken and a child slips past the point of no return. Published studies indicate that the extent of psychological damage suffered by a child depends in equal parts upon the victim's age and the duration of disruption in the bonding cycle. Interruption of the bonding process is more detrimental in the early months of life, and longer periods of separation, spanning days or weeks, inflict more psychic damage than a break of several hours.

In the worst scenario, detachment produces individuals afflicted with antisocial personality disorder (APD). Once commonly described as psychopaths, such individuals are now more often labeled sociopaths, to distinguish their affliction from the separate — and more severe — condition of psychosis. The American Psychiatric Association's Diagnostic and Statistical Manual offers the standard description of APD.[6]

> The central feature is a personality disorder in which there is a history of continuous and chronic antisocial behavior in which the rights of others are violated; persistence into adult life of a pattern of antisocial behavior that began before the age of 15; a failure to sustain good job performance over a period of several years (although this may not be evident in individuals who are self-employed or may not be in a position to demonstrate this feature, such as housewives or students); the antisocial behavior is not due to severe mental retardation, schizophrenia or manic episodes.

Lying, stealing, fighting, truancy and resisting authority are typical early childhood signs. In adolescence unusually early or aggressive sexual behavior, excessive drinking and the use of illicit drugs are frequent. In adulthood these kinds of behavior continue, with the addition of the inability to sustain consistent work performance or to function as a responsible parent and failure to accept social norms with respect to lawful behavior.

How many sociopaths are currently at large in the United States? "Expert" guesses range from five to 15 percent of the adult population, with the *low* estimate exceeding 13 million individuals.[7] Most sociopaths admittedly stop short of murder, working their mischief as con men and thieves, corrupt politicians or brutal policemen, "sharp" salesmen and philandering spouses. Some may kill "by accident," in the commission of another crime. A few go on to slay repeatedly, without remorse, apparently for sport.

Despite their relatively slender ranks, sociopaths have a dramatic impact on crime in the United States. A classic study of 9,945 Philadelphia males born in 1945, conducted by Marvin Wolfgang and colleagues, revealed that 35% had logged at least one confrontation with police by age 18. Of those, six percent were chronic offenders, judged responsible for 52% of all reported crime within the city limits.[8]

In some cases, monster-making begins in the womb, with critical damage incurred by a fetus from the moment of conception. Malnutrition during pregnancy, for instance, may result in abnormal brain development, with teenaged mothers especially at risk. Teen mothers are 92% more likely to suffer from anemia while pregnant, 23% more likely to deliver high-risk premature babies, and their offspring suffer accordingly.[9]

Likewise, maternal alcoholism or drug abuse is another hazard to fetal development. Physical birth defects aside, the children of alcoholics and addicts are likely to enter the world with damaged brains or nervous systems, limiting the child's — and future adult's — ability to control violent, impulsive behavior. In the fall of 1990, a CBS News report on "crack babies," born in New York City to cocaine-addicted mothers, profiled one small boy who had already beaten and bloodied every member of his kindergarten class — including the teacher — at age five.

Prenatal damage is not always self-inflicted, by any means. The father of British slayer Patrick Mackay was seen to kick his pregnant wife in the stomach, and strangler Earle Nelson lost his mother to advanced venereal disease when he was only nine months old. While neither murderer was tested for organic brain dysfunction, it is not beyond the realm of possibility that damage or infection in the womb may have influenced their subsequent bizarre behavior.

It appears from recent evidence that even an unwanted or unhappy pregnancy, without physical damage, may jeopardize the future of an unborn child. Physicians do not fully understand the impact of a mother's mental state on fetal development, but they *do* know that maternal tension or anxiety result in secretion of hormones that affect the fetus. Malformation of the brain is possible if such reactions take place early in the second quarter of pregnancy, when the brain and autonomic nervous system of the fetus are developing.[10]

Beyond gestation, the delivery itself may further jeopardize an infant's chance at normal life, especially where complications interrupt the crucial flow of oxygen to the baby's brain. Brain death may result from an interruption of three minutes or more, and irreversible damage is possible after a much shorter time. Likewise, premature infants and those of low birth weight (below 5.5 pounds) are especially at risk for serious mental, physical, or developmental problems. It is significant, perhaps, that Christopher Wilder received last rites in the delivery room when he was born. And in the case of William Heirens, sexually-motivated slayer of three persons in his teens, use of high forceps at birth left the infant with a four-inch cranial swelling that endured through his second month of life.

Environment kicks in the moment that a child is born, and nothing breaks the bonding cycle quite like parental abandonment. As noted by author John Bowlby, "In psychopaths the incidence of illegitimacy and the shunting of the child from one 'home' to another is high. It is no accident that (Ian) Brady of the 'Moors' murders was such a one."[11]

Nor was Brady unique in his experience of maternal abandonment. Repeat killers David Berkowitz, Joseph Kallinger, and Steven Catlin were all given up for adoption as infants. Hillside Strangler Kenneth Bianchi, rape-slayer Martin Kipp, and killer-arsonist Bruce Lee were all children of prostitutes, passed off to relatives, foster care, or adoption at an early age. Poisoner Dorothea Puente grew up in an orphanage. German sex-slayer Juergen Bartsch was yet another "love child"; his mother died when he was five months old, and Bartsch spent the next eleven months in a foundling home before he was adopted. Ted Bundy, Charles Manson, Mary Bell, Barry Prudom, Richard Tingler, Max Gufler — all these and more repeat killers were the products of fleeting encounters, deprived of nurturing contact with one or both biological parents.

The problems of abandoned children are frequently compounded in foster care, with temporary "parents" more concerned about their monthly paycheck than the welfare of the child, while social workers frequently are young and inexperienced, habitually overworked and underpaid. Professional guidelines recommend a maximum of 30 children per case worker, but the American average in 1981 ranged from 70 to 90 children each.[12] The ultimate, inevitable outcome of an overloaded system is neglect, with children falling through the cracks and suffering abuse or deprivation in their crucial growing years. As an example, Florida authorities report that 200 children in foster care sexually assaulted other children in the twelve months ending November 1990; many of the victims were also foster children.[13]

Nor should it be supposed that mere legitimacy guarantees stability. The product of a forced marriage, Hugh Morse was abandoned by his father at an early age, leaving himself and his mother in the "care" of a brutal, domineering grandparent. William Cook and his seven siblings lived for months in a filthy mine shaft, before their alcoholic father finally hit the road and left the state to place his brood in foster homes. Future cannibal-killer Albert Fish was placed in a Washington orphanage by his own mother, at age five. Larry Eyler's mother considered a similar move when her son was two and a half years old; relenting for the moment, she waited until sixth grade before placing him in a home for unruly boys. Carlton Gary spent his childhood and adolescence with various paternal relatives, frequently running away in search of the father who abandoned him. Strangler Kenneth Erskine was discarded on the streets of London by his parents, left to starve or grow as best he could. In Georgia, Terri Rachals was two years old when her mother suffered a mental breakdown and her father gave her up for adoption; at age 11, her adoptive mother was crippled by a stroke and her second "father" sought refuge in an alcoholic haze.

At that, the children given up to foster care or the adoption system may be luckier than some who stay at home. Dysfunctional families are potential crucibles of crime, as indicated by the FBI's three-year study of 36 sexually motivated killers, including 29 killers with multiple victims.[14] Bureau analysts noted the failure of social bonding with caretakers who ignore, rationalize, or normalize antisocial behavior in a developing child, often supporting the child's distorted perception through their own deviant behavior. Rather than nurturing and protecting the child, such parents or guardians impose adult expectations and fail to intervene on the child's behalf in threatening situations. Specific misbehavior may be punished — even severely — but the overall ineffective social environment prevents the child from registering societal prohibitions at a cognitive level. Too often, the social breakdown extends beyond the child's immediate family to include negligent or nonresponsive teachers, counselors, clergy, physicians, and members of the legal establishment.[15]

When the FBI's sampling of sex-killers were quizzed on their family backgrounds, 69% reported histories of alcohol abuse, 53% listed relatives with psychiatric problems, 50% noted criminal histories, 46% admitted family sexual problems, and 33% detailed histories of familial drug abuse.[16] We have already noted the high risk of brain damaged children in families where alcoholism and drug addiction are prevalent; it should be noted here, as well, that drunken or addicted parents are typically dysfunctional across the board. Some types of mental illness, including schizophrenia and manic-depression, are now considered hereditary, and there is persuasive evidence that exposure to criminal forebears may incline a child toward the pursuit of violent crime. Dr. C. Robert Cloninger, a psychiatrist at the University of Washington School of Medicine, has done extensive research on adoptees, indicating that children whose biological parents have criminal records are four times more likely than others to become criminals themselves, even when their adoptive parents are law-abiding citizens.[17]

The annals of serial murder are rife with examples that prove the rule. George Putt's father was a drifter and habitual criminal, whose visits home were marked by heavy drinking and domestic violence. Henry Lucas was the son of bootleggers, his mother supplementing the family's liquid income via prostitution. Gordon Northcott's father died in a California lunatic asylum; a paternal uncle finished his days in San Quentin, sentenced to life on a murder charge. Poisoner Jane Toppan also lost her father to an asylum, living briefly with her grandmother before she was consigned to an orphanage. Florida's William Mansfield, Jr., was the son of a convicted child molester. German slayer Christa Lehman was a teenager when her mother was committed to a mental institution. Charles Manson's mother was an alcoholic prostitute, jailed for robbery soon after her son's fifth birthday; she often left him with relatives for weeks at a time, and once traded the child to a cocktail waitress in payment for a pitcher of beer. In England, Mary Bell boasted a similar background, with a criminal father and mentally unstable mother, who once gave the girl to a stranger she met at an abortion clinic. A two-generation survey of Albert Fish's family

reveals at least seven relatives with severe mental illness, including two who died in asylums. Juergen Hein's father was a chronic alcoholic, and his mother was mentally retarded. Two years after the divorce that split his family, Gary Heidnik was removed from his mother's custody because of her incessant drinking. Himself the son of a condemned serial killer, Gerald Gallego never met his father, but he was overexposed to his prostitute mother, plus an uncle, three cousins, and a half-brother serving time for murder, attempted murder, and robbery.

Within the context of such families, it comes as no surprise when bonding fails and children spend their early years in turmoil, often logging negative emotions toward their parents, guardians, and siblings. Of the FBI's sampling, 68% recalled frequent changes of residence in childhood; 47% reported their fathers absent before age 12, and 66% described their mothers as the dominant parent; 53% felt themselves treated unfairly in childhood and 72% acknowledged negative relationships with adult caretakers, including 44% who described negative relationships with their mothers.[18]

Dr. Manfred Guttmacher, a forensic psychiatrist who spent over 25 years as a medical advisor to trial judges in Baltimore, described sociopathic killers as the product of stormy marriages, with cruel, rejecting fathers and hysterical, seductive mothers,[19] but documented cases are as varied as the individuals themselves. Carroll Edward Cole grew up hating his adulterous mother and despising the father whom he regarded as "less than a man." Ed Gein's father was equally ineffectual, but Gein worshipped his domineering mother, preserving her bedroom as a kind of shrine after she died. George Putt, John Gacy, and Joseph Franklin lived in fear of their brutal, abusive fathers. Carlton Gary's mother changed dwellings each time she acquired a new lover, frequently leaving her son in the care of female relatives. Young Charles Manson watched his mother bring home lovers of both sexes. Henry Lucas's mother confined herself to men, the "tricks" interspersed with violent assaults on her paraplegic husband. Jerry Brudos, Ed Kemper, and Bobby Joe Long detested their carping, overbearing mothers, even though Long shared a bed with his until the age of 13 years.

For what it may be worth, religious training offers no apparent remedy for fledgling killers. Herbert Mullin, slayer of 13, was the product of a staunch Catholic home. Child-killer Arthur Bishop was raised a devout Mormon in Utah, and Eli Stutzman came from solid

Amish stock. Gary Schaefer's devotion to the fundamentalist Christadelphian sect did not prevent him from raping and killing three teenage girls. British vampire-slayer John Haigh was reared according to the strict precepts of the Plymouth Brethren, and New York sniper Yusef Rahman considered himself a devout follower of Islam.

If anything, a twisted or excessive emphasis upon religion may exacerbate the problems of a random killer in the making. Earle Nelson was clearly influenced by his custodian's religious fanaticism, compulsively underlining passages in the Bible he carried with him everywhere, quoting the Good Book to lull his chosen female victims. Fritz Klenner absorbed his father's apocalyptic brand of Catholicism so completely that rational thought was eclipsed by fantasies of impending Armageddon. In Jacksonville, Florida, young Ottis Toole was hopelessly torn between the teachings of his "born-again" mother and his maternal grandmother, a reputed Satanist who branded him "the devil's child."

While poverty is widely touted as a cause of crime, with correlation to the ethnic background of the criminals, serial killers reverse the national trend with a vengeance. Current FBI figures reveal that suspects arrested for murder average 56% black and 42% Caucasian (including Hispanics), with Orientals and American Indians accounting for less than one percent each.[20] In serial murders, however, a review of 500 American cases with identified suspects shows 84% Caucasian killers (of whom 17% were Hispanic), and only 16% blacks. One American Indian and one Asian killer are included on the list, with the Asian acting as accomplice to a white man.

Beyond the general family environment itself, each child is influenced by crucial formative events. The FBI's review of 36 incarcerated sex-killers points out certain common factors in their early lives, including: (1) trauma, often in the form of physical or sexual abuse; (2) developmental failure stemming from that trauma; and (3) interpersonal failure on the part of caretaking adults to serve as positive role models for the child.[21]

Some portion of the trauma suffered during childhood may be accidental, as with incidents of injury or illness that result in damage to the brain. A relatively minor injury may lead to lapses in control, with episodic or impulsive violence the result. Research confirms that damage to the hypothalmus, limbic region of the brain, or the temporal lobe may alter individual behavior to the point where self-control is jeopardized by the random discharge of electrical energy, producing episodes of bizarre, aberrant behavior. One Polish study noted lesions to the central nervous system in 14 of 24 killers examined.[22] And, as Dr. Mortimer Gross confirms, "There is a large body of evidence pointing to an association between organic brain disease and violence, particularly of the sudden-impulsive kind."[23]

The roster of 20th-century serial slayers is replete with brain-damaged victims of accident or disease. Earle Nelson was struck and dragged by a streetcar at age 10, emerging from a six-day coma with dramatic personality changes and debilitating headaches which lasted the rest of his life. Carlton Gary was knocked unconscious by a schoolyard swing, and John Gacy sustained an identical injury, suffering violent headaches for five years, until doctors diagnosed and treated a blood clot in his brain. Gary Heidnik tumbled from a tree in grade school, suffering an injury that prompted classmates to call him "football head." Bobby Joe Long suffered a series of head wounds between the ages of five and seven, including a fall from a pony which left him dizzy and nauseous for weeks afterward. Struck on the head with a rock at age nine, Max Gufler was thereafter subject to outbursts of unpredictable violence. Chicago sex-slayer William Heirens survived a series of falls between the ages of seven months and 12 years, twice knocking himself unconscious and suffering grim headaches into his teens; at age eight, he briefly "turned black" following a tonsilectomy accompanied by high fever and heavy bleeding. Christopher Wilder survived a near-drowning at age two, and one year later he was stricken with convulsions requiring medical resuscitation. Death nurse Robert Diaz was forced out of school in tenth grade by chronic illness. Eight-year-old Wesley Evans lay comatose for eight days after he was hit by a truck, waking with a limp and slurred speech, paralysis of his left side, and recurring hyperactivity which prompted his removal from school.

More often than not, the trauma sustained by future serial killers is deliberately inflicted during their formative years. When the FBI quizzed its sampling of captive murderers, 42% reported incidents of physical abuse in childhood, while 74% harbored memories of psychological abuse.[24] Whereas the physical abuse ranged from sporadic beatings to life-threatening assaults, psychological abuse was often more subtle, running the gamut from chronic neglect to overt cases of deliberate intimidation and humiliation.

One long-term study, carried out by members of the Minnesota Mother-Child Project, clearly demonstrates the link between abusive parents and a breakdown in the social bonding process. Without prior knowledge of their histories, 200 children were selected at random from lower-income urban families, their mothers mostly young, unwed, and poorly educated. Researchers tracked their subjects from pre-birth to the age of two years, with abusive or neglectful treatment registered along the way. From observation, the mothers were divided into five categories: (1) physically abusive; (2) verbally abusive; (3) neglectful or uncaring; (4) emotionally withdrawn or unresponsive; and (5) normal. After one year, the physically abused children were less than half as likely as normal children to have formed secure attachments; victims of abuse were three times as likely to be "anxious/avoidant," with corresponding displays of pent-up anger and frustration. The same pattern was evident at 18 months, while the children of emotionally withdrawn mothers showed even weaker attachments than the physically abused. At 18 months of age, *no* children of emotionally unresponsive mothers demonstrated bonding, while 75% of the normal children had formed solid attachments. The abusive and unresponsive mothers also produced offspring with lower performance on various measures of infant intellectual and verbal development.[25]

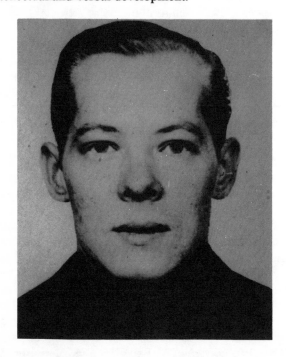

Richard Tingler's mother interspersed brutal beatings with reminders that her son was "born in sin." *(Credit: FBI)*

Abuse sustained in childhood by modern serial killers ranges from the mundane to the bizarre and sadistic. Edmund Kemper was locked in the basement for disobeying his mother. Marybeth Tinning's father preferred a closet, in between whippings administered with a flyswatter. John Gacy was beaten, thrown against walls, and branded a "sissy" by his brutal father. German slayer Kuno Hoffman lost his voice after one particularly savage beating by his father. Richard Biegenwald, George Putt, Thomas Braun, Albert DeSalvo, and Joseph Franklin all suffered similar thrashings from "the old man." Robert Tingler's mother did the beating in his family, punctuating blows with terse reminders that the boy was "born in sin." Eddie Cole was singled out for torture to insure his silence, after witnessing his mother's adultery. Michael Herrington's mother whipped him regularly till the age of 12, when he was big enough to take her favorite belt away. Henry Lucas was beaten so often by his prostitute mother that the assaults became routine, until the afternoon she clubbed him with a two-by-four and left him semiconscious for three days; when Henry's eye was gashed by a knife-wielding brother, Viola Lucas let him suffer for weeks, until infection demanded surgery. A hammer assault by his grandmother left rape-slayer Hugh Morse scarred for life. Joseph Kallinger's adoptive parents also favored hammers, alternating with a cat-o'-nine-tails and threats of castration.

In the realm of psychological abuse, parents sometimes seek to kill or maim the living thing their child loves most. Viola Lucas quizzed little Henry in detail, confirming his affection for a pet mule before she fetched her shotgun and blasted it dead in the yard. Leonard Maine was forced to shoot his own dog, on an allegation of chicken-stealing. Hugh Morse's grandmother slaughtered the boy's white mice, after he went to the movies without her permission. Steven Judy was forced to watch while his father skinned the family dog alive.

Considering their later crimes, it comes as no surprise that many of the childhood traumas suffered by serial killers are sexual in nature. In the FBI's limited sampling, 43% of those surveyed reported sexual abuse in childhood, while 28% had histories of sexual injury or disease. Thirty-five percent of those interrogated had witnessed acts of sexual violence in childhood; an equal number witnessed "disturbing" sex between their parents, while 42% observed unsettling acts between other adults or their friends. A whopping 73% reported some childhood involvement in "sexually stressful events."[26]

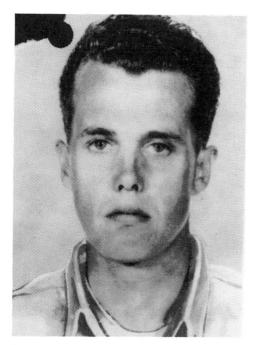

Hugh Morse was scarred for life when his maternal grandmother beat him with a hammer, during childhood. *(Credit: FBI)*

Childhood sexual abuse has been documented for numerous serial killers, without regard to gender. Velma Barfield and Gwendolyn Graham were molested by their fathers. An adoptive parent attempted to rape Terri Rachals, while Nanny Doss endured sexual assaults from relatives and neighbors alike. Young Donald Harvey was molested by an uncle and a male neighbor between the ages of six and ten. Arsonist Bruce Lee was abused by a male teacher at a school for the handicapped, and Juergen Bartsch was introduced to gay sex by a priest at parochial school, the assaults interspersed with tales of torture from the Inquisition. Ottis Toole and Pedro Lopez were both raped by pedophiles in early childhood, with Lopez enduring new assaults as a young man in jail. Forcible sodomy at age 13 taught Bruce Davis to despise the homosexuals he stalked in later life. Joseph Kallinger was molested by a gang of boys who held him captive at knifepoint. Child-killer Gordon Northcott was sodomized by his own father at age 10, while Gary Schaefer points the accusing finger at his older sister (an accusation she staunchly denies to this day). Rumors of mother-son incest persisted through Gerald Gallego's rocky childhood, while Charles Manson was raped and tortured by cellmates in various junvenile facilities. John Gacy was molested by a con-

struction worker, in an eerie preview of his own later crimes. A neighbor boy taught Eddie Cole to masturbate at age seven, while Harvey Carignan recalls adult women trying to "smother" him with their breasts and vaginas.

As for "disturbing sex" observed in childhood, it is worth noting that killers Charles Manson, Eddie Cole, Henry Lucas, and Gerald Gallego all watched their mothers performing with strangers on numerous occasions. Indeed, Lucas and his crippled father were sometimes beaten if they *refused* to watch; on the side, one of Viola Lucas's lovers taught Henry the "pleasures" of bestiality, raping and killing barnyard animals for sport. Peter Kurten's father forced his wife to strip for sex in front of the assembled children, later serving prison time for the attempted rape of his daughter; Peter likewise molested his sisters on occasion and was further influenced by a neighbor, a sadistic dogcatcher, who taught him to torture and masturbate dogs. George Williams watched his mother die in childbirth, later witnessing the murder of an infant brother by his stepmother. Leonard Lake's mother taught him to honor the human body by snapping nude photos of his sisters and various neighborhood girls. Observing a homosexual encounter at age 13, William Heirens reported the incident to his mother and was told: "All sex is dirty. If you touch anyone, you get a disease."

Under the vague heading of "sexually stressful events," it is worth noting that seven unrelated sexslayers, at least, were subjected to the identical trauma of compulsory cross-dressing in early childhood. In every case but one, the masquerade was orchestrated by a female relative or guardian, and while their motives varied, the results were strikingly consistent. An exception to the rule of torment by a brutal mother figure was Charles Manson, sent to elementary school in dresses by an uncle, with the sage advice that it would teach him "how to fight and be a man." Henry Lucas was also sent to school in skirts and dainty curls, until administrators filed injunctions to prevent his mother from abusing him in public. It is curious — and probably irrelevant — to note that Manson and Lucas both suffered their peculiar torment in Virginia, through the early 1940s. Further south and ten years later, Ottis Toole was dressed in petticoats and lace because his mother *wished* that he had been a girl. As an adult, ironically teamed up with Lucas for a murder spree that spanned the continent, Toole still dressed up in drag from time to time, when he was not consuming meals of human flesh. In California, Eddie Cole was forced to dress as "Mama's little girl" while serving coffee to his mother's female friends. A wicked stepmother was the culprit in the case of Rodney Beeler, her favorite dress-up "punishment" producing a serial rapist, presently sentenced to die for the one murder California authorities are able to document. Yet another Californian, Gordon Northcott, was habitually dressed as a girl by his mentally-unbalanced mother until age sixteen. And worlds away, in Ecuador, child-killer Daniel Barbosa bitterly recalled the way his mother dressed him as a girl to "keep him out of trouble" in the seedy barrio they occupied.

A sadistic uncle dressed Charles Manson as a girl for his first day of school, hoping he would "learn to fight and be a man." *(Credit: Los Angeles County Sheriff's Dept.)*

Children subjected to trauma of this sort are prime candidates for developmental failure, characterized by negative social attachment and resultant loss of control by adult caretakers. Where children are psychologically deprived or neglected, they frequently exhibit a diminished emotional response, including atrophy of what is commonly termed the conscience. Conversely, some abused children experience sustained levels of emotional and physical arousal in conjunction with their trauma. When arousal interacts with mental replays of the traumatic event — as with Albert Fish, reliving the beatings he suffered and witnessed in a Washington

orphanage — the child's perception of interpersonal relationships may be permanently skewed.

Thus, traumatized children tend to develop negative, rather than positive personality traits, disrupting formation of social relationships. The cycle feeds upon itself, with increased isolation prompting reliance on fantasy as a substitute for human interaction. Personality traits noted in the FBI's sampling of sex-slayers include rebelliousness, aggression, chronic lying, preference for autoerotic acts and fetishes, plus an exaggerated sense of privilege and entitlement — in short, the right to do exactly as they please, regardless of the consequence to others.[27]

The process of early personality development is known to professionals as "cognitive mapping," a gradual chain of events that determine the structure of future thought patterns, providing control of emotions and linking the individual to his social environment. In serial killers, the process is frequently fixed and repetitive, moving the child or adolescent toward an unrelieved antisocial view of the world. Fantasies and thought patterns are geared toward self-stimulation and relief from anxiety, thereby generating a primitive self-image and further alienation. Common manifestations of this condition include chronic daydreams or nightmares, along with highly visual fantasies featuring themes of dominance, revenge, sadistic violence, rape, mutilation, and death.[28]

Dysfunctional or abusive parents encourage this negative development in children, either by default — through failure to provide positive role models — or by actively setting examples for aberrant conduct. Adult caretakers may fail in their duties through physical absence, simple inadequacy, or their addiction to drugs and alcohol. Beyond mere neglect or the sorry example set by criminal parents, children also take cues to their future behavior from violent home environments. Where violence melds with sex — as in an atmosphere of prostitution, spousal rape, or sexual abuse of children in the family — the growing child soon loses track of the distinction between sex and mayhem.

If serial killers do not emerge from a vacuum, neither do they spring full-blown upon society without a hint of warning. Countless "symptoms" are proposed by experts in the field, some contradicting one another, but the warning signs described below appear on nearly every list.

(1) *Social isolation*, stemming from early abuse and detachment, typified by lack of friends and resistance to

physical contact. Seventy-one percent of the FBI's test subjects reported strong feelings of childhood isolationism, and specific case histories bear out the trend.[29] Charles Starkweather reacted to teasing in grade school with "a hate as hard as iron." Eddie Cole was so sensitive to jokes about his "sissy" name that he fought, maimed, and eventually murdered his elementary classmates. The social adaption of Henry Lucas and Charles Manson were doomed from the moment they turned up at school dressed as girls.

(2) *Learning disabilities*, frequently paired with juvenile delinquency. Physical and mental damage, early deprivation, and pervasive lack of trust in others all contribute to failure in school which is common to numerous serial killers. Of the FBI's sampling, 36% had repeated elementary grades, while 60% did poorly in high school and 47% dropped out entirely.[30] Eddie Cole was one such, failing every subject in his junior year despite a tested "genius" IQ of 152, and Gerald Stano's school records note a history of learning and "adjustment" deficits. A partial list of other dropouts who went on to kill repeatedly includes Christine Falling, Henry Lucas, Charles Manson, Velma Barfield, Ottis Toole, William Smith, Bruce Davis, Steven Catlin, Nannie Doss, Richard Biegenwald, Charles Starkweather, Wesley Evans, and Larry Eyler, to name only a few.

(3) *Symptoms of neurological impairment* linked to injury or illness, including headaches and seizures, poor muscular coordination, and incontinence. Of the sex-killers responding to FBI questionnaires, 68% reported histories of enuresis (bedwetting), 29% described themselves as accident prone in childhood, 29% suffered from persistent headaches, and 19% were subject to occasional convulsions.[31] We have already noted the childhood convulsions experienced by Christopher Wilder, along with the headaches suffered by brain-damaged killers John Gacy, Earle Nelson, and William Heirens. Ottis Toole was also stricken with seizures as a child. Gerald Stano was known to teachers and classmates as a boy who often fell down for no apparent reason. Alton Coleman lost control of his bladder so often in childhood that playmates tagged him with the nickname "Pissy." When Gary Heidnik wet the bed, his father hung the sheets outside a second-story window to amuse the neighbors; sometimes he hung Gary out the window, too, or sent him off to school with a bull's eye painted on the seat of his pants.

(4) *Deceptive behavior*, characterized by chronic and pointless lying, hypochondria, and chameleonlike behavior adopted to mask social deviance. Seventy-one percent of the FBI's test sample admitted habitual lying in childhood, and all of them refined deception to an art form over the course of their criminal careers.[32] John Gacy, Christine Falling, and John Christie all demonstrated hypochondria in early life, manufacturing imaginary symptoms to win attention, or to shirk responsibilities in school or at home. Habitual lying is so pervasive among future serial killers that a list of examples would easily fill the rest of this volume.

The only known Eskimo serial killer, William Tahl logged his first confrontation with police at age three. *(Credit: FBI)*

(5) *Problems with authority and self-control*, including constant challenges to parents, teachers, and the like, along with inability to tolerate restrictions and extreme reactions to the most trivial disappointments. Of the FBI's 36 test subjects, 67% admitted rebellious childhood behavior, 58% confessed malicious destruction of property, 48% described a history of temper tantrums, and 36% had run away from home on one or more occasions.[33] By age 11, Kenneth Bianchi's tantrums reached the point that both his home life and his education were disrupted. William Tahl began smashing neighborhood windows at age three, while Dayton Rogers preferred sniping at cars with a BB gun. Henry Lucas and Carlton Gary were chronic runaways, early behavior foreshadowing their rootless life styles as adults.

(6) *Precocious or bizarre sexual activity,* with emphasis on autoeroticism or violent and abusive demonstrations toward others. Of the FBI's test sampling, 71% confessed childhood involvement in voyeurism, with an equal number reporting various fetishes; an overwhelming 82% recalled compulsive masturbation starting at an early age and carried out through the remainder of their lives.[34] Masturbation became "an everyday thing" for Eddie Cole, after a neighbor introduced him to the practice at age seven. Joe Kallinger, conditioned by an early assault, preferred to masturbate while clutching a knife in his free hand. Henry Lucas and James Ruzicka each practiced bestiality, before moving on to rape and murder in later years. Gerald Gallego may have learned the sexual mechanics in his mother's bed; by age 13 he was charged with raping a younger girl. Leonard Lake graduated from photographing his nude sisters to coercing sex within the family. German slayer Heinrich Pommerenke reported his first act of sex at age 10, moving on to forcible rape five years later. Peter Kurten followed his father's example in molesting his sisters. Strangler Harvey Glatman practiced on himself in childhood, achieving orgasm as he choked himself to the point of unconsciousness. Vera Renczi, slayer of two husbands and 32 lovers, was notorious for her early promiscuity. William Heirens achieved climax while committing burglaries, amplifying his pleasure with the theft of women's panties which he wore at home. Jerry Brudos was so enamored of women's shoes that he burglarized homes to augment his collection, later knocking strangers down on the sidewalk to steal their footwear.

The FBI sampling also reveals that 81% of the sex-killers surveyed were stimulated by pornography, beginning in childhood, but a cautionary note is necessary here.[35] The anti-pornography crusade got a shot in the arm from Ted Bundy's eleventh-hour confessions, in February 1989 — and crusader James Dobson reportedly banked $1 million hawking videotapes of the Bundy sermonette[36] — but there are risks involved with taking such statements at face value. Bundy biographer Ann Rule describes the Dobson tape as "another Ted Bundy manipulation of our minds. The effect of the tape is to place, once again, the onus of his crimes — not on *himself* — but on us."[37] It is also worth noting that Bundy's definition of "soft-core pornography" included pulp detective magazines, replete with crime photos and staged "jeopardy" scenes which also fueled the masturbatory fantasies of killers Eddie Cole and John Joubert. It comes as no surprise that rape-

slayers enjoy pornography, but that enjoyment does not brand any given magazine or film as a "cause" of violent crime. Strangler Earle Nelson apparently limited his reading matter to the Holy Bible, and Heinrich Pommerenke killed his first victim after a viewing of *The Ten Commandments* convinced him women were the root of all evil. Leonard Lake so loved *The Collector,* a novel by John Fowles, that he christened his search for sex slaves "Operation Miranda," after a leading character in the book. Eddie Cole and Edmund Kemper both doted on gruesome horror movies. In short, the list of stimuli for random murder is as long and varied as the list of murderers themselves.

(7) *Obsession with fire, blood, and death,* characterized by fantasies of mayhem, frequently accompanied by outbreaks of arson which transcend the normal childhood incidence of playing with matches. Eighty-two percent of the FBI's subjects admitted frequent daydreams, focused primarily on rape or violence, and 56% were linked to acts of arson in childhood.[38] Ted Bundy was three years old when his teenaged aunt awoke from a nap to find herself surrounded by kitchen knives, Bundy grinning at her from bedside. Edmund Kemper fantasized about necrophilia while beheading his sister's dolls; he also enjoyed "playing gas chamber," writhing in simulated death throes as an older sister "threw the switch." John Joubert's childhood fantasies ran more to murder and cannibalism of his imaginary victims. John Haigh was singing in a church choir when he experienced visions of a forest, the trees spurting blood. Ottis Toole set fire to the first of some 20 Jacksonville homes at age six; questioned about his motive for burning houses years later, he replied, "I just hated to see them standing there." George Adorno torched his sister at age four, and Richard Biegenwald tried to burn the family home when he was five. Ten-year-old Gerald Gallego retaliated for a burglary charge by burning the complainant's home. Incarcerated for robbery at age 11, Carl Panzram set fire to the reformatory where he was confined. Robert Segee's long-running career in arson began at age nine.

(8) *Cruelty to animals and other persons,* with the acts of violence frequently concealed, disguised as "accidents," or blamed on others. Results from the FBI's survey of sex-slayers reveal that 36% practiced sadism toward animals in childhood, 54% were cruel or violent to other children, and 38% were assaultive toward adults.[39] Eddie Cole conceived the idea of strangling his enemies after choking a puppy to death, at age seven. Ian Brady was notorious for torturing strays in his slum

neighborhood of Glasgow. Bobby Joe Long was so jealous of his mother's dog that he once forced a .22-caliber bullet into the animal's vagina. Edmund Kemper soon graduated from decapitating dolls to beheading family pets, while Henry Lucas raped the animals he killed, before and after death. German slayers Peter Kurten and Bruno Ludke both grew up torturing animals for sport. Christine Falling tested the nine lives of cats by dropping them from high altitudes. British psychopath Patrick Mackay mutilated neighborhood pets before he graduated to beating and bullying children at school. Fighting and assaultive behavior is common among such children, sometimes escalating into homicide. Peter Kurten was nine years old when he claimed his first victim. Eddie Cole was eight when he drowned a boy who joked about his "sissy" name; a year later, he staged an accident that maimed the child who beat him in a yo-yo contest. In England, little Mary Bell was charged with two murders and one serious assault at age 11.

(9) *Stealing, hoarding, and gorging*, viewed by some analysts as symptoms of the child's emotional emptiness.[40] Fifty-six percent of the FBI's test sample admitted stealing in childhood, while 27% recalled histories of eating disorders.[41] When not torturing animals or beating his classmates, Patrick Mackay was a notorious neighborhood thief. Gerald Gallego began shoplifting around age five, soon graduating to burglary with his prostitute mother's encouragement. Germany's Werner Boost began stealing at age six, and his fellow countryman, Bruno Ludke, was likewise known for his sticky fingers. William Heirens missed his junior-high graduation due to a burglary arrest, while Jerry Brudos used theft to support his shoe fetish. Eddie Cole's first juvenile arrest involved the looting of a liquor store. For Henry Lucas, burglary and auto theft were simply ways to spend more time away from home. Carl Panzram's long career in violent crime began with childish robberies and escalated into random homicide.

(10) *Self-destructive behavior*, variously ascribed by different sources to an early death wish, sadomasochism, preoccupation with gore, or a simple craving for attention. Nineteen percent of the FBI's test subjects admitted incidents of self-mutilation in childhood,[42] and while few of them carried it off to the extent of Richard Biegenwald, setting himself on fire at age 11, various others were known to cut, burn, bruise, or brand themselves in repeated incidents.

(11) *Early substance abuse,* as a form of psychic escapism or emulation of parental behavior. The FBI's

test subjects were not questioned on substance abuse, but modern case histories demonstrate the pattern. Eddie Cole found it "cool" to steal liquor and show up drunk at school. Raised by alcoholic bootleggers, Henry Lucas found drinking a natural part of his life style, as well as a handy escape from the rigors of his abusive home. Carl Panzram logged his first arrest, at age eight, for being drunk and disorderly. Experimentation with drugs contributed to James Ruzicka's early arrests, beginning at age nine.

Generalities are often dangerous, and it would be a grave mistake to brand any child as a potential killer on the basis of the warning signs listed above. At the very least, however, children who display these symptoms of severe emotional disturbance — and especially where several warning signs are present in a single child — demand referral to responsible professionals for care and therapy. A parent, guardian, or teacher who ignores such symptoms does so, literally, at the risk of life and death.

As violent children translate fantasies to action, they begin to learn from their mistakes. The FBI's psychologists describe this process as a "feedback filter," letting individuals evaluate their actions, justifying aberrant behavior in their minds while sorting out mistakes, fine-tuning their performance to avoid restraint or punishment in future escapades. Improved techniques insure a greater margin of success in future crimes, which further fuel the individual's internal fantasies, demanding even greater stimuli... and so on, 'round and 'round.[43]

At the other end of the "expert" spectrum are those who relegate family environment to mere background noise, blaming genetic and medical factors for the modern rash of episodic violence. The "bad seed" hypothesis notes that various health conditions — including thyroid dysfunction, hemophilia, diabetes, heart disease, manic-depression, and schizophrenia — are passed down through family ties, suggesting that these or other inherited diseases may predispose certain victims toward impulsive, unpredictable violence.

In the 1960s, researchers ardently pursued the "XYY syndrome," so called after individuals born with a surplus "Y" — or male — chromosome. An estimated 100,000 males come so equipped in the United States, and it has been suggested that the extra dash of "maleness" makes them more aggressive, even violent, with a greater tendency toward criminal activity. The theory got a boost in 1966, when random killer Richard Speck was diagnosed — mistakenly, as it turned out —

as one such "supermale." Eager researchers cited his stature and facial acne as sure-fire symptoms of XYY syndrome, but genetic tests failed to bear out their suspicion. In the meantime, it was noted that XYY males comprise a larger percentage of the nation's prison population than the male population at large, but such figures are easily skewed. As researchers Jack Levin and James Fox point out, the XYY males who wind up in prison or mental institutions accused of violent crimes constitute a miniscule segment of the group at large.[44]

Another proponent of the "bad seed" theory, psychologist Joel Norris, lists 23 symptoms of genetic damage found in a select listing of modern serial killers.[45] They include:

1. Bulbous fingertips
2. Fine or electric-wire hair that won't comb down
3. Very fine hair that is soon awry after combing
4. Hair whorls
5. Head circumference outside a normal range of 1.5 cm
6. Epicanthus (upper and lower eyelids join the nose)
7. Hyperteliorism (abnormal distance between tear ducts)
8. Low-seated ears
9. Adherent earlobes
10. Malformed ears
11. Asymmetrical ears
12. Very soft or pliable ears
13. High-steepled palate
14. Roof of mouth steepled or flat and narrow
15. Forward tongue with deep ridges
16. Speckled tongue showing smooth or rough spots
17. Curved fifth fingers
18. Singular transverse palmar crease
19. Third toe longer than second toe or equal in length
20. Partial syndactyly of two middle toes
21. Abnormal gap between first and second toes
22. Abnormal teeth
23. Abnormalities in dermatoglyphics

Serial killers with documented backgrounds of genetic problems include Georgia strangler Carlton Gary and Florida's Bobby Joe Long. In Gary's case, physical examination reveals various symptoms from the Norris checklist, including adherent earlobes, claw-like fingers with bulbous tips and partial webbing, plus malformation of the toes. Bobby Long, on the other hand, carried an extra "female" chromosome, triggering abnormal production of estrogen which caused his breasts to grow with the approach of puberty. Surgeons removed six pounds of excess tissue from Long's chest, but he continues to experience protomenstrual symptoms linked to a strict lunar cycle.

With various serial killers reporting convulsions or seizures from childhood, it is logical to ask if epilepsy plays a role, however minor, in cases of episodic violence. Without indicting epileptics as a class, it is noteworthy that electroencephalogram (EEG) tests reveal "spiking" patterns of random, uncontrollable electrical discharges during seizure activity. Their source, the limbic brain, controls primitive emotions like fear and rage, triggering the "fight or flight" response when we are frightened or surprised. Serial killers Bruce Lee, Christine Falling, Fritz Haarmann, and Paul Minow were all diagnosed epileptics, while others demonstrate epileptoid symptoms only under the influence of drugs or alcohol. Twenty-four hours after his parole in 1967, Charles Manson was dropping LSD and "innovating" to the music of the Grateful Dead in San Francisco, lapsing into a seizure-like state with strobe lights flashing in his eyes.

Another target of modern research into episodic violence is the hypothalmus, sometimes described as the brain's "emotional voltage regulator." Dr. Helen Morrison, a Chicago psychiatrist whose interview subjects include serial slayers John Gacy, Richard Macek, and Peter Sutcliffe, cites damage to the hypothalmic region of the brain as a potential cause of violent crime. This portion of the brain regulates the hormonal system, including the adrenal and thyroid glands, with corresponding influence on individual response to real or perceived threats. In essence, Dr. Morrison contends that damage to the hypothalmus may prevent an individual from growing toward emotional maturity. When threatened or insulted, even if the threat is mere illusion, individuals with hypothalmic damage may respond with childish tantrums... and the grown-up weapons of adults.[46]

Neuropsychologist James Prescott champions the "deep brain dysfunction" theory of antisocial behavior, pointing to the septal region of the midbrain as a regulator of emotion and an individual's awareness of the world outside himself. Lying adjacent to the hypothalmus, this portion of the brain, once damaged or impaired, may produce episodic hallucinations or bizarre dreamlike states, where fantasy fuses with reality.[47] There is at least a chance that damage to the septal region helped produce the disembodied talking head — dubbed Charlie — which supposedly advised Joe Kallinger on when and who to kill. Likewise, a similar dysfunction may have helped to generate the lethal alter egos blamed by killers William Heirens and Carlton Gary for their various crimes. And we can only speculate upon the impact of the brain disease lepto-meningitis, belatedly diagnosed from the autopsy of Australian serial killer Arnold Sodeman. In the case of Henry Lucas, CAT scans and nuclear magnetic resonance testing revealed frontal lobe contusions, further damage to the temporal lobe, pools of spinal fluid at the base of the brain, and enlargement of the Sylvan fissures at the expense of surrounding tissue, indicating a significant loss of basic judgmental functions.[48]

Chemical imbalance may also affect human attitude and behavior, whether that imbalance results from brain damage, glandular dysfunction, environmental contaminants, or the deliberate ingestion of drugs and alcohol. Manic-depression, schizophrenia, and some forms of psychosis are treatable with medication to varying degrees, since they originate within the body, rather than within the mind. As an example, the chronic hormonal imbalance suffered by Mauricio Silva is cited as a contributory factor in the outbursts of temper that claimed four lives between 1978 and 1984.

Something as simple as a killer's diet may contribute to his crimes, if large quantities of refined carbohydrates — white flour, white sugar, and junk food — are absorbed by a body already out of kilter. Refined sugar's impact on hyperactivity is well established by modern research, and "loaded" diets are likewise blamed for causing or aggravating other forms of aberrant behavior.

On the other hand, research by Diane Fishbein and Robert Thatcher, at the University of Maryland School of Medicine, turn the spotlight on toxic trace elements — including lead, cadmium, arsenic, aluminum, and mercury — which may impair brain function and impede socially adaptive behavior.[49] Toxicological tests on one subject, serial slayer Henry Lucas, revealed abnormally high levels of lead and cadmium in Lucas's nerve tissue, the damage possibly compounded by decades of drug and alcohol abuse.[50]

In the classic suspense novel *Red Dragon*, by Thomas Harris, serial killer Francis Dolarhyde's murder ram-

page is sparked in equal parts by childhood abuse and the humiliation of a physical deformity. In real life, there is persuasive evidence that early embarrassment linked to physical defects may warp the future course of an individual's life. Repeat killers Mauricio Silva and Eric Cooke, an Australian practitioner, both suffered from the same cleft palate that plagued Harris's fictional stalker. Robert Hansen's youthful acne was so severe that he recalls his face as "one big pimple"; shunned by the attractive girls in school, he grew up hating them and nursing revenge fantasies that claimed 17 lives. William Cook's drooping eyelid prompted numerous taunts, until he beat one of the jokers half to death with a baseball bat. Charles Starkweather's bowed legs and runty stature prompted numerous schoolyard battles, building up the "hate as hard as iron" that prompted him to slay 11 victims. British arsonist Bruce Lee suffered from partial paralysis and a deformed right arm, frustrating his desire to match the exploits of the kung fu star whose name he legally adopted in his teens.

There are substantial risks involved in trying to predict an individual's adult behavior from specific childhood symptoms, and it must be granted that the vast majority of children from abusive homes do not go on to kill for sport. Predictive theories are often based on tiny samplings — sometimes on a single case — and subjects chosen for review have typically drawn much attention to themselves by means of their bizarre behavior. Many children who display the classic warning signs of future episodic violence stabilize in adolescence or adulthood, even in the absence of corrective therapy.

Where, then, do serial killers *really* come from?

A review of modern cases indicates that most are products of a grim convergence in their early lives, with several different factors joining forces to create a twisted specimen. Abandonment or early brain trauma are no more guarantees of serial violence than are child abuse or malnutrition, but a combination of such factors clearly amplifies their impact on the body and the mind.

Consider Henry Lucas, brain-damaged from childhood beatings, subjected to cross-dressing and other extremes of psychological abuse, blinded in one eye, witness to his mother's promiscuity and schooled by her lovers in sadistic bestiality, drinking heavily by age nine or ten. Or Ottis Toole, an early seizure victim, dressed as a girl and raped as a child, torn between his grandmother's Satanism and his mother's fundamentalist Christianity. Or Bobby Long, traumatized by repeated head wounds, feminized by genetic hormonal imbalance, a child of divorce who shared his domineering mother's bed until age 13. Or Charles Manson, abandoned, tortured, raped, incarcerated and humiliated almost from the moment of his birth.

The list goes on, with endless variations, but the killers who have left their bloody tracks around the world in recent times appear to share one common trait. To quote David Heise, professor of sociology at Indiana University in Bloomington, each and every killer on the list was "socially assassinated" in the early years of life by factors they could not control.[51] A few of them would kill while still in grade school, but for most, the trigger incident still lay ahead. Their silent rage had yet to reach the point of no return.

To understand exactly why they killed, we must pursue them into adolescence and beyond. It is a journey fraught with peril, littered with the bodies of the innocent, but no one has devised a short-cut yet.

Our trek, like theirs, proceeds with one step at a time.

Chapter 2

Silent Rage

It is impossible to estimate how many children come of age in violent, loveless homes across the land. Each year, Americans officially report more than a million incidents of child abuse or serious neglect, including some 120,000 cases of sexual abuse, but those figures are merely the tip of the iceberg, consisting of criminal cases reviewed by police.[1] The numbers fail to make allowance for innumerable other children who are subject to neglect, humiliation, and brutality in circumstances hidden from the public eye.

If every child produced from a dysfunctional relationship was homicidal, the United States would be one giant charnel house by now. It is apparent, then, that most are somehow capable of overcoming their traumatic origins and functioning within the ranges of behavior which society regards as "normal." They may not be happy, but they manage to adapt.

And so, unfortunately, do the children who grow up to kill.

It is an old refrain. When bodies are discovered and arrests are made, the television cameras roll, recording neighborhood reactions for posterity: "I can't believe he'd ever do a thing like this." "She wouldn't harm a fly." "He was the last one in the world that anybody would suspect, the gentlest man you'd ever want to meet."

In practice, sociopaths are emotional chameleons, hiding lethal rage and morbid fantasies behind what some psychologists refer to as a "mask of sanity." In public, they are often animated, charming, even charis-matic, with a kind of extrasensory divining rod that helps them pick out weaknesses in others. As renowned psychiatrist Hervey Cleckly points out:

> It must be remembered that even the most severely and obviously disabled psychopath presents a technical appearance of sanity, often one of high intellectual capacities and not infrequently succeeds in business or professional activities for short periods, some for considerable periods... Although they occasionally appear on casual inspection as successful members of the community, as able lawyers, executives, or physicians, they do not, it seems, succeed in the sense of finding satisfaction or fulfillment in their own accomplishments. Nor do they, when the full story is known, appear to find this in any other ordinary activity.[2]

The annals of modern serial murder are replete with examples of killers who passed unnoticed as the boy or girl next door. Ted Bundy was a Boy Scout in his youth, later a charming political activist who presented the image of a successful law student despite slumping grades. Repeat killers Arthur Bishop, Richard Angelo, and John Joubert were all Eagle Scouts in their teens. John Gacy was famous for his holiday theme parties, performing as a clown at children's hospitals when he was not immersed in local politics. Dean Corll was another charmer, luring young victims and accomplices alike with gifts of homemade candy. Rape-slayer Albert DeSalvo frequently posed as a talent scout, persuading dozens of women to open their doors and submit to intimate fondling while he recorded their measurements for nonexistent modeling assignments. Despite a life style of cannibalism and "unparalleled perversity," Albert Fish was bland enough to win the trust of total strangers, waltzing off with their children to "birthday parties" from which they would never return. Ed Gein was known around his home town as a simple-minded handyman and local "character"; no one suspected he was also killing, robbing graves, and crafting household decorations out of human body parts.

Ironically, the random killer's mask of sanity is often manifested in benevolent behavior, frequently extending to the choice of a career in public service. Various psychologists are prone to argue over whether such behavior constitutes a quest for power or a simple craving for attention, but the overall result supports an outward image of the killer as a good Samaritan, devoted to the welfare of his fellow man. In 1969, Ted Bundy earned a police commendation for capturing a purse-snatcher; the following year, he rescued a drowning three-year-old from Seattle's Green Lake, subsequently volunteering his services to a crisis clinic hot line and writing a pamphlet for women on rape prevention. Child-killer Andre Rand worked as a physical therapy aide at a school for the handicapped. When not engaged in murder, Ralph Nuss earned his living as a psychiatric social worker. Marybeth Tinning passed time as an ambulance driver between the murders of her eight children. Richard Angelo joined a volunteer fire department at the earliest permissible age, before moving on to a nursing career.

Indeed, careers in medicine seem to hold a special appeal for serial killers, granting free access to potential victims while allowing egocentric predators to pose as "heroes" or "angels of mercy." The modern list of healers-turned-killer includes physicians Roland Clark, Joseph Emory, Sohrab Khan, Marcel Petiot, Michael Swango, John MacGregor, Robert Clements, Morris Bolber, and Colin Campbell. In Stockholm, Dr. Teet Harm used his position as chief criminal pathologist to confuse police investigations of the mutilation-slayings he committed with the aid of an accomplice, Dr. Thomas Allgren. Dentists Glennon Engelman, Arthur Waite, and Tony Protopappas all claimed multiple victims before they were exposed and prosecuted. Poisoner Severin Klosovski, better known to British authorities as "George Chapman," gained his skill with lethal potions as a surgeon's apprentice. Californians Robert Diaz and William Archerd each harbored dreams of a medical career, but neither could afford the education; they went on to serve — and kill — in lesser capacities, Diaz as a vocational nurse, Archerd as a state hospital attendant. Nurses Genene Jones, Bobbie Sue

Terrell, Ann Green, Anthony Shook, and Carol Bundy (no relation to Ted), all stand convicted of multiple homicides in the United States, while Fritz Rudloff, Cecile Bombeek, and Michaela Roeder carried on the lethal tradition in Europe.

Nor is formal education mandatory for would-be medical assassins. In March 1991, four Austrian nurse's aides were convicted of slaying 20 patients between 1983 and 1989; the four defendants earlier confessed to 49 murders, and various official estimates of the body count exceeded 300. In Malmo, Sweden, Anders Hansson poisoned 23 of his elderly charges, accusing his victims of "harassing the staff." Nurse's aide Donald Harvey holds the American record for serial murder, with 87 documented victims spanning two decades. Equally vicious, if less prolific, were Jeffrey Feltner, Randy Powers, Catherine Wood and Gwendolyn Graham. Anthony Joyner did maintenance work at the Philadelphia nursing home where he raped and murdered six elderly women. In New York, Annette Washington murdered the clients she served as a home health care worker. Dorothea Waddingham preyed on residents of the British nursing home she operated, and hospital manager Arnfinn Nesset holds the Norwegian record for multiple murders, with 27 confessed slayings and 35 others suspected. In America, Velma Barfield, Anna Hahn, and Dorothy Matajke were all self-styled "nurses" and "companions," preying on the elderly who trusted them for daily care.

In addition to the killers named above, unsolved serial murders at various hospitals in France, Canada, and the United States have claimed more than 200 lives since World War II. No suspect was ever identified in the deaths of 17 patients at the Town Hospital in Macon, France, in the mid-1940s. Two nurses were suspected of poisoning infants at Toronto's Hospital for Sick Children, but authorities could never agree on a final body count, much less the identity of their prime suspect. In Ann Arbor, Michigan, a pair of Filipina nurses were convicted in five of 14 similar slayings at a veteran's hospital, but the convictions were overturned on appeal and charges were dismissed. Nurse Terri Rachals confessed to a half-dozen hospital murders in Albany, Georgia, then recanted her statement and claimed faulty memory; convicted on one count of aggravated assault, she was sentenced to 17 years in prison. Another nurse, Mary Robaczynski, was allowed to surrender her license in lieu of criminal prosecution, despite her admission of four Maryland homicides. Police were investigating 22 suspicious deaths at Prince

George's Hospital, in a Maryland suburb of Washington, D.C., when nurse Jane Bolding confessed to three of the killings and seven attempted murders; her trial ended in acquittal, after the confession was ruled inadmissible as evidence. In New Jersey, Dr. Mario Jascalevich was charged with using curare to poison patients at Riverdell Hospital; jurors acquitted Jascalevich, and the crimes remain unsolved today. And in the Chicago suburb of Downer's Grove, a series of lethal insulin injections ended abruptly after hospital administrators dismissed one of their night-shift nurses, suspected of committing the crimes.

Behind the mask of sanity, most random killers are impulsive, irresponsible, and totally devoid of conscience. A minority profess remorse when they are captured, and a handful halt their killing sprees by means of suicide or a surrender to police, but for the most part they are quite content to kill and kill again, without a thought of breaking off the game. Easily bored with their everyday lives, they seek distraction and stimulation in morbid fantasy, drug and alcohol abuse, promiscuous sex, and the thrill of the hunt.

With such unstable personalities involved, it comes as no surprise that psychopaths experience substantial turmoil in their private lives. Marital problems are a recurring theme, with typical reports including numerous short-term marriages, violent arguments, chronic infidelity, aberrant sexual demands, and spousal abuse. Strangler Earle Nelson's bride was so appalled at his perverse sexual appetite that she fled their home and sought refuge in a sanitarium. Steven Catlin was married five times, while Gerald Gallego made seven trips to the altar by age 32, molesting the daughter he sired from one union. Eddie Cole married — and occasionally murdered — women who reminded him of his drunken, promiscuous mother. Charles Brown was forced into marriage at age 16, fathering four children before he finally hit the road. Joseph Kallinger's two marriages were marred by suicide attempts and brutal child abuse. Ottis Toole married a woman 24 years his senior, then abandoned her when she objected to his homosexual liaisons. Henry Lucas and Harvey Carignan saw marriages dissolve after they molested their stepchildren. Transient slayers Johann Hoch, Edmund Cody, and James Watson claimed some 90 brides between them, killing off the majority for profit or pleasure.

Many psychopaths also have problems with employment, changing jobs frequently, clashing with peers and employers, sometimes falling back on a parasitic lifestyle, bilking friends and family for their support. Of the FBI's cooperative sampling, only 20% reported steady employment prior to committing their first murder; 69% recalled sporadic unemployment, and 11% were jobless.[3] British slayer John Christie lost his first job, as a police dispatcher, over accusations of petty theft. Gordon Cummins was dismissed from several jobs for being dishonest and unreliable. For habitual drifters like Henry Lucas, Ottis Toole, and William Guatney, odd jobs and handouts from the nearest rescue mission are a way of life. Others — like truckers Edmund Cody, Benjamin Boyle, and Peter Sutcliffe, or traveling salesman Gary Robbins — take advantage of their transient jobs to troll for victims while they earn their pay.

As noted in the previous chapter, criminal behavior is common among psychopaths, particularly males, and incidents typically escalate through adolescence. Of the FBI's captive sampling, 94% had prior convictions for sexual offenses prior to the commission of a murder, with 13% of those boasting four or more convictions.[4] In terms of adolescent crime, the U.S. Department of Justice reported 50,000 juveniles detained for criminal offenses during 1986. Of that number, 90% were charged with acts that would have been considered serious for an adult; nearly one in five stood accused of murder, rape, robbery, or aggravated assault.[5]

The early crimes attributed to antisocial personalities may not be violent or sexual in nature, but they demonstrate the overall contempt for law and society which typifies psychopaths as a class. Scotland's Peter Manuel logged his first arrest at age 12, escaping from custody 11 times over the next three years. Henry Lucas and Charles Manson were also escape artists, repeatedly fleeing from juvenile facilities. Repeat killers Patrick Mackay, Carlton Gary, Ian Brady, David Bullock, Paul Knowles, Tyrone Bridges, Steven Catlin, and Ottis Toole were among those who began compiling long arrest records in their teens. Eddie Cole recorded his first arrest in high school, topping 45 before his final conviction on charges of multiple murder. In New Orleans, John Brooks was sought by police on 16 felony counts when he died at age 20. Arthur Bishop was a fugitive from embezzlement charges when he began killing children in Utah. Henri Landru compiled a long record of fraud convictions before he turned to murdering his fiancees.

The sociopathic behavioral traits noted in Chapter 1 continue to manifest themselves through adolescence and adulthood, frequently becoming more severe with age. In terms of social isolation, 77% of the FBI's sampling reported such feelings in adolescence, with 73% regarding themselves as isolated adults.[6] With transient killers like Lucas, Toole, and Charles Hatcher, isolation from other humans may be a literal fact. British slayer Dennis Nilsen compensated for the loss of a live-in companion by "killing for company," stashing his lifeless roommates in cupboards and beneath the floorboards of his home. In other cases, social isolation may present itself in the form of a "double life," with the killer's murderous side concealed from family and friends. John Gacy's wife and neighbors had no inkling of the graves beneath his house, in spite of fetid odors emanating from the property. Randall Woodfield was a star athlete, whose coaches helped conceal his penchant for indecent exposure. David Berkowitz was a mild-mannered postal employee by day, stalking human prey by night as New York's "Son of Sam."

Learning disabilities are downplayed in later life, but we have already noted the high percentage of high school dropouts among serial slayers. Of those who make the cut for college, some — like Ted Bundy and David Dowler — are mediocre students, changing majors frequently and fading in the stretch without obtaining their degrees. Others survive college and graduate school, even the rigors of medical training, by sublimating their lethal urges, putting homicide on hold and finding their diversion through sex or alcohol and drugs. For those who persevere, the mask of sanity is vital, and a whole new world of victims lies in store.

Symptoms of neurological impairment continue to plague many sociopaths throughout their lives. Thirty-three percent of the FBI's test subjects reported chronic headaches during adolescence, with 45% suffering regular pain through adulthood. A full 32% of those questioned described themselves as accident prone in adolescence, with 27% sustaining frequent accidents as adults. Seizure activity declined from adolescence, when 21% of the subjects suffered convulsions, but 13% of the adult killers were still affected. Bedwetting plagued 60% of the adolescent subjects, dropping sharply to 15% in adulthood.[7]

At the same time, various slayers incurred new injury or crippling abuse beyond their childhood years. Bobby Joe Long, already the victim of several childhood head injuries, shattered his skull in a motorcycle accident, emerging from his latest trauma with an irrepressible desire for constant sex. Max Gufler suffered his second major head wound as a wartime ambulance driver, thereafter exhibiting violent mood swings. John Christie was wounded and gassed by the Germans in World

War I; blind for five months after the attack, he suffered from hysterical mutism for three and a half years. Child-slayer Pedro Lopez was gang-raped in prison at age 18, killing three of his four attackers in retaliation. Ottis Toole and Danny Figueroa were both diagnosed as retarded in their teens, while British strangler Kenneth Erskine possessed the mentality of an 11-year-old at age 24.

Deceptive behavior remains a way of life for random killers, with 75% of the FBI's correspondents admitting to chronic lying in adolescence and 68% carrying the trait through adulthood.[8] In Texas, Genene Jones alternated tales of her relationship to rock stars with descriptions of her own near-death in nonexistent car wrecks and the shooting of an abusive brother-in-law. Marybeth Tinning reported innumerable threats and crank calls from anonymous enemies, once vandalizing her own home and filing false burglary reports in an apparent bid for sympathy. Kenneth Bianchi borrowed an old friend's name for the phony psychiatric diploma he used to deceive various "patients" in Los Angeles. David Dowler and Fritz Klenner regaled acquaintances with lurid tales of their performance as CIA agents and contract killers; Klenner went further, duping the population of his Carolina home town by posing as a graduate of Duke University's medical school — a deception tolerated and encouraged by his physician father. Christopher Wilder, though deeply in debt, maintained the image of a "millionaire businessman" and professional race car driver. In California, death nurse Robert Diaz insisted that friends and relatives address him as "Doctor." While a fugitive from Alabama murder charges, Audrey Hilley married a man in New Hampshire, then staged her own death and returned in the guise of a twin sister to console her grieving "brother-in-law!"

Another manifestation of the deceptive phenomenon is chronic hypochondria, employed by certain random killers to evade responsibility or as a magnet for attention. John Gacy's elusive "heart condition" spared him from the drudgery of many chores, but never interfered with digging graves beneath his house. When not employed at Texas hospitals, Genene Jones was herself a chronic patient, logging 27 visits in one two-year period; her complaints ranged from chest pains and itching hands to belching, diarrhea, and "burning up" constipation. Florida's Christine Falling was another frequent visitor to emergency rooms, checking in on an average of twice per month with untraceable "red spots," "abnormal menses," and imaginary "snakebites."

Since 1951, psychologists have labeled such excessive hypochondria as "Munchausen's syndrome," a compulsive bid for sympathetic attention named after Baron von Munchausen, the renowned 18th-century purveyor of tall tales. A curious parallel condition, first described in 1977, is "Munchausen's syndrome by proxy," wherein those responsible for care of children, invalids, and the like seek attention by harming their charges. The latter condition has been cited as a possible explanation for serial murders committed by various nurses, as well as some mothers like Marybeth Tinning, who killed eight of her own children between 1972 and 1985.[9]

Problems with authority and self-control are the lifelong earmarks of the sociopath. FBI questionnaires reveal that 84% of the sex-killers tested were openly rebellious in adolescence, with 72% carrying the trait into adulthood. Sixty-two percent of the adolescent subjects engaged in malicious destruction of property, with 35% following suit as adults. Temper tantrums were a common form of self-expression for 50% of the correspondents in adolescence, and of 44% in adulthood. A full 46% of the Bureau's subjects ran away from home in their teens, with 11% deserting families as adults.[10] For chronic drifters like Lucas and Toole, Charles Hatcher, and Anthony Goodin, the very thought of "home" was enough to put them on the road. Eddie Cole's explosive temper led to countless fistfights, in and out of jail. Indeed, the roster of arrests and criminal convictions logged by random killers for comparatively "minor" crimes is proof enough that few of them can live for long within the strictures of a civilized society.

Aberrant sexual behavior is yet another trademark of the killer breed, with extreme promiscuity recorded among 90% of identified female sociopaths.[11] Of the FBI's limited test sample, 82% described compulsive masturbation during adolescence, and 81% continued the practice through adulthood.[12] The Bureau's questionnaire did not follow up on childhood reports of voyeurism and fetishism, but documented case histories show random killers addicted to vicarious stimulation, inexorably graduating from panty raids and peeping incidents to sexual assault and murder in their endless quest for a better, more powerful "fix."

Sex-slayers Eric Cooke, Charles Floyd, and Rickey Brogsdale all began their lethal careers as night-prowling "peeping Toms." In Oregon, Jerry Brudos escalated from stealing women's shoes and underwear to beating a girl who resisted his teenage sexual advances; in later life, he kept his victims' shoes with feet intact and fashioned paperweights from their severed breasts. By age 17, William Heirens had learned to enhance the sexual thrill of burglary by beating, shooting, and stabbing female victims whom he found at home. Gregory Davis was another youthful voyeur, developing a fixation on older women in his teens. A thousand miles and twenty years apart, Eddie Cole and John Joubert each masturbated over the staged bondage photos in pulp detective magazines. Randall Woodfield's compulsion for self-exposure led to arrests in high school and finally scuttled his career with the Green Bay Packers. Michael Lupo, stricken with AIDS, filled his diary with the names of several hundred homosexual lovers. Bobby Joe Long masturbated habitually to relieve his sexual tension, unsatisfied by intercourse with his wife on an average of four or five times per day. Albert DeSalvo branded his wife as "frigid" when she balked at making love six times a day; his alternate outlet included raping some 2,000 women and slaying 13. German cannibal Joachim Kroll masturbated while strangling an inflatable doll with his free hand. Leonard Lake conceived his plan for the abduction of sex slaves after years of coercing his sisters into incest. In England, Peter Sutcliffe joked about molesting female corpses during his employment at a Yorkshire funeral home.

With such pathology at work, many serial killers log their first arrests for sexual offenses. Steven Judy was twelve years old when he invaded a neighbor's home and raped her at knifepoint. Peter Manuel and Heinrich Pommerenke were each 15 when they launched their careers in forcible rape; John Brooks was the same age when police charged him with molesting an eight-year-old girl. In Australia, Christopher Wilder was a teenager when he joined in his first gang rape. Arthur Goode, also a teenager, confined his advances to younger, smaller boys. John Roche inaugurated a series of violent rapes at age 17. Alton Coleman plea-bargained his first rape charge to a simple robbery conviction at age 19; in prison, psychiatrists described him as "a pansexual, willing to have intercourse with any object, women, men, children, whatever." Another 19-year-old, Milton Johnson, was first convicted of raping an Illinois woman and torturing her with a cigarette lighter. Joseph Bryan, jailed at 19 for molesting two younger boys, confessed arousal at the sight of children "tied up and screaming." Freeway killer William Bonin logged his first arrest for kidnapping, sodomy, and child-molesting at age 21. John Gacy was a relative late-bloomer, recording his first conviction at 26, for sodomy under coercion.

Child-killer Joseph Bryan told psychiatrists he liked to see little boys "tied up and screaming." *(Credit: FBI)*

The sociopath's childhood fascination with fire, blood, and death typically worsens with age. Sixty-one percent of the FBI's test subjects admitted fantasies of rape, with a full 50% dating the first such fantasies from ages 12 to 14; a lethal few began to fantasize sexual assaults as early as age five.[13] Such fantasies play a crucial role in sexually motivated murders, sometimes with the killers reenacting traumas suffered by themselves in early life. In other tested categories, 81% of the FBI correspondents admitted habitual daydreaming in both adolescence and adulthood; cruelty to children declined somewhat, from 64% among adolescents to 44% as adults, but attacks upon adults increased slightly — from 84% to 86% — as the perpetrators gained stature and strength.[14] Incidents of arson declined from 52% in adolescence to a still-significant 28% in adulthood; likewise, sadism toward animals showed a drop from 46% to 36% in the relevant age categories.[15]

In practice, arson remains a favorite sideline of some serial killers. Germany's Peter Kurten began torching barns in his early twenties, hoping to incinerate homeless tramps; twenty years later, at the height of his murder rampage, he took time off to burn 17 separate buildings in Dusseldorf. William Heirens, charged with burglary at 13, confessed setting fire to some of the

dwellings he robbed. In New York, David Berkowitz reportedly set thousands of "benevolent" fires to help the city fire department justify its budget requests. Joseph Kallinger twice set fire to his family home. Marybeth Tinning set fire to the trailer she shared with her husband, moving on from there to demolish a church and a nearby barn. Ottis Toole's love affair with fire was a lifelong relationship; he was serving time on a Jacksonville arson charge when Henry Lucas blew the whistle on their joint murder spree. Rape-slayer Anthony Spencer logged his first arrest on an arson charge, at age 15. Australian Eric Cooke burned down a church where he had been rejected in a choir audition; later, he destroyed a theater, apparently for spite. In New Jersey, Robert Zarinsky warmed up for murder by setting fire to lumber yards. British arsonist Bruce Lee achieved orgasm by lighting the fires that claimed 22 lives. In New England, Robert Segee confessed to setting 25 major fires in seven years, including the blaze that destroyed a circus tent and trapped 169 helpless victims inside.

While sadistic treatment of animals wanes slightly with age, some serial killers never lose their taste for the game. Peter Kurten practiced bestiality from age 13, and he especially enjoyed knifing sheep to death as he climaxed; in later years, when he ran short of human victims, Kurten satisfied himself by decapitating swans in an urban park. California vampire-slayer Richard Chase ate living birds and smeared himself with blood from slaughtered cattle over several years before he started tracking human prey. The prevalence of such attacks is further illustrated by three cases reported during a six-day period in March 1991. On March 14, authorities in King County, Washington, aired reports of an unidentified gunman who had killed four house cats — and ruined one stuffed toy — in a series of drive-by shootings through residential windows. The following day, police in Fairfax County, Virginia, announced their search for a man who had raped ten ponies around Great Falls, injuring one of the mares so badly that it died of internal hemorrhaging. And on March 20, the sheriff of Yalobusha County, Mississippi, reported the poisoning of 72 animals — including dogs, opossums, bobcats, and vultures—within a span of eight days.[16]

Violent behavior escalates as sociopaths become more proficient and confident, with many serial killers claiming lives before they are old enough to vote. In Washington state, detectives suspect Ted Bundy of committing his first murder at age 12. Robert Segee's confessions include the admission of two homicides committed when he was 13 years old. Ottis Toole, Gary Krist, and Richard Delage were all 14 when they claimed their first victims; in Alabama, Raymond Brown was the same age when he slaughtered three members of his

Future "Top Ten" fugitive Gary Krist committed his first known murder at age 14. *(Credit: FBI)*

own family. Henry Lucas managed to conceal his first rape-slaying at 15. In New York City, Willie Bosket had killed two persons and stabbed 50 others by his fifteenth birthday. Harold Jones and Edmund Kemper each claimed two victims at age 15, with Kemper murdering his own grandparents for personal amusement. Yet another 15-year-old, Martin Rutrell, joined two older accomplices for a murder spree that left four persons dead and three others wounded. New Yorker George Adorno killed three persons at age 15, claiming a fourth victim when he was paroled three years later. Wayne Horton committed the first of his five known murders at age 16. In New Jersey, 16-year-old Daryl Hayes was convicted of two murders and four sexual assaults. Georgia's Clinton Bankston murdered five victims during his sixteenth year. Notorious 17-year-old killers include: Dwain Little (first of five victims); Sean Sellers, Carl Richardson, Dwayne Wright, and William Heirens (three victims each); Juergen Bartsch (four killed); and Leslie Torres (six slain in New York). Karl Warner was a San Jose high school student when he hacked two female classmates to death. Four hundred miles to the

south, in Santa Barbara, Thor Christiansen murdered three women while still in his late teens. Richard Biegenwald committed his first murder at age 18, in New Jersey; Thomas Braun and Leonard Maine were the same age when they shot and killed three victims in Washington state. Another 18-year-old, cannibal-slayer Reginald Oates, mutilated four young boys and assaulted several other children before his arrest in 1968. Hoosier Calvin Perry, also 18, reportedly confessed four murders before he hanged himself in jail. Strangler Kenneth Bianchi boasted to friends of his first murder at age 20; two years later, he was suspected of killing three girls around Rochester, New York.

Theft, hoarding, and gorging are more symptoms which persist with serial killers through adolescence and adulthood. Eighty-one percent of the FBI's limited sampling confessed to stealing in their teens, with 56% continuing the larcenous behavior as adults. Reports of eating disorders were remarkably consistent, including 36% in adolescence and 35% in adulthood.[17] Peter Manuel, Eric Cooke, and Henry Lucas all tried their hands at burglary before they made their mark as repeat killers; Lucas and Charles Manson also dabbled in auto theft on the side. Harvey Glatman graduated from purse-snatching to a robbery conviction years before he started strangling models in Los Angeles. Arthur Bishop preferred the less violent art of embezzling cash from his employers. In New York, Marybeth Tinning stole aimlessly and without reason — cash from a relative's purse, the treasury of her bowling club, and the "Resusci baby" from a neighborhood ambulance crew.

Self-destructive behavior actually escalates among serial killers with advancing age. Among FBI test subjects, 21% confessed incidents of adolescent self-mutilation, while 32% deliberately scarred themselves as adults.[18] In Wyoming, Wayne Nance heated a coat-hanger to brand himself with Satanic symbols. Nurse Bobbie Sue Terrell was twice hospitalized after slashing her own vagina; on yet another occasion, she stabbed herself in the side to substantiate pointless claims of a false robbery. In South Carolina, Mitchell Sims liked to call himself a "human ashtray," grinding out cigarettes on his bare chest. In addition to the self-mutilators, various serial slayers have taken the ultimate step of committing or attempting suicide. Repeat killers Gary Robbins, Michael Player, Fernando Cota, Carmelo DeJesus, Robert Clements, Fritz Klenner, Norbert Poehlke, Barry Prudom, and Joe Ball killed themselves in lieu of submitting to arrest; others — including Mack Edwards, Leonard Lake, Antone Costa, Charles

Hatcher, Robert Succo, Gloria Tannenbaum, Richard Macek, Karl Denke, Henri Gerard, Georg Grossman, and Calvin Perry — committed suicide in custody. Unsuccessful suicide attempts have been recorded for Henry Lucas, Donald Harvey, Eddie Cole, Richard Biegenwald, Gary Heidnik, and Joe Kallinger, among others.

Drug addict Enrique Estrada bludgeoned elderly women to death in their southern California homes. *(Credit: FBI)*

Alcohol and drug abuse among sociopaths predictably increase with age, and many serial murders are fueled by artificial stimulants. Ted Bundy was a chronic drunk who joined Alcoholics Anonymous on death row. Eddie Cole committed all his adult murders under the influence of alcohol, several times blacking out in the process and waking hours later, with another female corpse in his bed. John Gacy habitually drank before trolling for victims; in prison, alcohol produced such a violent reaction from Gacy that a straitjacket was used to prevent self-injury. Herbert Mullin began sampling hallucinogenic drugs in his teens. Random killers Carlton Gary, Leslie Torres, and Richard Ramirez were all addicted to cocaine at the time they committed their crimes. Bobby Joe Long was a frequent user of LSD and marijuana in the 1970s; a decade later, he admitted drinking heavily while stalking Florida prostitutes. Rape-slayer James Ruzicka began abusing drugs at age

nine. In Massachusetts, Antone Costa was an outspoken disciple of the 1960s drug culture; three of his dismembered female victims were unearthed from shallow graves in his rural marijuana garden. Poisoner Velma Barfield was hopelessly addicted to prescription drugs, four times hospitalized for accidental overdoses in the 1970s. Charles Manson's bizarre "family" elevated drugs and rock music to the status of a twisted religion. Other notorious serial killers identified as alcoholics and/or drug addicts include Steven Catlin, Lawrence Bittaker, Patrick Mackay, Richard Chase, Hoyt Cobb, Harrison Graham, Enrique Estrada, Steven Hurd, Calvin Jackson, and Henry Lee Lucas.

Regardless of their sobriety, a majority of serial killers are driven by the need to dominate and control others, thus compensating for the pent-up frustration, rejection, and fear in their own early lives. Different sociopaths express the yearning for power in various ways. Some join the military, while others collect powerful cars. A significant number gravitate toward careers in law enforcement. Some who fail to make the cut as cops surround themselves with guns and paramilitary hardware, revering the century's ultimate authority figures from Nazi Germany.

While drawn to military service for the uniforms and weapons, sociopaths often founder on the jagged rocks of discipline. Among the FBI's sampling of sex-killers, 58% had been dishonorably discharged from the military, with 29% facing criminal charges while still in uniform.[19] Lady-killer Lloyd Greeson is an extreme example: convicted of crimes while serving with the Canadian army in World War II, he was later dishonorably discharged from both the U.S. Army and Marine Corps between 1946 and 1950. Bela Kiss sought refuge from murder charges in the Hungarian army, later deserting to join the French Foreign Legion. Mark Smith launched his career in sexual homicide while serving with the army in Europe. Gary Heidnik and Jerry Brudos were each discharged from service on the grounds of mental instability. James Hall was drafted by the Navy in 1943, then dishonorably discharged after eight weeks of basic training. Random killers Westley Dodd, Martin Kipp, Gary Rardon, Hugh Morse, Gary Schaefer, Richard Tingler, and Eddie Cole were all stripped of their uniforms following criminal convictions on charges ranging from theft to child-molesting and manslaughter. Death nurse Robert Diaz was discharged from the Marine Corps after going AWOL for six weeks. Joseph Christopher joined the army after a series of racist murders in New York; a short time later, he was jailed for stabbing a black GI at Ft. Benning, Georgia. Veterans of military service who went on to kill repeatedly include William Bonin, Patrick Kearney, Leonard Lake, Henri Landru, Severin Klosovski, Michael Lupo, Barry Prudom, Dennis Nilsen, Charles Brown, Albert DeSalvo, Billy Waldon, and Japan's Kodaira Yoshio. Others launched their murder sprees while still in uniform, including John Joubert, Gordon Cummins, Eric Craig, Anthony McKnight, Thomas Rath, William Hance, Edward Leonski, George York and James Latham, Ronald Gray, Bruce Shreeves, and the French thrill killers, Moujot and Janin. Larry Eyler never got around to enlisting, but he enjoyed donning Marine Corps paraphernalia and boasting of combat service in Vietnam.

Police work, with its trappings of violence and authority, exerts an irresistible attraction for some sociopaths. Dennis Nilsen, England's record-holding serial killer, progressed from service as a London patrolman through a string of civil service jobs. In Florida, Gerard Schaefer — convicted of two murders and suspected of 32 more — was an ex-sheriff's deputy. David Rogers, Matthew Quintiliano, Stephen Smith, Manny Pardo, Jack Scully, and Norbert Poehlke all committed their murders while still employed as policemen; in the cases of Smith, Pardo, and Scully, the murders were linked to rabid vigilantism. Gennadiy Mikhasevich, strangler of 33 women in the Soviet Union, worked part-time as a volunteer patrolman. John Gacy, Fritz Haarmann, and the Hillside stranglers all posed as detectives on occasion, to entrap their victims. Horace Kelly and Kenneth Bianchi fell short of recruiting standards, taking alternate jobs as security guards. Ed Kemper's violent record kept him out of uniform, but he enjoyed buying drinks for off-duty detectives, gleaning details of their progress on outstanding murders — including his own.

Hitler's Germany stands as a leading example of authoritarian violence in modern times, and various random killers are drawn to the Nazi mystique like moths to a flame. When William Heirens was arrested in Chicago, shortly after World War II, police seized glossy photographs of Nazi leaders along with numerous guns and stolen articles of women's underwear. In Miami, killer-cop Manny Pardo referred to Jews as "parasitic leeches." Joseph Franklin found the Ku Klux Klan and the American Nazi Party too moderate for his taste, dispensing with formal organizations to launch his own one-man war against blacks and Jews. Cleveland transvestite Frank Spisak was another self-styled "Aryan warrior," gunning down victims on the basis of their skin color or supposed Judaism. Ian Brady studied German to enjoy Hitler's original *Mein Kampf*, dressing his girlfriend/accomplice in black leather and dubbing her "Myra Hess." After spending several adolescent years in Germany, Richard Clarey fantasized Nazi voices commanding him to slay Americans. In England, Patrick Mackay imagined himself as a fascist world dictator, "Franklin Bollvolt the First." New Jersey slayer Robert Zarinsky vandalized Jewish cemeteries while referring to himself as "Lieutenant Schaefer, leader of the American Republican Army." Fritz Klenner, Leonard Lake, and Charles Ng were creatures of the far-right "survivalist" movement, stockpiling weapons and corresponding sporadically with neo-Nazi cultists. California's Danny Figueroa carried his obsession with "Rambo" paramilitary trappings to a lethal extreme in 1986, when he stalked and killed five strangers in as many weeks.

A correlative of racial bigotry in psychopaths is hyperreligiosity. Already divorced from reality in varying degrees, some random killers draw their strength from gods — or demons — who endorse their random violence in the service of a "holy cause." Earle Nelson never traveled far without his Bible, quoting passages from memory to lull the female victims he would later rape and strangle. James and Susan Carson seized upon a passage from the Book of Exodus to justify the deaths of strangers they mistook for "witches." In Stamford, Connecticut, Benjamin Miller was expelled by a local congregation for his outspoken fanaticism; months later, as a self-ordained street preacher, he "carried the message" to black prostitutes by strangling five with their own brassieres. Velma Barfield attended services three times a week, taking off work to volunteer time in the church office, meanwhile skillfully concealing her own drug addiction and murders of at least five persons. A viewing of *The Ten Commandments* inspired Heinrich Pommerenke to murder ten women and rape 20 others, as punishment for their "sins." In New York, convicted kidnapper Devernon LeGrand founded his own church, impregnating numerous "nuns" and dismembering those who displeased him. Charles Manson could never seem to decide if he was Satan, Jesus Christ, or a peculiar hybrid of the two. The list of self-styled witches, sorcerers, and Satanists who killed and killed again in modern times includes Sean Sellers, Antone Costa, Bobby Maxwell, Richard Ramirez, Michael Swango, Wayne Nance, Donald Harvey, Marti Enriqueta, Anjette Lyles, Robert

Berdella, and Vaughn Greenwood. In custody, such murderers as Susan Atkins, Henry Lucas, and Charles "Tex" Watson often demonstrate a tendency to "find the Lord," although it may be argued that their born-again conversions are a ploy to win the sympathy of conservative parole boards.

In terms of racial or religious violence, random killers sometimes draw their inspiration from established, semi-secret cults or fringe political societies. The First Amendment's blanket coverage of propaganda and religious dogma has encouraged the proliferation of bizarre, fanatic sects and parties in America for some 200 years. The vast majority are satisfied to wring their members dry of cash and fade away, but others actively contribute to the atmosphere of what some sociologists have termed a "counterculture," fueling violent fantasies with doctrines that support a twisted individual's prerogative to torture, rape, and murder on a whim.

Where racial hatred is concerned, America has well-established outlets in the form of white supremacist and neo-Nazi cells from coast to coast. The Ku Klux Klan has been providing violent misfits with a place to hide since 1866, and in the years since World War II, at least 100 Nazi splinter factions have been publicly identified. Nomadic slayer Joseph Franklin spent years absorbing racist propaganda from the KKK, American Nazis, and the lunatic National States Rights Party before he murdered 15 "racial traitors" in the 1970s. Frank Spisak was on his way to death row when the Idaho-based Social Nationalist Aryan People's Party stepped forward to claim him as a dues-paying lieutenant; the party's leader, ex-convict Keith Gilbert, announced that Spisak was "acting under direct orders of the party" when he murdered three victims in Cleveland. The orders, according to Gilbert: "Kill niggers until the last one is dead."[20]

Nor are racist fanatics exclusively white. In 1973, the California State Attorney General's office compiled a list of 45 murders, the victims exclusively white, committed by members of a Black Muslim splinter group dubbed the Death Angels. Prospective members earned their "wings" by killing four white children, five women, or nine men, documenting their crimes with Polaroid photographs. Eight would-be members of the cult were jailed in April 1974, linked to San Francisco's six-month string of "Zebra murders," with five defendants convicted at trial and sentenced to life imprisonment. An estimated 15 Angels managed to escape the dragnet and presumably remain at large. A decade later,

several members of the all-black Hebrew Israelites — who also called themselves Death Angels, in what may or may not be coincidence — were charged with 14 murders, most of them involving whites whose ears were severed as an offering to the leader of the cult. And in the suburbs of Chicago, angry blacks returned from Vietnam to organize a terroristic gang they called De Mau Mau, named for Kenya's revolutionary movement of the 1950s, gunning down Caucasian targets in their homes and on the street.

A rather different cult phenomenon has troubled the American Southwest, where excommunicated Mormons clinging to the doctrine of polygamy were organized and armed by "prophet" Ervil LeBaron. Christening themselves the Lambs of God, LeBaron's followers preached "blood atonement," defined as the execution of defecting cultists, and one of the first victims was LeBaron's own daughter, strangled in 1962. LeBaron died in prison 19 years later, serving time for the murder of rival polygamist leader Rulon Alred, but his disciples linger on, blamed for at least 22 murders and numerous other crimes spanning several states. As recently as 1988, LeBaronites shot and killed three Texas victims in a single afternoon of violence; one of the dead was an eight-year-old girl.

In theory, the ideal "religion" for a homicidal psychopath would champion self-interest over group responsibility, exalting selfish, carnal whims above the rights of others. Such a doctrine is, in fact, embodied in the magical pursuit of the occult. Regardless of the label — Wicca, voodoo, Santeria, Satanism, "black" or "white" — the search for "hidden knowledge" stresses one practitioner's or one cult's quest for power and advancement, with protection from (or the destruction of) perceived opponents, be they Christians, law enforcement officers, or rival wizards.

Organized Satanic groups, especially, are quick to draw the public line at criminal behavior, loudly disavowing those who cite their published literature as inspiration for a spree of human sacrifice. Founded on the egocentric doctrines of Aleister Crowley — "Do what thou wilt shall be the whole of the law" — the Church of Satan and its several splinter factions invite all comers to indulge their deepest, darkest desires... within reason, of course. It is convenient to dismiss "misguided" Satanists who maim and kill, much as the Ku Klux Klan is prone to disavow its members jailed for lynching, but responsibility is not so easily erased. *The Satanic Bible* tells its readers that "the most simplified description of Satanic belief is: *indulgence instead of abstinence.*"[21] If this is not enough, we are informed that "Satan stands for vengeance, instead of turning the other cheek," and "Satan represents all of the so-called sins, as they all lead to physical, mental, or emotional gratification."[22] Bearing in mind that those "so-called sins" include murder, some converts to Satanism understandably have problems grasping the "symbolic" aspects of a special chapter "On the Choice of a Human Sacrifice."[23]

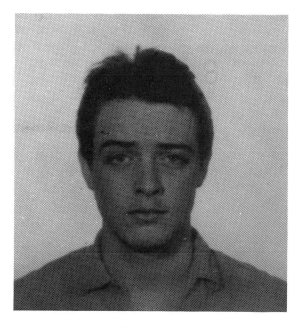

Bobby Beausoleil dabbled in Satanism before attaching himself to the Charles Manson "family." *(Credit: Los Angeles County Sheriff's Dept.)*

Since the mid-1960s, six percent of America's reported serial murders have involved practitioners of Satanism or ritual magic. Charles Manson's "family" is a prime example, drawing at least two members — convicted killers Susan Atkins and Bobby Beausoleil — directly from the Church of Satan, freely mingling with other Satanic cults that included the Ordo Templi Orientis and the sinister Process Church of Final Judgment. Another offshoot of The Process, calling itself the Four P Movement — a name apparently derived from the Process "power sign," consisting of four P's arranged in the shape of a swastika — has been linked with homicides in several states; David Berkowitz, New York's "Son of Sam," is a self-described ex-member of the cult, and authorities are pressing their search for

Satanic accomplices in his murder spree. Chicago authorities cracked a vicious Satanic coven in 1982, jailing four young men who made a habit of abducting, raping, and murdering women, afterward eating the flesh from their breasts. In Massachusetts, Carl Drew kept his stable of prostitutes in line with Satanic mumbo-jumbo, sacrificing those who offended him and raping their headless bodies while the other "worshippers" looked on. Houston's Harold Smith collected teenage disciples, leading them on a rampage of torture and murder in 1985. Four years later, the world was stunned by news from Matamoros, Mexico, where drug-dealing cultists had slaughtered at least 15 victims, quaffing the blood in an effort to make themselves bulletproof. Similar mutilation-slayings have been reported from the Florida keys, where federal officers suspect that killer cults are dealing in cocaine.

It should not be supposed that random killers universally progress from troubled childhoods into homicide without a second thought. For many, their pathology is manifest in suicide attempts, self-mutilation, or direct pleas for help from the authorities. Between 1961 and 1970, Eddie Cole repeatedly committed himself to mental hospitals in California and Nevada, confessing his urge to rape and strangle women; in each case, he was dismissed by psychiatrists as a hoaxer, no danger to society at large. After the trauma that shattered his skull, Bobby Joe Long spent years describing his new, uncontrollable sexual urges for incredulous doctors. Repeat killers Charles Manson, Henry Lucas, Carlton Gary, and Edmund Kemper were all freed from custody over their own objections, parole authorities flying in the face of stated intentions to commit more violent crimes.

When psychopathic killers meet the modern psychiatric system, they are frequently ignored, misdiagnosed, and freed to kill again. They learn to manipulate doctors and tests, donning the mask of sanity time and again to deceive professional therapists and wriggle out of custody. Joseph Baldi spent ten years in various mental institutions before he was jailed for multiple murder in New York. Christopher Wilder survived years of therapy and shock treatments with his homicidal urges intact. Bobbie Sue Terrell was committed for psychiatric observation after repeatedly stabbing herself. German vampire-slayer Fritz Haarmann spent six months in an asylum before he escaped. Joseph Kallinger was committed twice, following arrests for arson and felony child abuse. Gary Taylor spent 11 years in therapy for shooting and assaulting women on the street. James Grace was committed by his mother, then released by psychiatrists after brief observation. Herbert Mullin, Patrick Mackay, Steven Judy, and Anthony Spencer were all familiar with asylums in their teens. Henry Lucas, Eddie Cole, Lawrence Bittaker, Roy Norris, and Harvey Glatman were each treated by psychiatrists in prison, without effect. Repeat slayers Gary Walker, Joseph Bryan, Gary Heidnik, and Jerry Brudos were all discharged from military service on grounds of mental instability; subsequent treatments in civilian life failed to divert them from slaughtering women at random. Psychiatrists twice observed Albert Fish without detecting his appetite for human flesh. Westley Dodd and James Ruzicka conned their way through court-ordered treatment for mentally disordered sex offenders. William Day and Winford Stokes each escaped from mental institutions with the help of misguided staff members. Serial slayers William Steelman, Erno Soto, Robert Liberty, Arthur Goode, and Jeffrey Jones were all committed for treatment at various times, without result. Albert DeSalvo was cooling his heels in a Massachusetts state hospital when he confessed 13 murders in Boston.

For all its failings — overcrowded jails and underfunded mental institutions; teachers, counselors, and social workers short on crucial expertise; a legal system that appears to favor violent criminals instead of victims and their families — society is not the only culprit in our modern murder epidemic. Ultimately, every random killer is responsible for his or her atrocious crimes, and once these predators have tasted blood — in some cases literally — there is no turning back short of death or prison. And, as we shall see, confinement in a cage is not enough for some.

The years of childhood trauma, torment, and humiliation call for a response in kind, producing specimens who look at human life and death almost as aliens, a breed apart. Behind the mask of sanity, their brooding rage awaits an opportunity to surface, granting them at least a temporary respite from frustration, anger, and contempt for all mankind.

But it is never good enough.

Inevitably, when the pain and rage return, the hunger follows.

There is always one more victim waiting, somewhere down the road.

CHAPTER 3

Voices of Death

A generation of Americans has grown accustomed to the cinematic image of the hulking psychopath, most often silent, sometimes wheezing through a hockey mask or growling like an animal as he pursues his human prey. It may be something of a shock, therefore, to realize that random murderers are neither mute nor incoherent. While their grammar may not always pass inspection, they have much to tell us... if we dare to listen. Hear the murderers among us as they speak.[1]

On life...

That's the way I grew up when I was a child — watching my mom have sexual acts. She wouldn't go into different rooms, she'd make sure I was in the room before she started anything, and she would do it deliberately to make me watch her, you know. I got so I hated it. I'd even leave the house and go out and hide in the woods and wouldn't even go home. And when I'd go home, I'd get beat for not coming home. I don't blame Mom for what she done. I don't blame her for that. It's the idea of the way she done it. I don't think any child out there should be brought up in that type of environment. In the past, I've hated it. It's just inside hate, and I can't get away from it.

Henry Lee Lucas

I can't remember being happy at any time since I was born.

Hugh Morse

I haven't blocked out the past. I wouldn't trade the person I am, or what I've done — or the people I've known — for anything. So I do think about it. And at times it's a rather mellow trip to lay back and remember.

Ted Bundy

Theodore Bundy, confessed slayer of 30 women, regarded murder as "a rather mellow trip." *(Credit: FBI)*

There is no doubt in my mind that a demon has been living in me since birth. All my life I've been wild, violent, temporal, mean, cruel, sadistic, acting with irrational anger and destructive. When I was a child I often had real and quite severe nightmares. I saw monsters often and I heard them, which often caused me to go screaming hysterically into my parents' room. Now I know they were real — just like now. I've been tormented all my life by them, never having peace or quiet.

David Berkowitz

My rebellion against the world started that first day in school, and from that first day I became rebellious. I had stayed in my rebellious mood even to this day. Why had I become rebellious against the world and the human race? Because that first day in school I was being made fun at, picked on, laughed at. Why were they making fun of me? My speech for one thing, and the other was my legs. I was a little bowlegged. In those younger years of my life I had built up a hate that was as hard as iron and when people tease, make fun of and laugh at a little youngster in her or his early childhood, that little youngster is not going to forget it. I wouldn't deny I was like a hound prowling for fights, quarreling, and doing wild things and placing everyone among my enemies. Kids picking on me and not having a thing to do with me caused me to have black moods. At least that's what I call them, 'cause most of the time, I would just sit in one place and stay motionless in a gloomy manner and it was obvious that there was no reasoning with me when in one of my black moods. Boys and girls that I knew didn't bother me while I was in my motionless and gloomy manner, they would just let me be and stay in my black mood, and even to this day I still have them melancholy moods.

Charles Starkweather

I have been told that my stepfather and mother died in Aurora, Missouri. I left home when a child. They used to task me to do work; in other words, they used to give me a task and they would never let me go out anywhere. I had to stay home as long as four months without being off the place and never visiting any of the other little neighborhood boys. There was a church meeting going on and all the children were going to the meeting. The folks never went to church, but I had been going to Sunday School at the school house. It was the first time in my life that I disobeyed my mother that I know of. I pleaded with her an hour upon Friday morning to let me go to church that night. The church was near our school house. I had been invited by one of the neighbor-

hood boys. There were two other boys that lived near us that came by my home. But she would not let me go as I pleaded with her at least an hour, and the last words I told her was that I was going if I was killed for it. I must have been 12 years old.

I went to church and I came back that night and we had a fireplace and they slept near the fireplace in one big room, and they told me that if I went to bed they would whip me to death and I sat up and began to get cold. There was quite a snow storm during the night. They wouldn't let me get by the fireplace. At last, they said if I would go to bed they wouldn't whip me until morning. Before breakfast my mother went around where she had a stick hid, and when I saw her make for it I made for the door and ran from home.

James Watson

I have no feelings, ladies and gentlemen. My heart is a block of ice.

Dennis Webb

He was a very good man, Mr. Sheinfeld, to me. I do not blame him for anything, only blame myself, and what Mr. Sheinfeld said was true. I was taking awful risks and I was certain to bring disgrace on myself and more misery to my family.

But I don't know, I couldn't see it as clear as some people who have had a better life. Mr. Sheinfeld, although he was a very good man, was the same as the guys from the probation and parole office. He was on the inside of something I'd been on the outside of all my life. Oh, I know that guys who have come from bad homes have made good, it's not that, it's just my own personal reaction to what my bad home was like — and it's this thing, this urge that I had — and now I see that it's true and that I've had it all my life.

You can believe it or not, but I was known as a good kid by everybody around the Chelsea neighborhood — except the cops, who saw me as trouble, mostly, I guess. You can go over to Chelsea now and find some people who knew me and see if they don't tell you: "Yes, Albert was a nice, polite boy." And few of them will believe that Albert DeSalvo is what he says he is: the Boston Strangler.

Albert DeSalvo

I felt close to the land and to all things animated upon it. I would be repelled by the shooting of crows and rabbits. A rabbit, to me, was one of the least offensive creatures which hopped about. I was horrified by the sight of rabbits infected with myxomatosis. I would kill them as they staggered blindly about with swollen eyes and dying of starvation. Adults told me that there were a lot of pests around that had to be destroyed. I was not allowed to have any pets, save once a white rabbit which I had to keep in a very small hutch with a wire window. It died in winter. I was accused by my parent and stepparent of starving it to death. This as a child hurt me deeply. My mother was very house-proud and I suppose she could not tolerate animal hair around the house on the carpet. I got the feeling sometimes that she didn't want me around on her carpet either.

Dennis Nilsen

When five years old I was placed by my mother in St. John's Orphanage, Washington, D.C. There I learned to lie, beg, steal, and saw a lot of things a child of seven should not see. Misery leads to crime. I saw so many boys whipped it took root in my head. I have many hundreds of times whipped and tortured myself, as marks on my behind will show.

Albert Fish

There is no happiness without tears, no life without death. Beware! I am going to make you cry.

Lucian Staniak

On sex...

I stopped the car. Got out and went to the bathroom. It seems to me that she followed me. I went to the bathroom, and I know she came up behind me, and that's when I lose all control. Changed it to Dorothy, and it just changes to the cemetery and just changes to the — I get very scared that she is going to hurt me again and that I'm not going to let that happen, and then I do the things to her that Dorothy did to me. It's — it's more than just that — it's not — it's just — everything. I lose control over everything. I mean everything just changes. It's not that I can start to breathe real fast and I get a rush or anything like that. It's just the whole scene changes and everything is different. I see myself getting hurt by my sister. I see that whole thing happening to me again, and this time I'm not going to let it happen like that. I make her lay down. I think she's on her belly. And I just do the same things to her that she — my sister — that she did to me. You see, it's not — it's not the little girl waiting there, I mean it's actually my sister that's there and that, I'm gonna, and I'm forcing her to do those things to me, just like she forced me to do them to her. And then I spanked her. It was all over and I spanked her.

Gary Schaefer

Sex is one of my downfalls. I get sex any way I can get it. If I have to force somebody to do it, I do. If I don't, I don't. I rape them; I've done that. I've killed animals to have sex with them, and I've had sex with them while they're alive.

Henry Lee Lucas

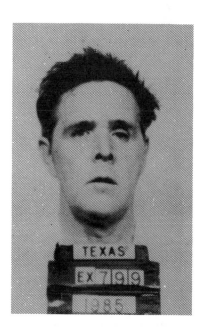

Henry Lee Lucas — "I've killed animals to have sex with them, and I've had sex with them while they're alive." *(Credit: Texas Dept. of Corrections)*

Q: *Do you know when you get up from your room to go out, when you have surrendered to the urge to go out, what you are going out for?*

A: *Yes, they always were burglaries.*

Q: *Would you prowl around the streets in a state of suppressed sexual excitement looking for an entrance?*

A: *It wasn't that way. Maybe it's not excitement. It feels like it's further away in the distance. You don't seem to have any feeling of anything.*

Q: *When you saw the window you made a decision? You went into a state of sexual excitement?*

A: *Yes, there was sexual excitement. I always had an erection.*

Q: *You told me the erection was sufficiently complete to interfere with your bodily movements. An emission never occurred before you went into the windows?*

A: *No, I am quite sure.*

Q: *It was the act of going through the window?*

A: *Yes.*

Q: *Sometimes you had an emission and sometimes not, but I think you must pretty often have had an emission; otherwise, you would have done more burglaries?*

A: *Sometimes there were oodles of them done a night; sometimes four a night.*

Q: *You wouldn't have an emission on each of the four?*

A: *No.*

Q: *But you did before the four were completed?*

A: *Most likely.*

Interrogation of William Heirens

When this certain thing comes on me, it's a very immediate thing. I get up in the morning and I get this feeling and I tell my wife I'm going out on my job, but I'm not. I could always get out of the house because of my work and the kind of work I was doing — for a construction company — kept me out a lot anyway on the streets.

I never went for no specific woman — what I had in mind was a picture of Woman, an image, you understand me? — not of anyone I knew, but just of all they had and what I needed to have the sex thing with them, you understand me?

Albert DeSalvo

What I did is not such a great harm, with all these surplus women nowadays. Anyway, I had a good time.

Rudolf Pleil

I wish there was a clear view on motive, conventionally speaking, then I could come to grips with the problem. Sex maniac? I suppose I could lie and say they refused to have sex and I killed them. No, that's not true. Robbery? No, impossible. Sadism? No, the thought of receiving or inflicting pain is abhorrent to me. Necrophiliac? The thought of sex within the sacredness or a dead body turns me right off.

Dennis Nilsen

I couldn't follow through with the male end of the responsibility, so my fantasies became... if I killed them,

you know, they couldn't reject me as a man. It was more or less making a doll out of a human being, and carrying out my fantasies with a doll, a living human doll. I suppose I could have been doing this with men, but that always posed more of a threat. They weren't nearly as vulnerable. Plus, like in the case where sex is involved, or the thrill of having a woman around, alive and dead, wasn't there with a man.

Edmund Kemper

In April or May of 1933, my son Henry drove me in his car to New Haven, Connecticut, to see a widow who had an ad in a friendship magazine for a husband. When we got there, she was gone to town. During these four years I wrote to about 20 widows who claimed to have money, but it was all hot air. I write as a habit — just can't seem to stop. A few months after I done that deed, I shoved five needles into my belly, legs, hip. An X-ray will show them. Three weeks ago I spilled alcohol on my behind and then lit a match. I can hardly sit still now.

Albert Fish

Q: *Would you describe what sort of feeling you have when you rape someone?*

A: *I don't know. Uh, nervous feeling, uh, I get excited. Uh, I just start speeding.*

Q: *Pardon?*

A: *I just start speeding. I get, get a high feeling.*

Q: *Does it affect your speech?*

A: *Yes, I get to stuttering. I get to talking real fast, uh, I get real nervous.*

Q: *Could you describe it as something that's very exciting to you?*

A: *Yeah.*

Q: *Are you able to control what you're doing once you get started in this type of behavior?*

A: *Once that gets started, there, there could be an army standing around and I don't think I'd stop.*

Q: *Have you felt the same way with other girls you raped?*

A: *Yes.*

Interrogation of Steven Judy

Yes, I went out with girls. Some were mild dates with nice Christian girls, but most of the girls I went out with were either the gibberty-gibbet type, that used too much makeup and dressed in expensive clothes, or they were the harlot type, that weren't hard to get a date with and were easy to get along with. I had my fights that seem to happen every other day, and like almost everybody, I had my dreams of things I wanted. But of all the dreams, fights, and women, none of them ever seemed to fit in this world.

Charles Starkweather

Q: *Did you ever have the thought that you would have liked to remove or cut off your penis and preferred to have it in the shape of the sexual organs of a woman?*

A: *Well, part of that is true.*

Q: *What part of that is true?*

A: *That like removing part of myself.*

Q: *Does that part mean your penis?*

A: *Well, that doesn't seem like. Well, that seems like that was before, when I was young.*

Q: *Do you ever have any recollection, Eddie, of taking any of those female parts, the vagina specifically, and holding it over your penis to cover the penis?*

A: *I believe that's true.*

Q: *You recall doing that with the vaginas of the bodies of other women?*

A: *That I believe I do remember; that's right.*

Q: *Was there a resemblance in some of these faces to that of your mother?*

A: *I believe there was some.*

Q: *How about the face? Have you ever placed the faces over your own face?*

A: *That I did. I'm pretty sure of that. The parts sort of like eyes — those parts of a head. There should be some parts of just a head, and I suppose there would be about two or three.*

Q: *Well, do you remember how you held the faces over your own face?*

A: *I believe there was a cord here.*

Q: *Do you think you would wear the face over a prolonged time?*

A: *Not too long; I had other things to do. Maybe about an hour or so.*

Q: *Would you ever put a pair of women's panties over your body and then put some of these vaginas over your penis?*

A: *That could be.*

Interrogation of Edward Gein

I don't have any feelings toward an individual's rights. Rape is the ultimate.

David Carpenter

Our humor is unusual. I wonder why others don't see the necrophilic aspects of existence as we do?

Veronica Compton to Douglas Clark

I hate a bitchy chick.

Gerald Stano

Gerald Stano murdered 41 "bitchy chicks" between Pennsylvania and Florida, beginning at age 18. *(Credit: Florida Dept. of Corrections)*

Anybody who knew me before the accident and knows me now would say that it's like I was two different people. I knew there was something wrong with my head when I was in the hospital after the accident. I was just out of it for months and then, while still in the hospital, I started thinking about sex. That's all I could think about day and night. I thought about it with my wife, with people I knew from before. It started driving me crazy.

I tried to tell the doctors at the hospital that there was something still wrong with me. I couldn't get these thoughts of sex out of my mind, and Cindy and I had gone from having sex two or three times a week to at least two times a day. And I was still masturbating to get relief. I thought about having sex with just about every girl I met or got to know.

Bobby Joe Long

Q: *Well, when you stick an instrument up a person's vagina or you cut a person or bite a person, that seems to indicate a certain amount of rage. That's getting even or something. What would it be? I mean, that's not normal sexual gratification. Can you dig a bit deeper?*

A: *Well, we've said... when we... we're not talking about normal sexual gratification. We're not talking about normal anything, okay? Certainly it's abnormal. You're not suggesting and I'm not suggesting, certainly, that it's normal.*

Interrogation of Ted Bundy

On murder...

Cannibal-slayer Ottis Toole — "Remember one time I said I wanted me some ribs." *(Credit: Florida Dept. of Corrections)*

HL: *See, we got so many of them, Ottis. We got to turn up the bodies. Now this boy and the girl, I don't know anything about.*

OT: *Well, maybe that's the two I killed my own self. Just like that Mexican that wasn't going to let me out of the house. I took an ax and chopped him all up. What made me... I been meaning to ask you. That time when I cooked some of those people. Why'd I do that?*

HL: *I think it was just the hands doing it. I know a lot of the things we done, in human sight, are impossible to believe.*

OT: *When we took 'em out and cut 'em up... remember one time I said I wanted me some ribs? Did that make me a cannibal?*

HL: *You wasn't a cannibal. It's the force of the devil, something forced on us that we can't change. There's no reason denying what we become. We know what we are. Ottis, you know everything you say is going on tape here.*

OT: *I know.*

HL: *And will be used in court against you.*

OT: *I know.*

HL: *Personally, I'd have preferred you not talk about that. I don't want people to look at us as that kind of person.*

OT: *Remember how I liked to pour some blood out of them?*

Henry Lee Lucas and Ottis Toole

She picked me up, really, I didn't go after her. She was a whore. She manipulated men, and she wanted to manipulate me. Once I had her in the car, I tied her up and raped her. Then I strangled her and dumped her body alongside the highway. I knew what I was doing, but I just couldn't stop myself. I hated her. I hated her from the time she picked me up, but I didn't plan to murder her. I don't even think I planned to rape her either. She was just sitting there in the front seat of the car, and I grabbed her, covered her mouth, and tied her up. I was sick, and I knew I was in real trouble. Then a few days later I met the Simms girl, and it was the same thing all over again. She was a barfly. She really picked me up, and I just turned on her in the car.

Bobby Joe Long

I have a problem. I'm a cannibal.

Stanley Baker

I love young 'uns. I don't know why I done what I done. The way I done it, I seen it done on TV shows. I had my own way, though. Simple and easy. No one would ever hear them scream. I did it like, you know, simple, but it weren't simple. I pulled a blanket over the face, just the right amount for the little 'un. A voice would say to me, "Kill the baby," over and over, very slow, and then I would come to and realize what happened.

Christine Falling

Every man has his passion. Some prefer whist. I prefer killing people.

Rudolf Pleil

It's an uncontrollable urge that builds and builds over a period of weeks until I have to kill.

Charles Hatcher

When I killed the cop, it made me feel real good inside. The sensation was something that made me feel elated to the point of happiness, for I achieved in putting to death one of my tormentors. After killing him, I wanted to kill some more. I needed money, so I drove the dead cop's police car into Mobile. I hid the car, and I waited in the Greyhound depot until the banks opened. I got a cab and had him drive me to a bank and I instructed him to wait. The crowd wasn't too big, so I robbed the bank. After that, I had this cab drive me into New Orleans, where I planned to take a plane to California to kill my older brother and also kill them cops that hurt me. But I was caught in Moss Point and while being guarded by two cops, I broke and ran, daring them to shoot me. They fired three shots at me but missed. I was caught a few minutes later and taken to jail, where I am now. For what I've done, I feel no regret or sorrow whatsoever, and if I die I'll know I was perfectly right in killing that cop. I honestly believe I've committed no wrong.

Gerald Albert Gallego

She was a hooker. Angelo went and picked her up. I was waiting on the street. He drove her around to where I was. I got in the car. We got on the freeway. I fucked her and killed her. We dumped her body off and that was it. Nothing to it.

Kenneth Bianchi

If I gave a shit about the parents, I wouldn't have killed the kid.

Clifford Olson

He was a kid. It was all there in front of him, his whole life, sex, fun, all of it. Why should he have it when I never did? I took it all away from him. Besides, I never killed a kid before. I wanted to see how it felt.

Stephen Nash

I figure, well, if I ever get a chance to kill somebody, I'll just kill them, even if it was just an old man.

Joseph Danks

Q: *When did you learn that woman was dead?*

A: *Well, when I read it in the paper. I think it was the next day I read it in the paper.*

Q: *You had never known the woman before?*

A: *No.*

Q: *Did you ever tell anybody that you had killed that woman?*

A: *No.*

Q: *You kept it a secret until this time, that is until your present arrest?*

A: *Yes.*

Q: *Did you attempt to have any sexual relations whatever with her?*

A: *No.*

Q: *Did you have any sexual satisfaction from that crime?*

A: *Just like when I go into the open doors, I get sexual satisfaction just from doing that.*

Q: *Did you wash her body after you cut her?*

A: *No.*

Q: *What did you say?*

A: *I don't know. I am quite sure I didn't.*

Q: *Could you have washed it and not remember it?*

A: *Yes.*

Interrogation of William Heirens

She opened the door and she turned around to take me to the kitchen to let me see what had to be done. As she walked to the kitchen, her back was to me. I hit her right on the back of the head with the pipe. She went down.

Now, let me say this, this was terrible and I don't like talking about it. She went down and I ripped her things open, showing her busts. She was unconscious and bleeding. I don't know why, but then I hit her again on the head with the pipe. I kept on hitting and hitting her with the pipe. This is like out of this world. This is unbelievable... oh, it was terrible, because her head felt like it was all gone... terrible. Then I took this fork and stuck it into her right bust and I left it there. I covered her with a sheet. It was bloody... oh, wasn't it, my God!

Albert DeSalvo

I thought of making this a demonstration to the authorities in Santa Cruz — how serious this was and how bad a foe they had come up against. I had a thought of annihilating the entire block that I lived on. Not only the block that I lived on but the houses approaching it, which would have included as many as ten or twelve families. It would have been a very slow, a very slow, quiet attack.

Edmund Kemper

Shooting people was, I guess, a kind of thrill. It brought out something.

Charles Starkweather

I did it all for me. Purely selfishly. I worshipped the art and the act of death, over and over. It's as simple as that. Afterwards it was all sexual confusion, symbolism, honoring the "fallen." I was honoring myself. I hated the decay and the dissection. There was no sadistic pleasure in the killing. I killed them as I would like to be killed myself, enjoying the extremity of the death act itself. If I did it to myself I could only experience it once. If I did it to others, I could experience the death act over and over again.

Dennis Nilsen

Q: Did you ever punish these six children by depriving them of food?

A: Yes.

Q: How long would you deprive them of food?

A: One or two days.

Q: Did you ever secure medical treatment for these children after you left New York in 1958?

A: No.

Q: Did you know that these five children, who are dead, were starving to death before they died?

A: I knew that they were not being properly fed.

Q: Did you and your wife ever eat, when the children had no food?

A: Yes.

Q: Why did you inflict such punishment on your children?

A: Because they would not behave or do what they were told.

Q: Did you ever burn Marjorie's hand over a gas stove, because she took something?

A: I slapped her hand and it was burned on the stove.

Q: Did you ever burn any of your children with a cigarette lighter on their private parts because they would not tell you when they needed to go to the bathroom?

A: Yes I did.

Q: Why did you dispose of the five children by throwing their bodies away?

A: I was scared and did not know where to go for help.

Q: Do you feel that you are responsible for the death of these five children?

A: Yes, because I did not provide proper care.

Interrogation of Kenneth Dudley

Q: What happened next?

A: I come around the end of the bar and I pulled a pistol, a .38 from my left-hand side that was in a shoulder holster.

Q: What did you do with the pistol?

A: Something scared the bartender and he started to run.

Q: Which way did he run?

A: Toward the front door.

Q: How many times did you fire at him?

A: Five.

Q: Did you hit him?

A: Five times, I thought.

Q: Did he get out the door?

A: Yes.

Q: Did you bring him back in again?

A: Yes, I dragged him back in.

Interrogation of Charles Brown

Q: *You say that it started with revenge, but that it also had to do with preventing earthquakes, which I guess other people had been doing. Other people were killing other people, which was keeping the earth quiet. In particular the San Andreas fault? Or in general? Or what?*

A: *All faults. We human beings, through the history of the world, have protected our continents from cataclysmic earthquakes by murder. In other words, a minor natural disaster avoids a major natural disaster.*

Q: *But if murder is a natural disaster, then why should you be locked up for it, if it's natural and has a good effect?*

A: *Your laws. You see, the thing is, people get together, say, in the White House. People like to sing the die song, you know, people like to sing the die song. If I am president of my class when I graduate from high school, I can tell two, possibly three young male homo sapiens to die. I can sing that song to them and they'll have to kill themselves or be killed — an automobile accident, a knifing, a gunshot wound. You ask me why this is? And I say, well, they have to do that in order to protect the ground from an earthquake, because all of the other people in the community had been dying all year long, and my class, we have to chip in so to speak to the darkness. We have to die also. And people would rather sing the die song than murder.*

Q: *What is the die song?*

A: *Just that. I'm telling you to die. I'm telling you to kill yourself, or be killed so that my continent will not fall off into the ocean. See, it's all based on reincarnation, this dies to protect my strata.*

Interrogation of Herbert Mullin

I married Bertha Goodrich in North Yakima on June 11, 1919. We were married and went to Tacoma, stayed a little while and went to Seattle. We were around the lake and the driveways practically where everybody goes, and we were out to the lake and discussing something and it just seemed like an impulse came over me and I hit the girl without provocation. I had to hide the body near the lake and then later went and got a boat and sank the body. We were both sitting and something came up and I just got up and took a medium-sized rock. Something just seemed to say "Do it," and when it is done something would seem to say, "Well, it is all right."

James Watson

I don't know why I do it. I get headaches, pass out, and hear funny noises.

Anthony Spencer

We had lunch. Grace sat on my lap and kissed me. I made up my mind to eat her. I took her to an empty house in Westchester I had already picked out. When we got there, I told her to remain outside. She picked wildflowers. I went upstairs and stripped all my clothes off. I knew if I did not, I would get her blood on them. When all was ready I went to the window and called her. Then I hid in a closet until she was in the room. When she saw me all naked she began to cry and tried to run down the stairs. I grabbed her, and she said she would tell her mama. First I stripped her naked. How she did kick, bite, and scratch. I choked her to death, then cut her in small pieces so I could take my meat to my rooms, cook and eat it. How sweet and tender her little ass was roasted in the oven. It took me nine days to eat her entire body. I did not fuck her, though I could have, had I wished. She died a virgin.

Albert Fish

I had gotten out of bed and I was in the kitchen making coffee. Evidently, I had done some cooking the night before. There was some meat on the stove in a frying pan. I think it was human flesh. I had gone to the bathroom and found her in my bathtub, and part of her buttocks was missing. The feet were gone, the hand, the arm. I found them in the refrigerator.

Carroll Edward Cole

If you commit a crime you should have a gun. There's nothing like the power of a gun to get what you want. Murder is the ultimate crime, and it's the ultimate thing to get away with. To get away with the act of murder is the ultimate challenge.

David Carpenter

In my lifetime I have murdered 21 human beings, I have committed thousands of burglaries, robberies, larcenies, arsons and last but not least I have committed sodomy on more than 1,000 male human beings. For all these things I am not in the least bit sorry.

Carl Panzram

On death...

I kept hearing her talking to me and telling me to do things. And I couldn't do it. I had one voice that was trying to make me commit suicide, and I wouldn't do it. I had another one telling me not to do anything they told me to do. That's what got me in the hospital, was not doing what they told me to do.

Henry Lee Lucas

What kind of future do you think I'd have throwing garbage and picking up a whore. How long do you think I'd have lived? Forty years? Too long. Ten years? Too long. Better a week with the one who loved me for what I was. Better to be left to rot on some high hill behind a rock, and be remembered, than to be buried alive in some stinking place.

Charles Starkweather

I want the chair. That's what I've always wanted. My lawyer told me there are a hundred men waiting to die in the chair. I'm asking the judge if I can have the first man's place. He's sitting there sweating right now. I'm not sweating. I'm ready for it.

Mack Edwards

You had better put me to death, because next time it might be one of you or your daughter.

Steven Judy

Even though this court may pronounce me guilty a thousand times, the higher court of our great Aryan warrior god pronounces me innocent. Heil Hitler!

Frank Spisak

My sexual and emotional aspirations became entrenched in creating and enhancing the "dead" image. I became "dead" in my fantasies. In the mirror I became dead. I did not regard the image as me at all but perhaps as a vision of me in a visually perfect state. I fear pain, but in a real sense I do not mind being dead because "dead" is a desirable image. I think that in some cases I killed these men in order to create the best image of them. It was not really a bad but a perfect and peaceful state for them to be in.

Dennis Nilsen

Hurry it up, you bastard. I could hang a dozen men while you're fooling around.

Carl Panzram, to his executioner

It doesn't bother me in the least. There are a hell of a lot worse things that can happen than to die in the gas chamber.

Douglas Clark

Part II

Pattern Crimes

"I wanted to know how it would feel... but I'm sorry about it now, of course."

— John Lawrence Miller

"I cannot bring myself to keep remembering these incidents over and over again. These are ugly images totally alien to me. I seem to have not participated in them, merely stood by and watched them happen — enacted by two other players — like a central camera."

— Dennis Nilsen

"The fantasy that accompanies and generates... the anticipation that precedes the crime is always more stimulating than the immediate aftermath of the crime itself."

— Ted Bundy

Chapter 4

Hunting Humans

The average man or woman typically regards compulsive killers as a breed apart, and so they are to some extent, but they are also sons and daughters, wives and husbands, neighbors, students, teachers, doctors, nurses, citizens of the community at large. Their life styles, motives, choice of weapons and prospective targets are as varied as the murderers themselves. In short, there is no standout "killer type" we can identify on sight and guard ourselves against. We can, however, pick out certain trends or similarities among the stalkers, charting patterns in the way they track their human prey.

Generalizations are always risky, in criminology or any other field, but systematic study of a recognized phenomenon demands a sense of order, guidelines and controls. We cannot hope to understand the killers in our midst until we recognize the traits they share in common and the points where they diverge.

After years of studying convicted felons, the FBI's Behavioral Science Unit has roughly divided serial killers under the headings of *organized* and *disorganized* offenders, based upon their mental state, behavior patterns, and the evidence retrieved from crime scenes. The categories are deliberately vague, and while Dr. Hannibal Lecter was overly harsh in blaming the system on "a real bottom feeder," FBI spokesmen have acknowledged its deficiency by creating an intermediate "mixed" heading to accommodate troublesome cases.[1]

In FBI parlance, organized offenders are those who plan their homicides ahead of time and carry out their strategy with fair attention to detail. They typically have

a high birth order status, and male killers are often the oldest son in a family. Their fathers generally have stable work histories, but childhood discipline is inconsistent, alternately harsh and lax. Organized killers possess good intelligence, with IQs ranging from average to genius levels. They prefer skilled occupations as adults, but frequently encounter problems on the job because they chafe at discipline. Most such offenders are socially adept and sexually competent, frequently residing with a spouse or lover who may have no knowledge of their crimes. Specific stressful incidents precipitate most homicides committed by the organized offender, and abuse of alcohol is common in advance of violent acts. Reports of anger or depression in the days before a murder are routine, but organized offenders normally describe themselves as calm and focused at the moment of the kill. A highly mobile predator, the organized offender typically maintains at least one vehicle in good condition, sometimes traveling compulsively in search of prey. The organized offender follows coverage of his murders in the media, and frequently collects newspaper clippings on the crimes. If there is too much heat, the organized offender may forsake employment and relocate in another city to avoid arrest.[2]

Predictably, disorganized offenders are described by federal spokesmen as the flip side of the coin in most respects. They have a low birth order status, and their fathers typically display unstable records of employment, when they work at all. Abusive treatment during childhood is the norm. Disorganized offenders are notably less intelligent than their organized peers, with

IQs ranging from sub-average to mentally retarded. Parental examples are reflected in a preference for unskilled labor, with spotty work records marked by periods of unemployment. Disorganized offenders are socially inept and sexually incompetent, normally living alone or sharing quarters with a parent well into adulthood. They are typically fearful of others, and sometimes develop intricate delusional systems to validate their paranoia. Specific stress is not required to trigger violence in disorganized offenders; rather, their preoccupation with obsessive thoughts creates confusion and an ill-defined anxiety precipitating homicidal incidents. With ready-made delusions on tap, disorganized killers are less likely to drink or use drugs in advance of a crime. Most live or work in close proximity to their crime scenes, so they rarely travel far in search of victims. Few are interested enough to track their cases in the media, and fewer still disrupt their tawdry life styles in an effort to elude police.[3]

Coral Watts, slayer of numerous women in Texas and Michigan, fit the FBI's profile of a "disorganized" killer. (Credit: Texas Dept. of Corrections)

The Bureau's cut-and-dried taxonomy breaks down when killers stubbornly refuse to play by rules prescribed from Quantico. John Gacy fit the guidelines of an organized offender perfectly, except that he brought all his victims home to kill. Ed Gein is cited by the FBI as a disorganized offender, but he traveled far and wide to find the victims he dissected. Eddie Cole appeared to match the "organized" prescription, based on childhood background, fantasy and alcohol abuse, but all his murders were impulsive acts, without precipitating stress. Ed Kemper, "organized" and highly mobile, was a virgin living with his mother when he launched his murder spree in Santa Cruz, incapable of sexual arousal with a living partner. Coral Watts fit the disorganized mold, with his borderline I.Q. and random home invasions, but he fled from Michigan to Texas when the heat was on. Joe Kallinger's alleged hallucinations clearly qualify as a "disorganized" trait, but they did not prevent his scouring a tri-state area in search of prey.

In short, the Bureau's system still has many bugs to be resolved.

A more efficient means of classifying random killers deals with how they hunt, instead of who they are. A global survey of recorded cases from the present century reveals three general types of human predators, referred to here as territorial, nomadic, and stationary. While a killer's motives, choice of weapons, and selected victim class may be revised from crime to crime, few ever change the style in which they hunt. In essence, the technique expresses who and what they are, their view of life and of themselves.

Territorial killers are those who stake out a defined area — a city or county, sometimes a particular neighborhood, street, or municipal park — and rarely deviate from the selected game preserve. The most common type of serial killer, territorial slayers represent 63% of all American cases and 70% of all foreign practitioners. In the United States, 51% of our female serial killers and 75% of all nonwhite slayers fall into this category. In some cases, like Seattle's "Green River killer" or the still-unidentified "Southside Slayer" in Los Angeles, territorial killers earn their media nicknames from their chosen hunting grounds. In notorious cases — "Son of Sam," the "Hillside Stranglers," or the Atlanta "child murders" — a territorial stalker may generate widespread panic, altering the social lives, behavior patterns, even the hair styles of prospective victims. Some killers are remarkably specific in their choice of hunting territories, as with cannibal-slayer Lester Harrison, who committed all but one of his murders in Chicago's Grant Park. Others may select a given campus, shopping mall, a lover's lane or elderly retirement neighborhood in search of easy prey. A few territorial killers pull up stakes in the face of intense heat, but they invariably put their lethal urge on hold until they find another hunting ground that suits their fancy. Strangler Kenneth Bianchi was suspected of three murders in Rochester, New York, when he fled across country to Los Angeles, joining his cousin for ten murders in L.A. before he moved on to Bellingham, Washington, and committed his last two crimes. Coral Watts was linked to five murders in Michigan before he eluded police surveillance and turned up in Houston, Texas, slaughtering another 22 women prior to his arrest. In no case has a territorial killer been found to commit random murders in transit, between established hunting grounds.

Nomadic killers are a rootless breed, traveling widely in their search for victims, often confounding police as they drift aimlessly from one jurisdiction to another. Frequently touted by "experts" as the dominant class of serial killers, nomads actually account for 29% of American cases and 15% of all foreign reports. Domestically, 20% of all female serial killers and 21% of nonwhite predators rank in the nomadic category. Some — like Henry Lucas, Ottis Toole, Charles Hatcher, and William Guatney — are professional drifters, endlessly roaming in search of handouts, part-time jobs, and easy prey. Others, exemplified by Earle Nelson, Johann Hoch, and Lydia Trueblood, travel deliberately in an effort to outwit local authorities. Transient slayers like Ted Bundy, Gerald Stano, Joe Fischer, Bruce Davis, and James Watson sometimes claim prodigious body counts, with a select few numbering their victims in the hundreds. Henry Lucas confessed to 360 murders before recanting his statements in a last-ditch bid to avoid execution; police around the country remain convinced of his guilt in more than 100 slayings. In South America, Pedro Lopez ranged over three countries, ultimately confessing the murders of 110 girls in Ecuador, another 100 in Colombia, and "many more than 100" in Peru; Ecuadorian authorities were skeptical of his claim until he led them to 53 graves in succession, finally concluding that an estimate of 300 victims was "very low." Where transient killers are identified and still at large, as in the cases of Charles Starkweather, Christopher Wilder, and Alton Coleman, dramatic manhunts ensue, complete with banner headlines and additions to the FBI's "Most Wanted" list.

Stationary murderers, conversely, crouch like spiders in the center of a web, committing homicides primarily at home or at their places of employment — clinics, nursing homes, and hospitals included. The rarest of all serial slayers, stationary killers contribute only 8% to the US total, while accounting for 15% of all foreign cases.

In America, a significant 29% of female serial killers fit the stationary profile, versus a mere 4% of nonwhite killers. Most medical slayers belong in the stationary ranks, victimizing helpless patients in major hospitals, suburban clinics, and sometimes — as with Dr. Roland Clark and dentist Tony Protopappas — in their own offices. Killing at home provides a built-in means of concealment for slayers like John Gacy, Dennis Nilsen, Eugene Butler, Dorothea Puente, and John Christie. With their masks of sanity firmly in place, stationary killers may be active for years, murdering under the very noses of wives, children, and neighbors, dismissing inconvenient screams and rancid odors with a semi-plausible excuse. Stationary killers are normally adept at covering their tracks, but some take advantage of dumb luck, as when official negligence helped Calvin Jackson claim seven victims in a New York hotel for elderly women; only when Jackson strayed off his range to kill an eighth victim outside the hotel was he finally traced and arrested. Self-protection and victim accessibility dominate the stationary killer's choice of murder sites, though some — like Nilsen, Vera Renczi, Ed Gein, and Philadelphia's Harrison Graham — derive apparent satisfaction from keeping their victims nearby. In rare cases, killers are drawn to a particular location time after time, as when Jerry Spraggins returned to murder three unrelated tenants of the same Montclair, New Jersey, apartment over a four-year period. Except in cases of hospital slayings, stationary killers rarely generate a public outcry, their victims dropping out of sight without a ripple, and their crimes are seldom recognized before a death or chance arrest reveals the grisly truth.

A demographic scan reveals some interesting comparisons between serial killers and "normal" murderers. As previously noted, racial breakdowns on American killers show that 56% are black, with 42% Caucasian; Orientals and Indians account for .7% and .6% of the total, respectively.[4] Serial killers, on the other hand, average 84% Caucasian (including Hispanics) and 16% black; one Indian and one Oriental have been accused of domestic serial murders in this century, with the Asian serving as accomplice to a white man. In terms of sex, American killers average 88% male and 12% female.[5] Serial slayers hold closer to the norm in this regard, with identified subjects running 90% male and 10% female. And, while successful serial killers may remain active for decades, they tend to start young. Reviewing 280 American cases where a killer's age is known at the time of his or her first murder, we find that: 1% killed before age 13; 26% murdered for the first time in their teens; 44% claimed the first victim in their twenties; 24% held out until their thirties before killing; a mere 4% killed for the first time in their forties; and only two killers — .7% of the total — committed their first murder past age 50.

In operational terms, 87% of American serial killers are lone wolves, spinning out their fantasies in lethal games of hide-and-seek. Multiple killers are identified or strongly suspected in 10% of domestic serial cases, with insufficient evidence for any firm conclusion in another 2%. Three curious specimens — Henry Lucas, Ottis Toole, and Kenneth Bianchi — have demonstrated their ability to murder with or without an accomplice, taking their pleasure as it comes, on the spur of the moment.

When serial killers join forces in stalking their prey, they follow well-defined patterns, driven by primal motives. Of America's "social" stalkers, 56% confine themselves to working with a lone accomplice — either male or female — while the other 44% feel more at home in larger groups. It comes as no surprise to learn that the brutality of random homicide increases with the number of participants, as heartless killers egg each other on to new extremes.

Male pairs are the most common form of "social" interaction among serial killers, representing 30% of all American cases with multiple slayers, and the deadly duos come in every form imaginable. Some are brother acts, like Kevin and Bernard Haley in Los Angeles, Gary and Thaddeus Lewingdon in Columbus, Ohio, or Thomas and William Penn in Richmond, Virginia. Others are cousins, like Hillside Stranglers Ken Bianchi and Angelo Buono, or Florida slayers Dave Gore and Fred Waterfield. Joseph Kallinger enlisted his son Michael as an accomplice for murderous forays in Pennsylvania and New Jersey. Walter Kelbach and Myron Lance, in Salt Lake City, Utah, were homosexual ex-convicts with a shared fondness for torturing their victims. Bisexual Henry Lucas and homosexual Ottis Toole were occasional lovers, as well as companions in crime, though Lucas now describes the sweaty interludes as simply "a favor" for Toole. James Latham and George York were teenage soldiers who went AWOL on a whim, traveling in stolen cars and murdering at least seven persons in an aimless trek from Florida to Utah. Leonard Lake and Charles Ng shared common interests in firearms and "survivalism," the occult, and homemade snuff films. Around Buffalo, New York, Theodore Simmons and Milton Jones teamed up to torture, rob, and murder Catholic priests.

In rural Kentucky, Philip Clopton and James Cable collected nubile sex slaves, killing several and scattering bodies over a tri-county area before an intended victim shot Clopton to death and made good her escape in April 1990. Nor is this lethal form of male bonding an exclusively American phenomenon. In France, Thierry Paulin and Jean-Thierry Mathurin joined forces to torture and kill at least 21 elderly women between 1984 and '87. In Germany, Kurt Lueking and Juergen Dohmeyer murdered at least three victims before their arrest in 1987.

Male-female couples account for another 25% of American serial cases with multiple killers. A slim majority of the reports involve unmarried lovers — Charles Starkweather and Caril Fugate, Mitchell Sims and Ruby Padgett, Alton Coleman and Debra Brown, James Marlow and Cynthia Coffman — who kill for kicks, cash, sex, or all of the above. Male dominance is normally assumed in such cases, but the charge may be a sexist slur against the lethal ladies who have minds and motivations of their own. "Lonely-hearts killer" Martha Beck clearly called the shots for Raymond Fernandez, stalking wealthy spinsters in the 1940s, and a Romanian killer named Tcaiuc blamed his 21 murders on a teenage girlfriend, who allegedly suggested the crimes and lured male victims to remote killing grounds for the pleasure of watching them die. California torture-slayer Gordon Northcott's mother confessed participation in one of his 20-odd murders and was sentenced to life imprisonment. There is no record of a brother-sister murder team, but husbands and wives have gone hunting together since the 1930s. John and Mary Creighton were sentenced to die for poisoning relatives in New York state, while James and Susan Carson cited scripture to justify the execution of suspected "witches" in California. Murder was a matter of economy for Missouri's Ray and Faye Copeland, paying off their ranch hands in hot lead, rather than cold cash. Alvin and Judith Neelley were thrill killers with a taste for violent sex, convicted of two murders in Dixie and suspected of 15 others. Like the Neelleys, Gerald and Charlene Gallego took turns sexually abusing their female victims before a bullet or a bludgeon ended the ordeal. Kenneth and Irene Dudley killed their own children, practicing murder as a form of birth control — a feat emulated in France by Andre and Yvette Lelievre.

A startling deviation from the norm of killer couples was revealed in December 1988, when Michigan authorities filed murder charges against lesbian lovers Catherine Wood and Gwendolyn Graham. Recognized as the first female murder team since British "baby farmers" Amelia Sach and Annie Walters were hanged in 1902, Wood and Graham were employed at a Grand Rapids nursing home when they devised a "game" of murdering their helpless patients. The object: To select victims based on the initials of their surnames, spelling out "M-U-R-D-E-R" as a private joke. A lover's quarrel and Graham's threat to murder infants in the next round of the game prompted Wood to unburden her conscience, resulting in life sentences for both women.

By nature and necessity, most serial killers are intensely private individuals. They require strong motivation to collect in groups of three or more, increasing their personal risk with the sharing of deadly secrets, and religious fervor provides the motive — or excuse — in 52% of such cases. Bastardized Satanism is the common theme in at least 71% of America's cult-related serial murders, from Charles Manson's "family" to the elusive Four P Movement, New York's "Son of Sam" murders and the beach massacres perpetrated by "Maxwell's Silver Hammer" in southern California, Carl Drew's Massachusetts menagerie and the cannibal-murders of young women around Chicago. John Kogut and his predatory accomplices scrawled Satanic emblems near the site where teenage victims were raped and murdered on Long Island, while Harold Smith's adolescent disciples were convicted of brutal torture-slayings in Houston, Texas. Elsewhere, polygamy and power-envy drove the Mormon Lambs of God to kill at least 22 victims in their quest for "blood atonement." Racial purity was the theme in a series of ax murders during 1911 and 1912, with authorities blaming the tiny Sacrifice Church after 49 mulatto victims were hacked to death in Louisiana and Texas. A different brand of racism merged with religion in more recent times, sending members of the all-black Hebrew Israelites and Muslim "Death Angels" out to sacrifice whites in the name of their respective gods.

All-male "wolf packs," ranging from three to a half-dozen members, have accounted for 10% of America's serial murders with multiple killers involved. Apparently unknown outside of the United States, these predatory bands are sometimes driven by sadistic sexual desires, as in the California "Freeway murders" or the Houston torture-killings instigated by Dean Corll, carried out with the help of teenage accomplices Elmer Henley and David Brooks. Other gangs are motivated by greed, as in the New York series of penny-ante robberies that claimed 11 lives in early 1980. Three gunmen were convicted in that case, but suspects remain

at large in Los Angeles, where seven victims were knifed to death by a trio of Hispanics, after surrendering their cash without protest. In Jasper County, Georgia, John Williams and his three sons enslaved numerous blacks in the years after World War I, murdering at least 18 when they rebelled or outlived their usefulness. Nor is a concrete motive absolutely necessary. During 1985, Dallas authorities jailed five teenage boys on charges of multiple murder, linking as many as seven senseless slayings to "a group of friends who liked to shoot people."

By contrast, when females join a predatory gang, they lean toward cults or the pursuit of cash. Birmingham, Alabama, was terrorized by a series of ax murders between November 1919 and October 1923, with 15 merchants robbed and hacked to death in their shops; the black perpetrators, arrested in January 1924, included four men and one woman. A few years later, in Philadelphia, Dr. Morris Bolber recruited the Petrillo cousins and a local "witch" to assist with his massive insurance frauds, killing an estimated 50 victims by the time of their arrest in 1937. In late 1989, Tracy Holland joined male accomplices Keith Goodman and Jon Mead for a ten-week murder spree, claiming at least five victims in New York, Tennessee, and Mississippi.

On rare occasions, whole families join forces to kill. In 1972, authorities linked Sherman McCrary, his son Danny, and son-in-law Raymond Taylor with a year-long series of kidnap-murders spanning the continent from Florida to southern California. The victims were invariably young women, abducted from the scene of minor robberies, then raped and shot to death. McCrary's wife and daughter saw no reason to object. As Ginger McCrary-Taylor told police, "I love my husband very much, and it never occurred to me to do anything other than to stay with him." Gary Tison was serving life for an Arizona policeman's murder when his three sons helped him escape from state prison, taking serial killer Randy Greenawalt along for the ride. Before the gang was cornered twelve days later, six more hapless victims had been added to the Tison body count.

Racism, stripped of the pseudo-religious trappings, motivated at least two other serial cases with multiple slayers. In 1970, black gunmen Martin Rutrell, L.L. Thompson, and Ben Chaney, Jr. — himself the brother of a victim murdered by the Ku Klux Klan — spent five weeks driving through Florida and the Carolinas, killing white victims wherever they stopped. Eight years later, in Illinois and Nebraska, black army veterans with a grudge against white society banded together as "De Mau Mau," claiming a dozen innocent victims between May and September 1978. Eight gunmen were arrested in a sweep that broke the gang, two of them murdered in jail before the others were tried, convicted, and sentenced to life. Another case with racial overtones, still unresolved, is the series of so-called Atlanta "child murders." Defendant Wayne Williams stands convicted of killing two adult ex-convicts, accused by the prosecution — without formal charges — of another 22 related homicides, but new evidence casts doubt on the jury's verdict. According to Williams' defenders and FBI documents procured under the Freedom of Information Act, two KKK members are linked with several murders in the series, and with the unsolved strangulation deaths of 17 black women in Atlanta; another dozen murders blamed on Williams may be the handiwork of a local black militant organization and a separate, unnamed white-supremacist group.[6]

The motives for serial murder vary as widely as the killers themselves, but an overwhelming 69% of American cases are sparked by sex and sadism. Regardless of their taste in human prey, sex and violence are inextricably linked in the minds of many serial slayers, their brutal crimes a demonstration of power and dominance over helpless victims. Many are prolific lady-killers, in the mold of Ted Bundy, Christopher Wilder, Coral Watts, Brandon Tholmer, Richard Cottingham, Marvin Irvin, and Eddie Cole. Alaska's Robert Hansen considered himself a sportsman, flying his prostitute victims into the wilderness, there demanding sex, and stalking those who failed to satisfy. Slayers Gary Heidnik and Andre Rand extended their personal power trips with a preference for mentally retarded victims, while karate expert Roland Steele used elderly women as practice dummies. A sick combination of sex, sadism, and self-loathing motivated homosexual killers John Gacy, Dean Corll, Patrick Kearney, William Bonin, Randy Kraft, Paul Bateson, Robert Berdella, and Michael Terry. Serial stalkers like Frank Davis, John Joubert, Mack Edwards, and Arthur Bishop displayed a preference for young children. Occasional rogues, in the style of Henry Lucas, Ottis Toole, and Dennis Webb, rape and murder their victims without regard to sex or age. New England's Jane Toppan provides the rare example of a female sexual sadist, poisoning an estimated 70 to 100 victims for the thrill of seeing them die. In England, arsonist Bruce Lee could only reach orgasm by setting fires, a quirk that claimed 26 lives before his arrest in 1980.

"Freeway Killer" William Bonin was driven to sadistic murder by revulsion at his own homosexuality. *(Credit: Los Angeles County Sheriff's Dept.)*

Motiveless "thrill killers" are a further addition to the ranks of sadistic serial murderers. Charles Starkweather and Caril Fugate created a national sensation with their murders of 11 victims in Nebraska and Wyoming. George York and James Latham were fed up with army life when they hit the road in 1959, killing seven victims in five states. Boredom was the excuse for teenagers Thomas Braun and Leonard Maine, killing three West Coast victims and crippling a fourth during August 1967. Six years later, Douglas Gretzler and Willie Steelman slaughtered 17 persons in Arizona and California, all without apparent motive. Two decades and a thousand miles apart, John Wable and Randy Greenawalt amused themselves by executing sleeping truckers in their cabs. In Tucson, Arizona, Charles Schmid told friends, "I want to kill a girl tonight. I think I can get away with it." In fact, he murdered three before his luck ran out and he was jailed for life. Ronald Hoffman, Chicago's "Sunshine Sniper," randomly gunned down pedestrians in the latter weeks of 1978. Dr. Sohrab Khan studied medicine in the United States, but he took his homicidal urges home to Pakistan, there slaying 13 victims in November 1986. Sydney Jones, confessed slayer of 13 persons, left a terse note behind when he mounted an Alabama gallows in 1915. It read:

"I'm sorry I missed Richard Moore Sept. 12, 1912. Just one more would have made an even number."

Professional assassins are not considered serial killers, since they murder on cue, dispassionately, leaving the selection of targets to their employers. Trigger-happy bandits in the Jesse James tradition are likewise excluded, regardless of body counts, because they kill primarily when cornered by police, or when a robbery goes wrong. That said, the fact remains that some 14% of identified serial slayers — and 41% of America's female practitioners—kill at least some of their victims with money in mind. They differ from common mercenaries in their susceptibility to what psychologist Stanten Samenow calls a "double voltage" — that is, the amplified thrill of killing for profit *and* pleasure. While most armed robbers are content to steal and slip away, employing violence only as a last resort, compulsive killers brutalize their victims even in the total absence of resistance, counting on another death before they make their first demand for cash. As Florida police described their suspect in a recent case, these predators are "killers who rob, not robbers who kill."[7]

Compulsive killers with an eye on profit serve their fantasies in different ways. Some — like John Brooks, Richard Tingler, Paul Rhoades, Leslie Torres, and Sacramento's unidentified "Thrill Killer" — execute victims at random during penny-ante robberies. Another Sacramento operator, Dorothea Puente, ran a boarding house for elderly indigents, poisoning several and cashing their Social Security checks for herself. In Philadelphia, Dr. Morris Bolber and company dispatched an estimated 50 victims and pocketed the life insurance payoffs. Anna Hahn and Dorothy Matajke each befriended senior citizens, posing as nurses or companions and looting bank accounts until they tired of the game and murdered their unwitting benefactors. Martha Beck and Ray Fernandez recruited their victims from the newspaper "lonely hearts" columns, with Fernandez pitching woo until they had the cash in hand and it was time to fill another shallow grave. Robert Daniels met his victims on the road, in rural campgrounds, robbing them before he gunned them down or injected them with powerful horse tranquilizers. In New York, Calvin Jackson amused himself by looting the apartments of women he raped and murdered. Massachusetts pimp Carl Drew used Satanic rituals and human sacrifice to keep his whores in line. In France, Marcel Petiot took advantage of the Nazi occupation to make serial murder a cottage industry, promising Jewish refugees safe passage out of Europe and obtaining payment in full before he gassed, dismembered, and cremated his "clients." Convicted of 26 murders, Petiot confessed to 150 before he was guillotined in 1946.

A notable subspecies of profit killer is the "Bluebeard" variety, renowned for the murder of wives, fiancees, and lovers. Henri Landru, French slayer of ten women and one boy, is the classic example of this century, but America has spawned no shortage of able competitors. Johann Hoch easily leads the domestic field, with 55 known wives and a minimum of 15 — some say 50 — victims slain. Alfred Cline dispatched eight wives between 1930 and 1945, including a male evangelist for variety when the clergyman wrote Cline into his will. In Bakersfield, California, Steven Catlin used the herbicide Paraquat to poison two wives and his adoptive father before he was jailed. Prolific bigamist Harry Powers, alias "Herman Drenth," spanned the continent in his search for new brides, bringing the lucky ladies home to Clarksburg, West Virginia, where he maintained a sophisticated gas chamber and dissection lab. Convicted of five murders and suspected of 50, Powers admitted deriving sexual pleasure from watching his victims die. As he told police, "It beat any cat house I was ever in."

No less industrious than their male counterparts, "black widows" earn their keep and satisfy their darker urges by eradicating husbands, in-laws, and assorted other kin. Indiana's Belle Gunness set the standard for the century, slaughtering two husbands, three women, four children, and at least ten suitors before she faked her own death and disappeared in 1908. An anonymous Cleveland practitioner was suspected of poisoning three husbands and two of her own children in the 1920s, but prosecutors lacked sufficient evidence for trial, and her name has disappeared from police records. Jane Quinn poisoned one husband and shot two others before she was finally apprehended. In Chicago, self-styled "psychic" Louise Vermilyea disposed of two husbands, two daughters, one granddaughter, a stepson, and two boarders — one of them a police officer — before detectives got wise. Nanny Doss collected insurance money from the deaths of four husbands, two children, one grandchild, her mother, and two sisters, but she staunchly described her true motive as a search for "romance." Anjette Lyles practiced voodoo in Macon, Georgia, when not feeding poison to two husbands, a daughter, and two mothers-in-law. In Florida, Judi Buenoano was sentenced to die for killing her husband, a lover, and her own son. Missouri-born Lydia Trueblood roamed the western half of the nation, dispatching four husbands, her only child, and a brother-in-law. In North Carolina, arsenic relieved Blanche Moore of her husband, her father, and a well-insured lover. Connecticut's Amy Gilligan married and murdered five inmates of a nursing home she managed, along with four female patients who signed over their worldly goods. Foreign competitors include South Africa's Daisy DeMelker (three dead), Germany's Maria Velten (four known victims), Belgium's Marie Becker (ten killed), and French slayer Marie Besnard (killer of 14).

Six percent of America's serial murderers kill for varied motives, each crime separate and unique from those that went before. South Carolina's Donald "Pee Wee" Gaskins alternately killed for sex, to settle private grudges, and to cover up his thriving trade in stolen cars; imprisoned for his crimes, he took a contract to assassinate a fellow inmate and was subsequently sentenced to die. Hoosier rapist David Roberts incinerated a family of three as revenge for the filing of theft charges; he was free on bond in that case, pending trial, when he murdered the infant son of a rape victim. Dennis Webb impartially raped victims of both sexes, murdering some in the process; other targets were killed under contract, in gang fights, during robberies, or because their race and homosexuality offended Webb. Thomas Creech confessed 42 murders following his 1975 arrest, the crimes variously described as human sacrifices to Satan and contracts ordered by an outlaw motorcycle gang. Another biker, Julian Kennedy, murdered one stranger as part of his gang initiation; others were slain during arguments, robberies, drug deals, and jailbreaks. Homicidal soul mates Henry Lucas and Ottis Toole reportedly murdered for sex, profit, and the sheer hell of it during a seven-year cross-country rampage.

Another 5% of identified serial slayers describe their bloodletting as religious ritual, appeasing Satan or their deity of choice. Sincerity is difficult to gauge in such cases, but their occurrence in modern times is amply documented by examples previously listed. Nor are killer cults exclusively confined to the United States. In Barcelona, Spain, self-styled sorceress Marti Enriqueta kidnapped and dismembered children to obtain ingredients for her costly "love potions." Indian authorities seized cult leader Laxman Giri in 1980, charging him with multiple counts of human sacrifice; the victims, local children, had been killed to invest Giri's followers with immortality. In Thailand, cultist Sila Wongsin was executed in June 1959, on charges of sacrificing five provincial leaders to demonic deities. Mexican authorities have had persistent trouble with death cults,

including one led by the Hernandez brothers in Tamaulipas, with eight victims sacrificed before the sect was suppressed in 1963. Two decades later, 15 cult murders at nearby Matamoros were publicly linked with a dozen other mutilation-slayings around Mexico City. Back in the United States, practitioners of the Hispanic witchcraft known as *santeria* stand accused of human sacrifice in Florida, New York, and California.

"Mercy" killing is a common theme with slayers in the medical profession, accounting for 2% of American serial murders. Donald Harvey listed many of his 87 killings in this category, though his weapons — including arsenic, rat poison, drain cleaner, and sharp wires inserted through catheter tubes — were seldom merciful. In Albany, Georgia, nurse Terri Rachals confessed to poisoning several patients because she "couldn't stand to see them suffering." Another nurse, Genene Jones, reportedly murdered children to stress the need for a pediatric intensive care unit in her Texas community. At Maryland General Hospital, in Baltimore, Mary Robaczynski admitted pulling the plug on selected "gorks" — hospital slang for "God only really knows" — in an effort to ease their pain. Another Maryland nurse, Jane Bolding, reportedly confessed to "mercy" killings in March 1985, but police misconduct got the statement thrown out of court. In North Carolina, Anthony Shook "helped out" elderly hospital patients, enabling them to "just finish dying." Nurse's aide Jeffrey Feltner dispensed a similar brand of mercy to residents of nursing homes around Daytona Beach, Florida. And breaking the medical mold, drifter Norman Bernard murdered three homeless transients and wounded a fourth in 1983, explaining to police that he was "doing them a favor" by putting them out of their misery.

Few serial killers are legally insane, but some are certainly irrational, and a rough 2% of American cases result from delusions or outright madness. In California, Herbert Mullin slaughtered 13 victims in an effort to prevent disastrous earthquakes. Charles Manson's personal interpretation of Beatles songs inspired him to foment race warfare between blacks and whites. If we believe Joe Kallinger, a disembodied head named "Charlie" ordered him to murder chosen males and mutilate their genitals. Gary Schaefer mistook one victim for the stepdaughter he sexually abused on a regular basis; even with the stranger in his car, Schaefer continued to address her by his daughter's name. In Medina, Ohio, Martha Wise blamed her murder spree on the devil, saying: "He came to me while I was in the kitchen baking bread. He came to me while I was working in the fields. He followed me everywhere." Arsonist Robert Segee's private vision was that of an Indian warrior on horseback, the horse in flames. Kentucky's Cleo Green III believed himself possessed by a "red demon" that ordered the murder of elderly victims. Melissa Norris, meanwhile, hallucinated a demon inhabiting her infant son and beat the child to death in an abortive exorcism; in custody, she also confessed the murders of her mother and sister. Edward Leonski, the so-called "Singing Strangler," killed three women while trying to capture their voices. Nathan Trupp suspected television actor Michael Landon of Nazi sympathies, gunning down five victims in a futile attempt to reach his main target. Ed Gein decorated his farmhouse with human body parts and dressed in women's skins to dance beneath the moon.

Racial bigotry provides the motivation for approximately 1% of American serial murders, including homicides by individuals and larger racist gangs. Chicago's Mau Mau killers are a prime example, black men stalking whites, but there is hate enough to go around. Joseph Franklin and Frank Spisak were fanatic neo-Nazis, committed to murdering blacks and suspected Jews or "nigger-lovers" in their solitary bids to "purify the race." Minnesota's Billy Glaze hated Indian women, raping and murdering three before his arrest. Joseph Christopher killed a dozen blacks in New York state, cutting the hearts out of two victims for good measure. In Dayton, Ohio, Neal Long gunned down six blacks and the white architect of a local school desegregation plan. Black gunmen Martin Rutrell, Ben Chaney, and L.L. Thompson killed three whites and wounded three more on a wild tour of Dixie.

The final 1% of domestic serial killings are inspired by feelings of revenge or jealousy. Texas housewife Ellen Etheridge poisoned four stepchildren in a vain bid for her husband's attention. Midwestern gunman Rudy Bladel murdered six railroad workers to avenge his dismissal from the Rock Island line. In San Francisco, William Hanson shot and killed middle-aged men who reminded him of his sister's rapist. Drifter Bruce Davis, traumatized by a rape at age thirteen, spent the next decade murdering homosexuals. When Erno Soto's wife gave birth to a black child, the product of an adulterous love affair, Soto exacted retribution by murdering and mutilating dark-skinned boys. South American slayer Pedro Lopez was violently sodomized in childhood, and again in prison ten years later. Determined to repay his

loss of innocence in kind, he murdered some 300 children in Colombia, Peru, and Ecuador.

Each act of serial murder proceeds through phases, delineated by FBI analysts as precrime and postcrime behavior, in addition to the actual killing itself. No two slayers demonstrate identical behavior patterns, some telescoping the phases of murder into hours or days while others spin them out over weeks or months, but careful analysis reveals common elements in almost every case. The most impulsive killer still has moments of reflection, and the most methodical inevitably finds himself beyond the point of no return, compelled to forge ahead at any cost.

A killer's state of mind is obviously crucial to the crime, and it should come as no surprise that members of the FBI's test sample recalled highly negative emotional states preceding their murders. A full 50% described feelings of frustration, while 46% experienced anger or hostility; 43% were visibly agitated, with 41% reporting some excitement or arousal.[8] At the same time, many captive slayers questioned by the Bureau pulled themselves together at the moment of the kill. A mere 17% were nervous in the act of murder; 15% reported depression; 10% recalled feelings of fear; and 7% experienced some confusion.[9] Killers in the "disorganized" category were more likely to feel confused or distressed, while their "organized" counterparts were dominated by ritualistic fantasies.[10] Psychologist Joel Norris describes this early stage of murder as the "aura phase," when some killers retreat from reality into a fantasy world of their own creation, sometimes complete with heightened sensory awareness of sounds, smells, and colors. With brain-damaged killers, such fantasies may intrude on waking reality without warning; for victims of hormonal dysfunction, like Bobby Joe Long, violent urges surface with the predictable regularity of a female's menstrual cycle.[11]

In human terms, each random killer is an individual, their mental states as diverse as the slayers themselves. Some, like Joseph Kallinger, Nathan Trupp, and Herbert Mullin, are mentally unbalanced, driven to kill by delusions beyond their control. Others, like Charles Starkweather and Henry Lucas, are so brutalized in childhood that they grow up nursing a pathological hatred for all mankind. Transvestite Frank Spisak turned to Naziism for a sense of order in his chaotic life, pursuing the message of hate through a series of brutal crimes. John Gacy and Eddie Cole emerged from traumatic childhoods with serious misgivings about their masculinity; in Cole's case, the anxiety was compounded by hatred of his shrewish, adulterous mother. Pervasive loneliness drove Dennis Nilsen to kill and kill again, keeping the corpses around his home as a form of "company."

Specific stress factors influence the behavior of serial killers to varying degrees, with members of the FBI's test sample reporting a wide range of personal conflicts or problems. A full 59% recalled conflicts with females prior to killing, with typical incidents including arguments, sexual rejection, or perceived humiliation. Conflict with parents was reported by 53% of the sampling, while 48% were beset by financial problems. Employment difficulties were admitted by 39% of the killers and strongly suspected with another 26%. Only 21% cited marital stress as a precipitating factor, but a majority of the FBI's test subjects were unmarried. Additional stress factors noted in the federal survey included legal problems (28%), conflict with another male (11%), physical injury to the killer (11%), the death of a significant person (8%), and the birth of a child (8%).[12] For killers with hormonal or genetic problems, on the other hand, stress factors may be chemical or biological, internalized, producing panic, fury, or an overwhelming sexual desire without environmental stimuli.

Precipitating stress attacks each individual in different ways. Styllou Christofi resolved family arguments by murdering her mother and daughter-in-law. Marie Becker's adulterous fling at age 55 prompted her to dispose of her husband and others who displeased her. Marital discord and fear of exposure as a thief drove Velma Barfield to eliminate one victim after another. Ed Gein and Ottis Toole each consoled themselves with murder following the death of a beloved parent. In Marybeth Tinning's case, the natural death of one child led her to murder eight others, thus validating her self-description as a "bad mother" while reaping the attention that comes with funerals. Sexual abuse in childhood drove Bruce Davis and Pedro Lopez to recreate the trauma with fresh victims, casting themselves in the aggressor's role. The infidelity of Vera Renczi's husband soured her on men, but not on romance; when her later paramours appeared to waver, Renczi poisoned them and stored their bodies in the cellar, close at hand. Ibrahim Allam employed his wife in sexual extortion schemes, but violent jealousy turned blackmail into homicide. Adultery and the birth of an illegitimate child sent Erno Soto out to mutilate boys

resembling his wife's bastard son. Dennis Nilsen compensated for the loss of a favorite roommate by populating his lonely flat with corpses.

The advance planning of serial murder likewise varies from case to case. Fifty percent of the FBI's test sample reported intentional planning of murders, complete with selection of the victim, time and place; another 34% recognized a mounting urge to kill and left themselves open to prime opportunities, while only 16% described their murders as wholly spontaneous and unplanned.[13] "Organized" offenders are more likely to plan their crimes in advance, staking out a particular hunting ground or type of victim, frequently striving to gain a victim's confidence through feigned friendship or the assumption of a "trustworthy" persona — outfitting themselves as police officers, talent scouts, repairmen, and so forth. The "disorganized" offender, conversely, leans more toward impulsive assaults on random targets, overpowering victims with a "blitz" attack in lieu of striking up a conversation first.[14]

That said, the planning undertaken by individual slayers ranges from minimal to meticulous. Lawrence Bittaker purchased a van, nicknamed "Murder Mack," to facilitate the abduction and torture of his female victims. Ed Gein spent hours crafting home decorations out of human remains, but clumsy errors at a murder scene led police to his doorstep. Carlton Gary staked out the homes of his elderly prey for days or weeks before a raid. Several random killers, including Fritz Haarmann, John Gacy, the Hillside stranglers, and Ted Bundy posed as policemen to snare their victims; on alternate occasions, Bundy donned a cast and feigned injury to allay suspicion. Harvey Glatman and Christopher Wilder introduced themselves as glamour photographers, murdering their compliant models. Boston strangler Albert DeSalvo charmed his way into scores of apartments, posing as the talent scout for a modeling agency. Gary Heidnik dug pits in his Philadelphia basement for the housing of captive sex slaves. Leonard Lake built himself a rural bunker to serve as a combination torture chamber and snuff film studio. Harry Powers and Marcel Petiot constructed gas chambers to liquidate their victims, while vampire-slayer John Haigh used an acid bath to dispose of corpses. In France, Henri Landru cremated his numerous fiancees, coming close to the perfect crime. Vera Renczi procured zinc coffins for her 32 victims, while Hungarian slayer Bela Kiss preserved his in oil drums filled with alcohol.

Precrime behavior offers valuable insight to a killer's state of mind. Few serial murderers kill without a background of preliminary violence, escalating over time through acts of vandalism, arson, theft and home invasions, random shootings, torture and mutilation of animals, or threats and assaults on other human beings. Of the FBI's test sample, 49% reported drinking prior to the commission of a homicide; another 35% recalled using drugs in advance of a crime, but only 12.5% described their drug use prior to murder as exceptional, compared to "normal" use.[15] In essence, random killers may be viewed as violence junkies, needing ever-greater "fixes" to achieve release and realize their morbid fantasies.

In general, the preliminary violence practiced by random killers sets the pattern for their later homicides. Sex-slayers like Anthony Spencer, Albert DeSalvo, Brandon Tholmer, Randall Woodfield, and Bobby Joe Long warmed up for murder with repeated sexual assaults, sometimes sparing chosen victims even after they began to kill. George Putt twice attempted to rape his own mother-in-law, afterward turning to strangers. David Bullock and John Brooks were proficient thieves before they turned to murder for sport. William Heirens committed his fetish burglaries for sexual satisfaction, killing when his fantasy was interrupted. Ernest Dobbert and Joseph Kallinger cruelly abused their own children, eventually lapsing from torture into homicide. In Oregon, Jerry Brudos graduated from assault, rape, and theft of women's shoes to murder and mutilation of selected victims. New York's David Berkowitz set numerous fires and shot a neighbor's dog before turning his gun on young women. Cecile Bombeek, a Belgian nurse and drug addict, sadistically abused numerous patients before she began to rob and kill. Eddie Cole proved his masculinity by beating and robbing homosexuals, later assaulting and murdering women who reminded him of his adulterous mother.

In every random killer's drift from fantasy toward lethal action, there invariably comes a moment when the line is crossed, some trigger incident demanding violence there and then. As murderers and motives vary, so the crucial spark differs from case to case. Slayers with a detailed fantasy involving death must kill to act it out, as Robert Hansen sought fulfillment stalking prostitutes like game in the Alaskan wilderness. Vampire-killers Richard Chase, John Haigh, Wayne Boden, and Fritz Haarmann could only quench their thirst with human blood. Ritual sacrifice was an integral part of Herbert Mullin's plan to save California from catastrophic earthquakes. In Eddie Cole's mind, strangulation and posthumous rape was the only fitting punishment for adultery. Dennis Nilsen discussed death in almost poetic terms, and Ed Gein could scarcely have fashioned his bizarre home decorations without fresh corpses on hand. Douglas Clark enjoyed shooting women through the head while they sucked his penis. For cannibals Albert Fish and Joachim Kroll, or devoted necrophiles like Edmund Kemper and Bernard Giles, death is merely a means to an end.

When a serial killer's fantasy hinges on dominance, victims have a marginally better chance of survival. Rape-slayer Bobby Long spared five women for each one he killed — including the victim whose testimony led to his arrest. Compliance *may* defuse a sex-slayer's lethal rage, but the gamble is risky at best. Resistance triggers escalating violence in some offenders, but others react brutally to submissive behavior, irrationally blaming the victim for preempting control of the encounter. For some rape-slayers, like Harry Lanham and Anthony Knoppa, murder is simply a means for silencing troublesome witnesses. Others search hopelessly for the "ideal" sex partner, slaughtering those who disappoint. Peter Sutcliffe, raping one of his victims as she lay dying from knife wounds, complained that the woman "didn't try very hard" to please him!

Yet another type of random killer operates without conscious planning, violent urges unrecognized or actively denied while the victims are blamed for explosive encounters. Fetish burglar William Heirens killed when his fantasies were interrupted, afterward covering his victims' wounds as if to negate the act of murder. Woman-haters like Gerald Stano and Eddie Cole habitually blame alcohol or the behavior of their victims for outbursts of homicidal violence. In Alabama, Raymond Brown knifed three relatives to death after he was caught stealing money from his grandmother's purse; paroled after a quarter-century in prison, he killed two more women in identical fashion. David Bullock murdered one victim for laughing at him; another fatally annoyed Bullock by "messing with a Christmas tree" while they conversed. Conflict with authority prompts some killers — like Bruce Shreeves, George York, and James Latham — to desert military service in favor of a homicidal rampage; others, like New Yorker Alex Mengel and British slayer Barry Prudom, impulsively murder police officers without apparent motive. The morbid self-loathing of homosexual slayers like John Gacy and Larry Eyler results in the murder and mutilation of successive victims.

In terms of the murder itself, the FBI's Behavioral Science Unit classifies "organized" and "disorganized" serial killers chiefly on the basis of technique. Control or dominance is crucial to the organized offender, with frequent evidence of sadistic sexual assault. Such killers typically manipulate their victims with controlled conversation, striving to win their confidence before they are subdued and bound in restraints. Sexual assault by an organized offender normally takes place before death, and the act of murder is frequently eroticized, prolonged by means of torture, slow strangulation, and so forth. Organized killers typically come prepared, bringing their own weapons to the murder scene, afterward removing or destroying crucial evidence to frustrate police.[16]

Disorganized offenders, on the other hand, commit spontaneous, impulsive crimes. Instead of wooing victims with a polished line, they favor swift attacks, killing their prey outright to avoid resistance. Mutilation or sexual contact with the victim is normally postmortem, with damage to the face or genitals inflicted to "depersonalize" the victim. If weapons are used, disorganized killers tend to find them at the murder scene — a tool or kitchen knife belonging to the victim, a convenient stone or piece of wood — and little or no effort is made toward concealment of evidence.[17]

When it comes to choice of weapons, serial killers again defy national norms. In 1989, 62% of American murders were committed with firearms, 30% were the result of hands-on violence — stabbing, beating, strangulation — and another 8% were committed by other means, including arson, poison, and explosives.[18] Serial slayers, by contrast, prefer the personal touch: 51% kill manually, versus 22% who rely exclusively on firearms and 10% who utilize "other" means; another 14% alternate between shooting and manual attacks, while 3% — including killers like Henry Lucas, Ottis Toole, and Robert Segee — switch off between manual and other forms of homicide.

Most serial murders include some sexual elements, but the representative acts vary widely in terms of significance to the killers. Traditional penetration may not take place at all, replaced in some cases by acts of torture, mutilation, vampirism, or cannibalism. Fifty-six percent of the FBI's captive subjects admitted raping victims prior to death; another 42% reported acts of necrophilia, while 33% confessed to torturing their victims as a form of sexual release.[19]

The sexual elements of serial murder provide journalists with their most sensational headlines. Some killers, like Ted Bundy, John Joubert, and Wisconsin's "Mad Biter," Richard Macek, gnaw the bodies of their victims as a substitute for rape. Insertion of foreign objects, frequently accompanied by other mutilation, replaces normal sex for killers like Harvey Carignan, Albert DeSalvo, John Norman Collins, and Texarkana's unidentified "Moonlight Murderer." The vampirism practiced by killers Fritz Haarmann, Wayne Boden, Richard Chase, John Haigh, and Peter Kurten takes on a sexual element, with the spilling and consumption of blood supplanting intercourse. In the same context, killers like Teet Harm, Ottis Toole, Albert Fish, Joachim Kroll, Lester Harrison and other practicing cannibals eroticize their crimes by literally consuming portions of their victims. Necrophilia may be the last resort of sexually incompetent slayers like Bernard Giles, Melvin Rees, Ed Kemper, and Horace Kelly; for others, like Eddie Cole, it is rationalized as a means of debasing and humiliating a despised victim. Mutilation of a victim's breasts or genitals is typically recognized as a sexual assault, but other killers are driven to disembowel or decapitate their prey. Karl Warner stabbed his teenage victims more than 150 times each, wielding his blade as a substitute phallus. New York's Erno Soto severed the genitals of dark-skinned boys resembling his wife's bastard son. In some cases, killers like Yorkshire ripper Peter Sutcliffe return to their victims days or weeks after the crime, inflicting fresh mutilations as a further demonstration of control.

Many — perhaps most — serial killers are driven by ritual fantasies, revealing their obsessions in the way they treat their victims and the evidence they leave behind. John Gacy recited the Twenty-third Psalm while strangling his victims, urging them to be brave in the face of slow, agonizing death. Seattle's Green River killer inserted pyramid-shaped stones in the vaginas of several victims, their significance unknown to this day. German slayer Manfred Wittman forced his women to strip, binding them with their own underwear before he stabbed them repeatedly. Cleveland's "Mad Butcher of Kingsbury Run" dissected his prey with near-surgical precision, treating some of the bodies with chemical preservatives. Gary Robbins charmed his way into suburban homes, forcing housewives to shower before he carried them away, bound with handcuffs and venetian blind cords; at least two of his victims were identically burned on the left breast and arm before they were shot and stabbed to death. Joseph Kallinger reenacted childhood threats of castration by sexually mutilating his male victims. Ed Kemper silenced his carping mother by shoving her larynx down a garbage disposal, afterward using her head as a dart board. "Night Stalker" Richard Ramirez gouged eyes and decorated his murder scenes with Satanic graffiti. Another unidentified killer, San Francisco's "Black Doodler," broke the ice with his homosexual targets by drawing their portraits in bars.

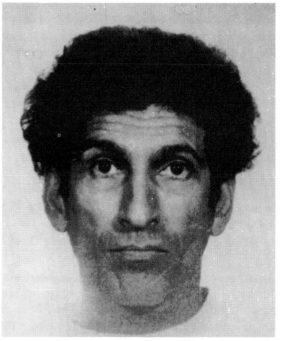

"Hillside Strangler" Angelo Buono experimented with caustic injections and electric shock to kill his hapless victims. *(Credit: Los Angeles County Sheriff's Dept.)*

Too often, random killers exercise their compulsions by torturing innocent victims. In Houston, Dean Corll and his accomplices tied boys to a special rack before raping and otherwise abusing them. Hillside Stranglers Ken Bianchi and Angelo Buono amused themselves with electric shock and caustic injections. Alvin and Judith Neelley injected one of their victims with drain cleaner, reducing her flesh to what a coroner called "the consistency of anchovy paste." Christopher Wilder traveled cross-country with Super Glue and bare electric wires, the better to torment his prey. Lawrence Bittaker and Roy Norris used hammers and pliers to produce the screams they craved. In Houston, Harold Smith's Satanic disciples tortured one of their victims to death in a cemetery, gouging his eyes out and scorching his

hair down to the scalp. Gary Heidnik's sex slaves were subjected to starvation, hanging by their wrists, electric shocks, and screwdrivers thrust in their ears. Wichita's unidentified "BTK" stalker coined his own nickname as an acronym for "bind, torture, and kill." In Italy, Giancarlo Guidice tortured his female victims for days at a time, snipping off fingers and toes, slashing their bodies with knives.

Another aspect of ritualism in serial murder is the frequent removal of keepsakes from various crime scenes. FBI analysts distinguish between *trophies*, collected by "organized" offenders to commemorate a successful hunt, and *souvenirs*, kept by "disorganized" killers as fuel for their fantasies, but the distinction is largely semantic.[20] Items collected by serial slayers range from the mundane — snapshots, items of jewelry or other personal effects — to ghoulish and bizarre, including amputated body parts. Joel Norris labels such behavior as the "totem phase" of random murder, wherein killers cling to symbols of their momentary triumph, hoping to sustain a satisfaction that eludes them in reality.[21] Other killers strive for the same result by following their cases in the media, saving news clips or jotting their thoughts in a diary, even revisiting crime scenes at great personal risk.

An interesting, if inconclusive, aspect of the FBI research suggests that random gunmen are more prone to certain types of follow-up behavior than are hands-on killers. Bureau analysts divided their captive subjects into two groups, one for killers who used firearms exclusively, the other limited to slayers with a preference for sharp or blunt instruments. Eighty-two percent of the gunmen admitted following their cases in the press, while only 50% of the hands-on killers were interested. Of the shooters, 64% saved news clippings about themselves and 56% kept diaries, compared to 26% of the beaters and hackers on both questions. Twenty-one percent of the gunmen photographed their victims, while only 11% of the manual killers brought cameras along. Likewise, 21% of the triggermen confessed their crimes to a confidante, versus 6% of the competition. Gunmen were also marginally more likely to revisit crime scenes, 44% to 34%, but no significant difference was noted in the collection of physical trophies.[22] FBI spokesmen stop short of drawing conclusions from their data, but logic dictates that gunmen crave reaffirmation of their crimes since shooting is a more remote act, lacking the physical contact — and thus satisfaction — of beating, stabbing, or strangling their victims to death.

For sheer outrageousness in souvenirs, no case can match Ed Gein's Wisconsin house of horrors — with skulls mounted on bedposts, faces hanging on the walls, human skin doubling as upholstery, nipple belts and hanging vaginas — but serial killers display no end of variety in their selections. David Berkowitz kept a journal of his many arson fires, while Randy Kraft filled a notebook with shorthand descriptions of his murders. Kraft also photographed his victims on occasion, a hobby shared by Jerry Brudos, Harvey Glatman, Lawrence Bittaker and Roy Norris, the Black Muslim "Death Angels," and Robert Berdella. When not snapping Polaroids, Bittaker and Norris recorded the screams of their victims for future enjoyment at home. In England, Ian Brady and Myra Hindley likewise taped the pathetic cries of a young girl they tortured to death. Cannibal Stanley Baker carried the knuckle bones of one victim in a belt pouch. In New York, Alex Mengel scalped one victim and wore the grisly relic as a disguise in his next attempted kidnapping. One California slayer, still at large, collected earrings and clothing from his female victims. Egyptian police retrieved the heads of 20 women from a killer's home in 1920; fifteen years later, Cleveland's Mad Butcher claimed the skulls of ten unidentified victims. Fetish-slayer Jerry Brudos loved women's shoes so much that he sometimes kept their feet as well; in other cases, he preserved their severed breasts as paperweights. In London, John Christie collected samples of pubic hair — which, curiously, matched none of his known victims. Another British slayer, nicknamed "Jack the Stripper," removed the front teeth of women he murdered. Members of the fanatical Hebrew Israelites reportedly severed the ears of their white targets to verify each kill. Leonard Lake videotaped the deaths of some victims, preserving the I.D. of others for personal use. Another name-dropper was Johann Hoch, habitually adopting the surname of his most recent bride. Besides planting bodies under his house, John Gacy also kept personal effects stripped from the pockets of his prey. Grave-robbing killer Alonzo Robinson saved heads, hanks of hair, and cured flesh. Greedy slayers like Vera Renczi, Harrison Graham, Fritz Honka, and Dennis Nilsen started corpse collections at home, keeping whole bodies on hand.

The final phase of serial murder is disposal, and again the methods used by random killers vary widely, from casual dumping on the roadside to elaborate dissection and concealment, even feeding the remains to animals. In FBI parlance, organized slayers often transport bodies away from the murder scene, taking pains to conceal the evidence; disorganized offenders, meanwhile, are prone to leave the corpses where they fall, with little or no attempt at concealment.[23] The comparison breaks down when "disorganized" slayers like Ed Gein and Harrison Graham bring their victims home for storage or other use, but in general terms, killers inclined toward concealment grow more proficient over time. Richard Kuklinski froze corpses for later disposal, thus defeating efforts to determine time of death. Leonard Lake and Gary Heidnik each boiled victims to remove flesh from bone, with Heidnik feeding some of the meat to his surviving captives, mixed in dog food. California rancher Joseph Briggen used human flesh to fatten his prize-winning hogs, while Texas nightclub owner Joe Ball fed wives and waitresses to his pet alligators. Incinerators, acid baths, and mobile crematoria have all been used by serial killers within living memory.

The placement and condition of a body provide valuable commentary on the killer's state of mind. FBI analysts specifically consider visibility, state of dress, positioning and final placement of the body when they view a crime scene, seeking clues to help them classify a killer and eventually clear the case with an arrest. Each factor plays its separate role in building up a profile of a killer still at large.

In terms of visibility, 58% of the FBI's test sample concealed their victims, while 42% left the bodies exposed.[24] For some killers — like the strangler in Sydney, Australia who left his female victims hanging from lamp posts — public display of the bodies may constitute a personal statement to society or the authorities. Other predators may be prevented from concealing the remains by circumstance, as when California traffic officers stopped Fernando Cota with a body in his van. For those who hide their victims, the location may have personal significance to the killer — a "totem place" in psychiatric terminology. Massachusetts slasher Antone Costa buried three victims in the same woodland "garden" where he cultivated his illegal marijuana plants. Eugene Butler and John Gacy planted bodies under their own homes, as much for the sake of proximity as for security. Jerry Dunbar spent four weeks in a motel room, with a woman's body rotting underneath the floorboards. Mack Edwards, building southern California's freeway system in the 1950s, hid his early victims under tons of asphalt and cement.

A victim's state of dress says much about the murderer's intent and motives, particularly in the case of sex crimes. Surveying victims of their captive correspondents, FBI analysts discovered that 47% were found nude, while only 28% were fully clothed. The other 25% were left in varying states of "sexual disarray"— 5% with genitals exposed, 9% with bared breasts, and 11% with their buttocks revealed.[25] Male victims of homosexual killers are frequently found with their pants pulled down, as in the Larry Eyler case. Australian slayer Eric Craig outsmarted himself by stripping his victims, then tying their clothes in an army-taught gunner's knot. John Gacy stuffed underwear into the mouths of several victims, and wadded panties were removed from the vagina of one woman murdered by John Norman Collins. Jerry Brudos enjoyed dressing dead women in lacy underwear, like life-sized Barbie dolls; he also severed one victim's breasts, redressing her in an oversized brassiere, cups stuffed with paper towels to take up the slack. At least five of Larry Eyler's 23 victims were found wearing white tube socks, supplied by their killer for reasons unknown. William Heirens, California child-killer Albert Dyer, and Michigan's unidentified "Babysitter" all washed their victims after death, laying them out in funereal style, complete with clean clothes.

The ritual positioning of bodies may reveal some aspect of the killer's private fantasy, or it may be intended to confuse police, as when a robbery or rape is simulated to disguise the slayer's true intent. Twenty-eight percent of the FBI's test sample deliberately posed their victims, while answers and motives remained ambiguous for another 17%.[26] Sex-slayers like Billy Glaze and Albert DeSalvo sometimes leave their victims exposed, with splayed legs; DeSalvo further dressed his women with elaborate bows around their necks and, on one occasion, a broom handle protruding from the vagina. Robert Liberty laid his victims out among flickering candles, dubbing himself the "Candlelight Killer." One of James Ruzicka's victims, in Washington state, was left hanging from a tree near the West Seattle Expressway. In Los Angeles, the Hillside Stranglers earned their media nickname by dumping nude bodies on highway embankments. Seattle's Green River killer, still at large, left one of his victims with a fish lying across her throat and another on her left breast; both hands were crossed over the woman's abdomen, the left weighted with a pile of fresh ground beef, her right grasping the neck of a wine bottle resting between her legs. In Gainesville, Florida, an unidentified slayer of five decapitated one female victim, propping her head up to face the bedroom door, while mirrors were positioned surrounding the corpse.

The final location of bodies may have significance to the killer beyond mere convenience. Besides preventing or postponing the discovery of crucial evidence, a dump site may contribute to the killer's private fantasy, thereby fulfilling dual functions for slayers like Renczi, Gacy, Nilsen, and Butler, who conceal their lifeless prey at home. Ritual placement of bodies may also highlight the killer's relationship to a third party, as when Ed Kemper buried severed heads, face-up, in his mother's flower bed, afterward sarcastically informing her that "People look up to you." Killer cousins Angelo Buono and Ken Bianchi discarded their victims in public as a gesture of contempt for the authorities. Rudy Bladel gunned his human targets down in railroad yards, to punish the company that discharged him. Julian Kennedy left one of his victims in a car, parked outside a Tampa, Florida, police station. In Los Angeles, Bobby Maxwell knifed his tenth victim to death on a bench 200 feet from police headquarters.

A peculiar aspect of serial murder is the tendency of some killers to dump their victims in clusters, at the private "totem places" noted earlier. Ted Bundy returned time and again to particular hillsides in Washington state, planting at least five victims at two sites. In South Carolina, Donald "Pee Wee" Gaskins came to grief when police followed up on his boasts of maintaining a "private graveyard." Jerry Brudos dropped two of his victims into Oregon's Long Tom River, weighted with automobile parts. Houston slayer Dean Corll buried 17 bodies under a suburban boat shed, with 10 others uncovered at two rural locations. Harrison Graham and Germany's Fritz Honka kept rotting corpses stacked in their apartments, somehow ignoring the stench. Farms made convenient burial grounds for John Williams in Georgia, Thomas McCormick in Colorado, and the Copelands in Missouri. Juan Corona planted 26 corpses in fruit orchards near Yuba City, California, while William Mansfield, Jr. used the junkyard surrounding his family's mobile home. Jack Scully folded his dead into oil drums, dropping them off in San Francisco's Golden Gate Park. In Poland, an unidentified slasher dumped 11 female corpses in the woods near Warsaw. England's Dennis Nilsen and Germany's Joachim Kroll each ran afoul of nosy plumbers when they tried to flush human remains down the toilet. Larry Eyler hid four bodies on an abandoned farm near Lake Village, Indiana; partially covered with dirt and leaves, the corpses were laid out methodically, three feet apart and facing north, with one black victim separated from the three Caucasians by a tree. Seattle's

Green River killer used at least four separate dump sites, alternating sporadically despite police surveillance. Many of the slayer's victims were covered with cut brush and branches, several stretched out next to fallen logs. Mark McAllister displayed less imagination, digging graves within an easy stone's throw of his West Virginia trailer park.

It should not be supposed, however, that the victims of a random slayer, though deceased, are totally without a voice. In fact, as we shall see, examination of a killer's chosen prey, specific preferences and methods of selection or exclusion, tell us much about that killer's state of mind.

With practice, it is even possible to pick out things the killer does not know about himself.

Chapter 5

Targets of Opportunity

In movies like *The Texas Chainsaw Massacre* and *Halloween,* the victims of serial murder are typically portrayed as lusty teenagers, butchered in the act of smoking dope or making love. Some fictional predators, like the title characters in *Red Dragon* and *The January Man,* select their prey by means so convoluted that it takes a psychic or computer wizard to unravel their design. The stalker is a manic genius or a mute, unfeeling beast; his chosen victims come across as cardboard replicas of humankind.

In fact, the real-life victims are as ordinary as their killers first appear to be. Their ranks include male and female, young and old, all races, affluent and penniless, well-educated and illiterate. They are drifters and debutantes, housewives and hookers, retirees and runaways. Some are aware of the risk when they take to the streets; others are hopelessly blind to their danger when murder comes calling at home.

The trait they share in common is their moment in the spotlight of a killer's twisted fantasy.

Male victims of domestic murders normally outnumber female victims three to one, but serial killers nearly reverse that trend, claiming 65% female victims and 35% male. Victims of both sexes range from infants to the elderly and all ages in between, depending on the killer's personal quirk. In terms of ethnic breakdown, serial murder victims are 89% Caucasian and 10% black; Orientals and American Indians divide the other one percent. (Thus far, no domestic serial slayer has deliberately confined himself to Oriental victims, though

one — Minneapolis killer Billy Glaze — murdered only women of American Indian descent.) Forty-two percent of American serial killers target victims of the opposite sex exclusively, while 16% kill only same-sex victims; 39% kill at least one victim of each sex, and the offender's sex remains unknown in 3% of all domestic cases, with the killers still at large. Ninety-four percent of America's "normal" murders involve killers and victims of the same race, but serial slayers fall below the norm, with 65% of their recorded murders in the same-race category. Another 10% kill only members of a different race, while 11% cross the color line impartially, from one crime to the next. A lack of evidence leaves the killer's race unknown in 14% of American cases.

Geography is another area where serial killers deviate from the norm. In an average year, some 43% of all domestic murders are recorded in the Southern states, while the West, Midwest, and Northeast average 20%, 19%, and 18% respectively.[1] Serial killers are less parochial: 25% strike in the South, with the West running a close second at 24%; the Midwest and Northeast lag behind with respective figures of 17 and 16 percent.

Serial murder is clearly a national problem — only Maine is untouched by the plague at this writing — but some states are safer than others. California is the worst by far, logging 97 cases in this century for 16% of the national total. New York runs second, its 45 cases since 1900 accounting for nearly half of all serial murders in the Northeast. Rounding off the top five are Texas (25 cases), Illinois (with 24), and Florida (reporting 20 cases to date). Author Ann Rule explains the geographic scatter by claiming that serial killers "run to the borders" in a physical expression of their mental extremity,[2] but her theory fails to explain why six "border" states — including Hawaii, Montana, North Dakota, Delaware, and Vermont — rank as the safest to date, with one case each in ninety years.

Upon further consideration, serial killers appear to choose territories rather logically. Their favorite hunting grounds include five of America's seven most populous states and seven of the nation's 11 most crowded cities. Aside from population density, cities like Los Angeles, San Francisco, Chicago, New York, and Miami share reputations as the most "liberal" in America where sex, alcohol, and drugs are concerned; all feature thriving subcommunities of prostitutes and homosexuals. In America's mobile society, these cities draw the vast majority of homeless transients, runaways, and would-be "stars"; they also rank consistently among the worst in terms of violent crime. Warm year-round climates and flourishing agriculture bring thousands — if not millions — of migrant workers and illegal aliens to California, Florida, and Texas every year, providing random killers with another ready source of prey. It is impossible to say if these states breed sadistic murderers in greater numbers or attract them like a magnet, from afar, but either way, the evident preponderance of random killers in the top five states should come as no surprise.

A hunter goes where there is ready game.

Psychologists and criminologists have long debated whether certain murder victims are "homicide prone," broadcasting silent, unconscious messages of vulnerability to potential assailants. The question is still unresolved, but serial murderers clearly prefer targets with a minimal capacity for resistance or self-defense. Whether the killer stalks all members of a given sex, selects his prey by race, or seeks specific "profile" victims, it is probable that he — or she — will try to stack the odds in favor of an easy kill.

Of the American killers reviewed for this study, 49% confined their attention to teenage or adult female victims. Twelve percent of the offenders specifically targeted adult males; of that killer class, 42% were homosexual, while the other 58% represented a potpourri of revenge and "thrill" killers, scheming "black widows," and hospital "angels of death." Infants and children were the victims of choice for 8% of America's serial killers, while another 2% preyed on the elderly. Transi-

ent or homeless victims were deliberately singled out in 2% of the reported cases. Finally, a full 27% of American serial slayers preferred a mixed bag, indiscriminately claiming victims of both sexes and various ages.

Traditionally, the majority of domestic murders have been — and still are — committed by a relative, "friend," or acquaintance of the victim, but the number of homicides by total strangers has increased dramatically since World War II. In 1989, 46% of the recorded murders in America were "stranger" slayings,[3] and serial killers exceed the national trend, murdering strangers in 56% of all known cases. Sixteen percent of identified serial murder victims knew their killers as friends, neighbors, coworkers, or casual acquaintances. Another 3% were related to their killers by blood or marriage: of the identified "family" victims, 49% were children killed by parents; 13% died at the hands of a spouse; 10% were parents murdered by their offspring; and 28% represented a wide range of grandparents, siblings, aunts and uncles, in-laws, cousins, nieces and nephews. One percent of the identified serial victims were killed as potential prosecution witnesses, and a single case — that of Dean Corll — involved a serial killer shot by one of his own accomplices, apparently in self-defense. With one or both parties unidentified at this writing, the killer-victim relationship remains unknown for 24% of America's serial murder victims.

The process of selecting victims — what author Joel Norris calls the "trolling phase" of serial murder — is highly individualized, serving the needs of a particular killer's compulsive fantasy. The several steps and choices may be automatic and instinctive or a product of deliberate, conscious thought, accomplished in a heartbeat or protracted over months, but every predator must choose a hunting ground, a victim, and a method of attack.

Selection of a hunting territory is the first prerequisite for a successful kill. A slayer's choice of stalking grounds may be determined by a private fantasy or vision, but it must include the basic elements of reasonable access, a supply of ready victims, and a decent prospect for evading capture. While some killers prefer the emotional rush of high-risk encounters, and a handful court arrest by leaving crucial evidence or living witnesses behind, none remain at large for long unless they take at least some rudimentary precautions to preserve their anonymity.

In short, the ideal hunting ground depends upon a given killer's personality and needs. Cannibal-slayer

Lester Harrison confined his prowling to Chicago's Grant Park and environs. Ted Bundy and Jerry Brudos displayed a mutual fondness for shopping malls and college campuses, with Brudos sometimes slipping into drag to stalk his female prey. For Carlton Gary, fixated on elderly widows, the Wynnton district of Columbus, Georgia, was an ideal game preserve. Homosexual slayer John Gacy did most of his trolling in Chicago's Uptown neighborhood, nicknamed "Lavender City" for the large number of male prostitutes. Christopher Wilder posed as a glamour photographer, approaching prospective victims at race tracks, shopping malls, and fashion shows. Malls and fairgrounds were also favored hunting grounds for the lethal husband-wife team of Gerald and Charlene Gallego. Rudy Bladel stalked his victims in midwestern railroad yards, while William Guatney rode the rails as a hobo, stopping only long enough to work odd jobs and kill young boys. In New York City, David Berkowitz and the still-unidentified "3X" gunman both haunted the borough of Queens. The elusive Green River Killer found most of his prostitute victims along the teeming Sea-Tac Strip, between Seattle and Tacoma, Washington. Los Angeles, meanwhile, produces so many territorial killers that it is sometimes difficult to tell them apart without a program: the Skid Row Slasher, Skid Row Stabber, Koreatown Slasher, West Side Rapist, Orange Coast Killer, Southside Slayer... each prowling neighborhoods known for their concentration of prostitutes, transients, elderly widows, or young women living alone.

In terms of victim selection, 40% of America's serial stalkers choose their prey on the basis of sex, with female victims outnumbering males by a ratio of ten to one. In Connecticut, mild-mannered Michael Ross raped and strangled six young women over 18 months in 1982 and '83. Richard Speck was linked to the murders of four women in Illinois and Indiana before his Chicago massacre of eight student nurses made international headlines. Harvey Carignan's 1949 death sentence for the murder of a woman in Alaska was overturned on appeal, paving the way for ultimate parole; in the early 1970s, he molested and murdered at least five more victims, cutting a bloody swath from Seattle to Minneapolis. New York's Joseph Baldi crept through open windows to stab women in their beds. In Florida, prolific killer Gerard Schaefer favored a hangman's noose, filling his journal with notes and sketches on the proper technique for stringing up "whores" and "fuck-sluts." Mark Smith began raping and strangling young women during his military service,

in Korea and West Germany, continuing the habit when he returned stateside. A quarter-century and several hundred miles apart, lady-killers Hugh Morse and Darren O'Neall earned dishonorable mention on the FBI's "Most Wanted" list. Strangler Jarvis Catoe drew little attention with black victims in New York, but the switch to white women in Washington, D.C., cost him his life. Sterilization by Hitler's SS did not prevent German slayer Bruno Ludke from raping and murdering an estimated 85 women. Further east, in the USSR, auxiliary policeman Gennadiy Mikhasevich strangled 36 victims in his quest for "revenge against adulterous women."

Rape-slayer Darren O'Neall was identified by a distinctive tattoo on his knuckles. *(Credit: FBI)*

The concept of women as submissive "sex slaves" drives some serial killers into a lethal frenzy. Ted Bundy was obsessed with the concept of "owning a female person," and Leonard Lake's diary described the perfect woman as "totally controlled; a woman who does exactly what she is told and nothing else. There is no sexual problem with a submissive woman. There are no frustrations, only pleasure and contentment." Charlene Gallego catered to husband Gerald's morbid fantasies by helping him abduct nubile "slaves," joining in sessions of sadistic abuse before the young captives were shot or beaten to death. Christopher Wilder traveled with one of his kidnap victims for nine days, repeatedly molesting her and using her to lure other prey before he ultimately set her free. In Kentucky, Philip Clopton and James Cable kept their teenage prisoners chained to trees between rapes. Gary Heidnik, bent on siring a prolific brood of children, converted his Philadelphia basement into a dungeon for captive prostitutes. Douglas Clark graded women on their sexual performance at gunpoint, reserving a fatal head shot for those who failed to satisfy.

Male victims are likewise selected on the basis of sex, where homosexual killers are involved. Outnumbered roughly six to one by heterosexual predators, gay killers sometimes manage to accumulate prodigious body counts. Randy Kraft leads the field among modern practitioners, linked with the murders of 67 victims in California, Oregon, and Michigan. Michael Terry, with six victims slain in Atlanta, seems a rank amateur in comparison with the likes of Larry Eyler (23 dead), Juan Corona (26 killed), Dean Corll (27 victims), and John Gacy (33 slain). Paul Bateson's string of mutilation-murders in New York inspired the controversial motion picture *Cruising*. Across the continent, Patrick Kearney mutilated and dismembered 28 young men in California's grisly "trash bag murders." London hairdresser Michael Lupo filled his diary with the names of influential male lovers before a diagnosis of AIDS pushed him over the edge; his victims were beaten and mutilated with razor blades, their tongues bitten off before Lupo defecated on the corpses. In Australia, William MacDonald — alias the "Sydney Mutilator" — stabbed his victims repeatedly before hacking off their genitals.

Potential profit ranks second on the list of prime criteria for victim selection in serial murder, accounting for 7% of American cases. "Bluebeards" and "black widows" are especially prone to kill for cash, most often in the form of an inheritance or life insurance payments, but not all profit-killers are related to their victims. Dr. Morris Bolber planned the deaths of 50 men in Philadelphia, using male accomplices to seduce dissatisfied wives, afterward splitting the insurance payoff with his latest victim's grieving widow. Dentist Glennon Engelman ran a similar murder mill in St. Louis, occasionally falling back on homicide to clear his backlog of bad debts. New York's Leslie Torres had a drug habit to feed, and he was terrified of leaving witnesses to any of his penny-ante stickups. In Sacramento, California, Dorothea Puente planted boarders in her flower garden and continued cashing welfare checks for those she killed. Velma Barfield looted the bank accounts of friends and relatives alike, covering her tracks with

strategic doses of arsenic. In California, rumors persist that Leonard Lake and Charles Ng may have offered their homemade snuff films for sale to black-market connoisseurs.

Age is the next most common factor in serial victim selection, with 6% of America's random killers preying on children or the elderly. Child-killers are among the most notorious of serial predators, terrorizing whole communities when their crimes make florid headlines. The unsolved "Babysitter" homicides in Oakland County, Michigan, are a prime example, surpassed four years later by the panic that engulfed Atlanta. Westley Dodd had a long record of child-molestation arrests before he murdered three boys in Washington. Real-life bogeyman Albert Fish claimed "credit" for molesting some 400 children, aside from the 15 he murdered and cannibalized. Mack Edwards killed at least six victims in California, before a guilty conscience led him to surrender and confess. John Joubert ambushed his prey on newspaper delivery routes, while Christine Falling smothered infants she was hired to baby-sit. Joseph Bryan told psychiatrists that he liked to see young boys "tied up and screaming," a quirk that cost three lives and placed him on the FBI's "Most Wanted" list. Arthur Goode walked away from a Maryland mental hospital and murdered two boys in March 1976. Ex-Eagle Scout Arthur Bishop was executed in 1988 for the murder of five Utah boys. Rhode Island's William Sarmento penned notes directing searchers to the bodies of his male victims, while Edward Holmes stalked children of both sexes in Maryland and the District of Columbia. In Baltimore, Reginald Oates confessed to drinking the blood and sampling the flesh of children he killed. Cincinnati's Charles Bischoff eluded detectives for 16 years, until the body of his fourth victim was discovered in his basement. Canadian Clifford Olson made a small fortune on his crimes, leading police to the graves of his victims at $10,000 a head.

Killers of the elderly are similar to child-slayers in many respects, including their preference for weak, defenseless victims. Pennsylvania's Roland Steele was a martial arts enthusiast who used old women as practice dummies, killing three and earning himself a death sentence in the process. "Stocking Strangler" Carlton Gary habitually blamed nonexistent accomplices for his crimes, escaping punishment for two New York murders and claiming seven more lives in Georgia before he was caged. In Jackson, Mississippi, Gregory Davis graduated from fondling elderly library patrons to lethal home invasions, mutilating his victims with kitchen knives. Anna Hahn, the first woman to die in Ohio's electric chair, posed as an angel of mercy, befriending elderly men whom she later poisoned... after they had "loaned" her large amounts of cash. Cleo Green III, of Louisville, Kentucky, took his marching orders from an invisible "red demon," butchering elderly women in their homes. Los Angeles police suspect rape-slayer Brandon Tholmer in the deaths of 34 senior citizens; some detectives also finger Tholmer as the elusive West Side Rapist, still at large after 33 attacks — with ten fatalities — in 1974 and '75. Paroled on a manslaughter conviction after the beating death of his first elderly victim, Indianapolis native Howard Allen claimed two more lives in identical fashion before he was captured and sentenced to die. In London, 24-year-old Kenneth Erskine was jailed for life on conviction of strangling seven seniors; prosecution in two other deaths was waived for lack of evidence. And in Paris, where the sadistic "Monster of Montmarte" terrorized elderly women from 1984 through 1987, immigrants Thierry Paulin and Jean-Thierry Mathurin were linked to a total of 21 slayings.

A victim's health or physical condition is the killer's prime consideration in 3% of America's serial murder cases, normally involving slayers from the medical profession. Donald Harvey holds the record, with 87 confirmed kills as a nurse's aide in Ohio and Kentucky, between 1970 and 1985. In Georgia, nurse Terri Rachals was charged with the murders of six patients and strongly suspected in the deaths of five others; her conviction on one count of aggravated assault was a concession to the jury's doubts about her sanity. Mary Robaczynski cited "mercy" as her motive for killing four Maryland patients, escaping prosecution with the surrender of her nurse's license. New York authorities are confident of Richard Angelo's guilt in ten hospital murders, while suspicion lingers in another 28 cases. In Florida, AIDS-stricken Jeffrey Feltner dispatched seven nursing home patients to "stop their suffering." California's Robert Diaz may have killed four times the dozen patients whose murders earned him a cage on death row. Genene Jones, convicted of one hospital murder and strongly suspected of some 30 others, committed her crimes as part of a one-woman campaign to promote construction of a pediatric intensive care unit. Dr. Mario Jascalevich was acquitted of six curare murders in Oradell, New Jersey, and the case remains unsolved today. Likewise, the 1977 conviction of two Filipina nurses in the serial murder of patients at a veteran's hospital in Ann Arbor, Michigan, were reversed on appeal,

leaving the crimes unsolved and unpunished. Canadian authorities cannot even agree on the number of victims killed at Toronto's Hospital for Sick Children between June 1980 and March 1981; "official" body counts range from eight to 43 infant victims, with no viable suspects in sight.

Race is the dominant factor in victim selection for 2% of America's serial murders, with killers crossing the color line to exorcise personal demons. In the past two decades, blacks have been targeted for execution by white supremacist gunmen like Joseph Franklin, Neal Long, Joseph Christopher, and "Aryan warrior" Frank Spisak. In Minneapolis, rape-slayer Billy Glaze confined his attention to the American Indian women he despised. Benjamin Miller, a postal clerk and self-ordained street preacher in Stamford, Connecticut, spent most of his time with black congregations after his own church expelled him for fanatical behavior; the apparent fondness for blacks, however, did not prevent Miller from strangling five black prostitutes between 1967 and 1971. Unlike their Caucasian counterparts, black racists tend to murder in groups — De Mau Mau in Chicago, California's Death Angels, the Yahweh cult of Hebrew Israelites in Florida. A unique case, recorded in 1911 and 1912, involved the ax murders of 49 mulatto victims in Texas and Louisiana, theoretically linked to a cult of militant blacks seeking to "purify" their race; one suspect was arrested and confessed to several of the crimes, but charges were dismissed for lack of solid evidence.

Another 2% of American serial murder victims are apparently selected on the basis of their residence, or lack of same. For predators like Montie Rissel, rape-slayer of five women in his own Virginia apartment complex, killing neighbors is a matter of convenience. New Yorker Calvin Jackson claimed eight of his nine victims at the seedy hotel where he worked as a maintenance man. "Night Stalker" Richard Ramirez showed a preference for one-story suburban homes with light-colored paint jobs. Jerome Spraggins is apparently unique in his obsession with a specific Montclair, New Jersey, address, returning time and again to murder three unrelated tenants between 1981 and '85.

A subclass of "residence" killers includes those who prey exclusively on transients or the homeless, banking on society to shrug the murders off as something less than top priority. Around the turn of the century, rancher Joseph Briggen murdered migrant farm workers in northern California, dicing their corpses into feed for his blue-ribbon hogs. Authorities were never certain whether sex or profit prompted Juan Corona to slaughter 26 migrants around Yuba City, California, but Missouri's Ray and Faye Copeland were clearly mercenary killers, luring transients into illegal livestock sales before the men were shot and dumped in shallow graves. Vagrants in New York's Bowery district were terrorized by random slasher Charles Sears in 1981, and life is especially hazardous for transients in Los Angeles, where killers Vaughn Greenwood, Bobby Maxwell, Michael Player, Joseph Danks, and Norman Bernard claimed 38 "skid row" victims in the span of a decade.

A victim's specific appearance — as opposed to general characteristics of sex, race, or age — seems to be the prime criteria for selection in 1% of America's serial murders. Ex-FBI agent Robert Ressler, writing in *Sexual Homicide*, notes the case of an anonymous slayer who victimized female drivers of two-door, light-colored cars, and similar cases are available with names attached. Ted Bundy showed a clear preference for young brunettes with long hair parted in the middle, more or less resembling a fiancee who rejected him before the onset of his adult murder spree. New York's "Son of Sam" likewise drew a bead on long-haired brunettes, prompting hundreds of women to clip and bleach their hair. Redheads were favored by Charles Floyd, in Tulsa, Oklahoma, during World War II, and by the unidentified strangler who scattered six bodies over five states in 1984 and '85. Vermont's Gary Schaefer preyed on girls resembling the stepdaughter he molested at home. In New York City, Erno Soto targeted dark-skinned boys whose appearance evoked painful memories of his wife's bastard son. San Francisco's "Paper Bag Killer," William Hanson, shot middle-aged men who walked with a limp, mistaking each victim in turn for the man who raped his sister.

Occupations doom another 1% of American serial victims, with prostitutes of both sexes dominating the list of job-related murders. College coeds are another favored target, stalked by the likes of Ted Bundy, John Collins, Edmund Kemper, Thor Christiansen, and Anthony Jackson. Slayers William Hansen and Bobby Joe Long lumped topless dancers together with the prostitutes they marked for extermination. Billy Gohl preyed on merchant seamen for over a decade in Aberdeen, Washington, killing dozens to supplement his income from the sailor's union with their pocket change and jewelry. The unidentified Ax Man of New Orleans showed a preference for grocers, chiseling through their doors at night to kill them in their beds. Randy Green-

awalt and John Wable shot truckers, while unidentified gunmen in San Antonio and New York city targeted cab drivers. Mitchell Sims and Ruby Padgett waged brutal war against employees of the Domino's Pizza chain. Rudy Bladel worked out his grudge against the Rock Island Line by shooting railroad employees. Hair-trigger coin shop robberies were Charles Sinclair's stock in trade, claiming 10 lives in seven states. Sex-slayers Herbert Coddington, Christopher Wilder, and Harvey Glatman set their sights on aspiring fashion models. Milton Jones and Theodore Simmons stalked Catholic priests around Albany, New York; elsewhere, authorities still seek the unidentified pattern-slayer of priests killed in four states since 1982. And in Belgium, Michel Bellen was so aroused by the sight of nurses' uniforms that even threats of death could not restrain him: sentenced to die for the rape-murders of two nurses in 1965, Bellen soon had his sentence commuted to "life," winning parole in May 1982; strangling a third nurse four months later, he received another death sentence... again commuted in 1984.

Thirteen percent of America's serial killers change their criteria for victim selection over time, sometimes from one murder to the next. Boston strangler Albert DeSalvo's first six victims were middle-aged or elderly white women, prompting manhunters to speculate on a possible mother fixation, but the next three women killed — including one black — were all in their twenties. Thereafter, DeSalvo seemed to lose track of his pattern entirely, murdering a 58-year-old, followed by victims aged 23 and 19, respectively. (So drastic was the strangler's shift, in fact, that some observers of the case still think a second killer was responsible for several of the crimes.) In New York state, Arthur Shawcross began his murderous career by killing two children, serving 15 years in prison on a manslaughter conviction for one of the slayings; paroled in 1987, he moved to Rochester and there murdered at least 11 women (with five more suspected) in a two-year period. Meanwhile, random killers like Henry Lucas, Ottis Toole, and Alton Coleman break all the rules, picking off victims without apparent regard to sex, race, or age.

Indeed, random selection accounts for a full 13% of America's serial murders, with pure bad luck placing victims in harm's way. Nomadic ax-killer Jake Bird murdered an estimated 42 victims in five years, wandering aimlessly across country before his arrest for a double slaying in Tacoma, Washington. Dennis Whitney reversed Bird's course, leaving California in 1960 with a vague plan "to kill maybe a dozen" persons on his way to Florida; in fact, he bagged seven, earning himself a death sentence in the Sunshine State. Rickey Brogsdale murdered four residents of Washington, D.C., without apparent rhyme or reason, and Danny Figueroa matched that body count in California, sniping random targets as he played "Rambo" with real guns. In New Orleans, John Brooks launched a one-man crime wave, claiming nine lives before he was caged in 1986. Senseless shootings in Oklahoma and California landed Billy Waldon on the FBI's "Most Wanted" list, while Richard Clarey gunned down three hapless victims— and confessed 100 other homicides — in Michigan.

Four-time killer Billy Waldon was severely beaten by cellmates, for refusing to murder a fellow prisoner in jail. *(Credit: FBI)*

Criteria for victim selection remains unknown in the final 12% of American serial murders, with numerous victims and a significant number of killers yet unidentified. One common theme in many cases, readily apparent, is the choice of "low-priority" victims, selected as a method of defusing public outrage and retarding a determined manhunt by police. For some predators, the targeting of prostitutes, homosexuals, or homeless "street people" is a kind of insurance, with the killer gambling on a sluggish response by authorities, journalists, and the general public. Skid row murders are buried in the back pages of most major newspapers, when they are reported at all, and police are doubly

handicapped in cases where "disposable" victims themselves remain anonymous. Cleveland's unsolved "torso murders" are a case in point, recorded in the midst of the Great Depression; five decades later, only three of the killer's 16 victims are positively identified, common links in the case as elusive as the headhunter himself. Ted Bundy, Juan Corona, Henry Lucas, William Bonin, John Gacy, Larry Eyler, Eddie Cole, Douglas Clark, Benjamin Boyle, Billy Mansfield, the Green River Killer — all these and more have nameless corpses charged to their credit, every unmarked grave a grim indictment of our "throwaway" society.

Worse yet are cases where police or members of the general public blindly overlook — or actively applaud — a killer's work. Authorities in San Diego, California, still reject Eddie Cole's confession to five local homicides, dismissing each case — including that of Cole's wife, found strangled to death in a closet, wrapped in a bedspread — as "death by natural causes." In Portland, Oregon, following the unsolved murders of several prostitutes, a police lieutenant voiced his opinion that violent death was an occupational hazard for streetwalkers. England's Yorkshire Ripper, Peter Sutcliffe, preferred to call himself "The Streetcleaner," purging his district of whores, and few complained about his crimes until Sutcliffe accidentally bagged an "innocent" girl on his fifth outing. Closer to home, similar feelings are echoed in Lake Elsinore, California, where some residents claim that a local prostitute-killer — as yet unidentified — is merely "cleaning up the trash downtown." Small wonder, in the face of such an attitude, that women's groups and gay rights activists complain of being short-changed by a legal system that evaluates a human life in terms of income, social status, sex, or race.

Selection of potential victims is the first part of a killer's task; it still remains for him or her to snare the human prey. A goodly number of our random stalkers opt for the simplicity of "blitz" attacks — a sudden blow or tackle from behind, an alley ambush, point-blank gunshots through the windshield of a car, perhaps a stealthy home invasion while the tenants are asleep. Some others, generally those the FBI would classify as organized offenders, utilize what author Joel Norris calls the "wooing phase," seducing their potential victims with an artificial bid for sympathy or trust. Ted Bundy sometimes wore a sling or hopped around on crutches, asking pretty girls to help him fetch some heavy object from his car, or from a house "just up the road." When national publicity unmasked Christopher Wilder's photographer persona, he switched tactics in mid-run, using a female hostage to put other women at ease. Alvin Neelley and Gerald Gallego both used their wives as decoys, luring nubile victims to "a party" where the booze and dope were free and plentiful. In Arkansas and Oklahoma, George Kent Wallace flashed a dime store badge at chosen boys and took them "into custody," from which a solitary victim managed to escape and testify. Several notorious killers have posed as police-men to snare their prey — and some have actually *been* policemen — but the list of alternate personas used by random killers to seduce their victims is virtually endless. Doctors, dentists, nurses, nurses' aides, a psychiatric social worker, janitors, repairmen, talent scouts, photographers, a security guard, gospel ministers, a nun, a babysitter, a Scout master, live-in companions for the elderly, potential employers, prospective buyers for advertised homes or automobiles, good Samaritans on a lonely stretch of highway... all these and more have lured hapless victims to untimely deaths in recent times.

An individual killer's technique depends in large part on his fantasies, the nature of his chosen prey, and the desired results of an attack, but general patterns are apparent from the mass of cases presently on file. With evidence in hand, we can begin to note which occupa-tions or activities place a potential victim at inflated risk of contact with a random predator.

Almost a third of the recorded cases in America — some 31% — involve audacious killers who approach their victims in a public place. Again, each killer has an individual technique. The contact may begin with idle conversation, or it may be swift and sudden as a blade between the ribs, but they are both means to a lethal end. In Los Angeles, Lawrence Bittaker and Roy Norris modified their van with a special sliding door, for snatching women off the sidewalk. Ted Bundy divided his time between campuses, shopping malls, and mountain ski resorts. Malls and other public gatherings, like races, fairs, and rodeos, provided fertile hunting grounds for Christopher Wilder, the Gallegos, and unidentified slayers of young women in Oklahoma and Wyoming. Jerry Brudos sometimes dressed in women's clothing prior to lurking in the shadows of an under-ground garage, but he preferred to pose as a Vietnam veteran when he made the college campus rounds. Child-killers regularly snatch their unattended prey from toy stores, ice cream shops, a corner playground, or the victim's own front yard. John Joubert and William Sarmento favored young boys out for an early morning bicycle ride. Where random snipers are involved, their victims are as likely to be shot down on the public street as anywhere. A killer with a grudge against the homeless typically assaults his victims anywhere that they are found, including one man stabbed to death within 200 feet of the Los Angeles Police Department headquarters. Taxi drivers shot or knifed in their cabs, women assaulted and slain on the walk home from work, hitchhikers casually run down on rural highways... all these and more fall victim to the killers who perform in quasi-public settings.

The next most common class of killers — accounting for 16% of the American total — dispatch their prey in homes or other private places where the victims feel at ease. Most of the classic "bluebeards" and "black widows" fall into this category, along with live-in companions or self-styled nurses like Velma Barfield, Anna Hahn, and Dorothy Matajke. Other killers, like Dean Corll, Gary Heidnik, Robert Berdella, John Gacy, and England's Dennis Nilsen, lure unsuspecting victims home with promises of liquor, drugs, or sex, surprising them with torture, rape, and death once they are trapped behind closed doors. The "homey" cast of killers would not be complete without consideration of the parents who destroy their own children: brutal fathers in the mold of Ernest Dobbert and Allen Washington; homicidal mothers like Debra Sue Tuggle, Marybeth Tinning, Martha Woods, and Paula Sims. In each case, bonds of trust are twisted to ensnare the chosen victim in a lethal web.

Ten percent of America's serial killers find their targets chiefly by invading private homes and either killing there, within the confines of a victim's residence, or dragging off their prey to preselected killing grounds. Satanic "Night Stalker" Richard Ramirez is probably the most notorious of the home invaders, sentenced to die in California on conviction of 13 sadistic murders and 30 related felonies. Another self-styled Satanist, Montana's Wayne Nance, stole keepsakes from the homes he violated, killing men and women indiscrim-inately, sometimes setting fires in an attempt to do away with evidence. Transient ax-killer Henry Lee Moore claimed 25 victims in 1911 and 1912, slaughtering whole families in their midwestern homes. In Boston, Albert DeSalvo charmed his way across the thresholds of countless apartments, murdering 13 women, raping as many as 2,000 others before he was brought to a semblance of justice. Ex-realtor Gary Robbins used his knowledge of the housing trade to strike up conversa-tions with prospective sellers, falling back on armed force to affect a capture when he found women home alone. Charles Floyd's voyeurism degenerated into lethal violence around Tulsa, Oklahoma, in the 1940s, claiming six lives in a series of brutal home invasions. Four decades later, Kim Brown murdered unsuspecting housewives in the Wisconsin Dells. In Richland, Georgia, police have all but given up hope in their search for a prowler who creeps into homes by night, unscrewing light bulbs to frustrate pursuit before snatching young girls from their beds.

Yet another breed of random killer — 5% of those recorded in America — confine themselves primarily to prostitutes, "exotic" dancers and the like, selecting those whose morals are in question by the very nature of their occupation. Those — at least where hookers are concerned — who offer themselves as the ultimate "targets of opportunity," climbing into cars with any stranger who has ready cash in hand. All of Europe's classic serial stalkers have been harlot killers, from Jack the Ripper to Yorkshire's Peter Sutcliffe, Italy's Giancarlo Guidice, Stockholm's cannibal team of Harm and Allgren, and London's "Jack the Stripper," presumed a suicide but still unnamed after nearly three decades. Closer to home, Louis Craine, Douglas Clark, and the Hillside Stranglers all stand convicted of murdering hookers around Los Angeles, while Raymond Singer terrorized prostitutes around Lancaster, California. Robin Gecht's team of Satanic cannibals, based in Chicago, preferred streetwalkers for their sadistic rituals. Richard Cottingham tortured and mutilated his prostitute victims in New York and New Jersey, while Ray Jackson plied his trade around Kansas City. Atlanta, Georgia, had its own "Jack the Ripper" in the early days of this century, and like his namesake, the slayer of 20 black whores was never identified. Across the country, in the past ten years, nameless predators have waged a war of attrition against hookers in Seattle, Washington (49 dead or missing); in Portland, Oregon (seven killed); in Los Angeles (15 murdered); in San Diego (42 reported slain); in New Bedford, Massachusetts (nine killed); in Washington, D.C. (15 slain in two distinct series); in Miami (31 dead and counting). Male hustlers, meanwhile, have fallen prey to the likes of Dean Corll, Larry Eyler, John Gacy, Patrick Kearney, William Bonin, Randy Kraft, and other denizens of the homosexual subculture.

An equal number of American serial slayers — 5% of the total — prey solely on patients in hospitals, clinics, nursing homes, and the occasional doctor or dentist's office. Nurses and nurses' aides are the most frequent offenders, but convictions have been returned on serial killers ranging from hospital maintenance personnel to veteran physicians. Dr. Michael Swango, rated a genius in high school, was suspected of killing at least seven patients during his internship at Ohio State University, in Columbus; fearful of lawsuits if Swango was dismissed, the university recommended him for a license to practice in neighboring Illinois, where he now stands convicted of attempting to poison several paramedics. In Detroit, Dr. Roland Clark weathered scores of official complaints, including cases of suspicious death, drug overdose and sexual assault; his medical license was four times revoked — and four times reinstated — before his ultimate conviction in the deaths of two office assistants. Successive convictions for second-degree murder and illegal abortion twice landed Dr. Joseph Emory in California prisons, but his medical license was restored by the state in 1974; two years later, he was jailed in connection with ten murder counts, linked to the deaths of infants at his cut-rate clinic in Los Angeles. Authorities are often slow to move against medical personnel, when they act at all, and numerous serial murders of hospital patients have gone unsolved from coast to coast, within the past two decades.

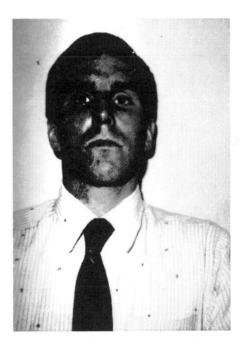

Dr. Michael Swango collected occult literature and poison recipes, practicing on patients and hospital paramedics. *(Credit: Quincy, Illinois, Police Dept.)*

Three percent of American serial stalkers target their prey on the job, typically mixing business with pleasure as they rob and kill. The vicious McCrary family is a classic case in point, suspected of kidnapping, raping and murdering 22 young women in a series of penny-ante heists across the country. (So notorious were the McCrarys, in their day, that they inspired a dramatic episode of the hit TV series *Hawaii Five-0*, with Slim Pickens starring as patriarch of the killer clan.) Paul Rhoades claimed at least six victims in Utah and Idaho, staging a series of robbery-murders in 1985 and '86, while Syvasky Poyner shot his five female victims in lunch-hour holdups around Newport News, Virginia. New York's Leslie Torres killed five persons and wounded six others in a week-long spree designed to feed his drug addiction. Charles Sinclair claimed twice as many lives, looting coin shops across the continent. Revenge, rather than profit, motivated Rudy Bladel's point-blank executions of railroad employees, and New York police continue their search for the unidentified slayer of seven cabbies, a gunman who "is getting into cabs and all he wants to do is shoot the driver."

Hitchhikers are another form of easy prey for random killers, climbing into cars with not-so-perfect strangers on the freeways, city streets, and urban back roads of America. An estimated one percent of domestic serial stalkers target hitchers as their victims of preference, and numerous others fall back on this resource sporadically, when they run short of hookers and homeless. Young coeds habitually hitchhike around college towns, providing ready meat for killers like Anthony Jackson in Massachusetts, John Collins in Michigan, Edmund Kemper and Thor Christiansen in California. An uncertain number of hitchhikers fell prey to the killer duo of Henry Lucas and Ottis Toole over the years, some picked up for purposes of sex and torture, others casually dispatched by random hit-and-run techniques. Harvey Carignan was constantly alert for hitchers, working his way east from Seattle to Minneapolis, and long-haul trucker Benjamin Boyle disregarded his company's ban on extra riders as he trolled the southwest for female victims. Robert Henderson sometimes thumbed rides himself, but he was death on wheels when he had access to a car; three of his hitchhiking victims were planted near Tavares, Florida, resulting in convictions that have placed him on death row. Homosexual slayer Randy Kraft was not above stopping for hitchers in southern California, and William Bonin's band of predators were so predictable in their approach that they were dubbed the "Freeway Killers," picking off a minimum of 21 young men in thirteen months. Thomas Rath carried the highway game to Germany in 1981

and '82, killing four young women and raping seven others before he was identified and brought to trial.

Another 1% of America's serial killers work primarily on lover's lane, targeting amorous couples parked in cars. New York's "Son of Sam" and California's "Zodiac" killer each prowled lover's lane on occasion, and "Sex Beast" Melvin Rees scored the first of his nine fatalities on a dark country road near Annapolis, Maryland. Two decades and a thousand miles apart, black gunmen Roy Mitchell and Clarence Hill amused themselves by victimizing white lovers in Texas and New Jersey, respectively. Working in darkness and catching their prey unaware, several notorious lover's lane killers have managed to remain at large: New York's "3X" gunman in 1930, bombarding police and the press with enigmatic notes from the "Red Diamond of Russia"; Texarkana's sadistic "Moonlight Murderer" in 1946; a black prowler in Atlanta, Georgia, who shot six victims and killed three in 1977. Overseas, the nocturnal display of casual sex triggered lethal violence from Germany's Werner Boost, a predator who used gunfire, gas-filled balloons, and cyanide injections to dispatch his human prey. And in Italy, the unidentified "Monster of Florence" has claimed 18 lives in a series of attacks on parkers and campers since 1968, typically shooting male victims to death and mutilating females with a knife, occasionally mailing their severed genitals to the police.

Classified advertisements provide live game for .5% of American serial slayers, with the lure working both ways. Some killers place their own ads, while others wait for their potential victims to shell out the money. At one time or another, random stalkers have gleaned their prey from the personal columns of matrimonial or "singles" publications, from offers of employment, and from advertisements of personal items for sale. Indiana's Belle Gunness made her living from the immigrant "lonely hearts" columns, paving the way for Martha Beck and Raymond Fernandez a generation later. (The same technique worked just as well for deadly Bela Kiss, in Hungary.) In Florida, Bobby Joe Long molested 50 victims as the "Classified Ad Rapist," before he turned to murdering suspected prostitutes and topless dancers. California's Leonard Lake picked off one of his numerous victims by scanning the daily papers for notices of cars on sale. In Seattle, Harvey Carignan murdered the first young woman who answered his advertisement for a gas station cashier. Harvey Glatman, in Los Angeles, divided his time between prowling "singles" clubs and advertising for would-be models, conning respondents with his spiel about the need for bondage shots to grace the covers of pulp detective magazines. Georgia's Earl Daughtrey victimized women who advertised household items for sale in neighboring Tift and Cook Counties, phoning ahead for appointments to strangle his prey.

Highway distress situations are the stock in trade for another .5% of America's serial killers, with women regarded as particularly vulnerable when their cars break down. California's "Zodiac" killer bagged his first victim by disabling her car on a college campus in Riverside, and one of the elusive slayer's rare surviving victims narrowly escaped death after he flagged her down, pretending that one of the wheels on her vehicle was wobbling erratically. Henry Lucas was especially fond of stranded motorists, offering a lift to the next available telephone, producing a knife or gun once they were safely in his car. At other times, when trolling with partner Ottis Toole, Lucas would sometimes deliberately ram other cars from behind, picking off the driver when she got out to investigate the damage. Hulking William Smith used an identical technique to bag his female prey in Salem, Oregon. California's latest "I-5 Killer," Roger Kibbe, offered one-way rides to stranded ladies in distress when he ran short of prostitutes to strangle. Steven Judy was executed in Indiana for the rape-slaying of a young mother and the drowning of her three children, after he stopped to help his victim change a flat tire. In Florida, Dade County authorities suspect one unidentified assailant in the murders of five women, each picked off after their cars were disabled with flat tires at area shopping malls.

It is important to note that a full 23% of America's serial stalkers vary their techniques of capturing victims from one crime or series of crimes to the next. A killer of prostitutes may switch to hitchhikers or motorists in distress if ready prey runs thin along his favorite trolling route. Texarkana's "Moonlight Murderer" staged his final raid on a rural farmhouse, after police stakeouts made lover's lane too dangerous for further hunting. In Chicago and environs, John Gacy alternated freely between the murder of male hustlers and his own construction employees. Roy Norris and Lawrence Bittaker abducted women from the streets by force, if no willing hitchhikers presented themselves in timely fashion. When Harvey Carignan was not advertising for victims or brutalizing young hitchers, he sometimes assaulted women at city bus stops. In short, most serial killers preserve a certain flexibility in their approach to the hunt, and in 4% of American cases — where victims and/or murderers are unidentified — the method of attack remains unknown.

The question of personal defense against serial killers is problematical, since many of the stalkers are complete strangers to their prey, striking at random and often by surprise. In theory, certain high-risk targets — prostitutes and the sexually promiscuous, hitchhikers and motorists who stop for hitchers — can reduce their odds of suffering assault by finding different occupations, modes of transportation, and means of private entertainment. Children can be watched more closely on the street, in yards, at shopping malls. Neighborhood watch programs can report suspicious strangers and watch out for elderly residents living alone. States can mandate sweeping background checks for all employees at a hospital or nursing home.

But what of victims who have taken all the "right" precautions to protect themselves from harm? What happens when the car breaks down, a bus is missed, or they are forcibly abducted from a parking lot at gunpoint? How should they respond?

The proper method of reacting to a criminal assault remains a highly controversial topic with selected experts in the field. Most such arguments revolve around techniques for coping with a sexual attack where the assailant is presumed to be nonhomicidal — a risky assumption in itself, as we have seen, since many random murderers begin as rapists, killing over time as they require a greater thrill, or even as a twisted form of "self-defense" against arrest.

Reliable statistics are hard to come by in this area, with so many rape victims murdered or declining to report attacks, but the FBI grilled its caged correspondents on the subject of victim resistance, with some interesting results. In the cases with relevant data, 28% of the victims offered no resistance, 31% tried verbal negotiation with their assailants, 6% verbally refused to submit, 10% screamed, 19% fought back physically, and 4% tried to escape.[4] The offenders responded to resistance in various ways: 34% professed no reaction whatsoever; 14% resorted to verbal threats; 25% escalated their aggressive behavior; and 25% became physically violent.[5] From this sampling, the FBI experts conclude that victim resistance will be met with increased force or aggression in 50% or more of all sexual assaults.

From the data collected in their study, Bureau psychologists have outlined six general methods of coping with criminal assailants, each of which has drawbacks in relation to particular offenders.[6] The techniques include:

1. *Escape.* Described as the optimum response where feasible, a victim's ability to flee from attackers clearly depends on a wide variety of circumstances. If the assailant is armed or mentally unstable, failed attempts to break away may escalate the brutality of the attack.

2. *Verbally Confrontative Resistance.* Screaming to attract help or shouting such things as "Stop!" and "Get away from me!" conveys an immediate message of noncompliance with the assault. Some attackers are frightened away by this tactic, while others may panic or become enraged to the point of using deadly force.

3. *Physically Confrontative Resistance.* Ranging from moderate to violent and potentially lethal, a victim's capacity for physical resistance is dictated by factors including the time and place of an attack, availability of weapons, and the size or number of assailants. Speed and surprise are generally critical when victims decide to fight, and some degree of counterviolence should be anticipated.

4. *Nonconfrontative Verbal Resistance.* This technique is divided by FBI experts into three subcategories, including efforts to dissuade the attacker, bids for empathy, and attempted negotiation. In the first category, a victim might claim "I'm a virgin" or "I have my period," in an effort to put the would-be rapist off, but allusions to pregnancy and venereal disease are strongly discouraged as possible fuel for the attacker's morbid fantasy of punishing "sluts" and "tramps." Pleas for empathy, through conversation and attentive listening, are sometimes effective, as in the case of a Florida victim who saved herself from rape-slayer Bobby Joe Long by describing her own background of childhood abuse. Negotiations are described by Bureau experts as the safest, most effective means of minimizing violence in a sexual assault, but it is frankly admitted that such conversations rarely prevent the rapist from proceeding with his conquest... in a "less brutal" manner, of course.

5. *Nonconfrontative Physical Resistance.* A true wild card, this technique may be feigned or the product of uncontrollable bodily functions — fainting, seizures, gagging or vomiting, involuntary urination, and so forth. Some attackers are repulsed or frightened by such symptoms, but the technique increases victim risk in dealing with sadists or "displaced-anger" offenders. On one hand, a sadist will be excited by involuntary physical spasms, viewing them as evidence of a successful assault, while the "displaced-anger" assailant — already seething from real or imagined insults by family members, friends, and total strangers — may interpret retching or seizures as the ultimate slap in the face, reacting with savage violence. Since few victims are capable of diagnosing their assailant on the spot, the risks inherent in this method seem to outweigh the rewards.

6. *Submission.* Recommended by FBI spokesmen as the last resort, when other methods have already failed, victim submission comes with its own risks attached. For some offenders, like the sadist, victim acquiescence is a part of the overall fantasy, calling for escalated brutality as the victim becomes a "willing" participant in the crime. Other assailants, counting on some measure of resistance to validate their mental image of the victim, may be so frustrated by compliance that they kill to erase a contradictory image.

In practice, victims have no way of knowing whether they are dealing with an "ordinary" rapist or a killer with a taste for violent sex, and the decision to submit or fight is highly personal. In robberies, it may be wise to let the money go and save yourself — though, even here, the rules are different where a serial offender is involved — but sexual assault can escalate from simple fondling or rape to torture, death and mutilation in a heartbeat. Clearly, if a victim *knows* that she or he is dealing with a killer — as where several victims of a given type or class have recently been murdered in the neighborhood — all-out resistance would appear to be the only option. Escape may be more likely in a public place — a city street or shopping mall, for instance — while defensive weapons are more likely to be found at home. In either case, the risk of dying from a sudden knife thrust or a bullet in the brain may be preferred to capture by the likes of Henry Lucas, Ottis Toole, or Lawrence "Pliers" Bittaker.

And sometimes victims *do* get lucky. In Montana, Wayne Nance was killed by one of his intended targets in September 1986. Harvey Glatman was disarmed by a female captive and held at gunpoint until police arrived, leading to his ultimate conviction and execution in San Quentin's gas chamber. Elsewhere, would-be victims are alive today because they fought back against such random stalkers as Ted Bundy, Alton Coleman, Robert Hansen, Harvey Carignan, Vaughn Greenwood,

David Berkowitz, Coral Watts, Richard Ramirez, Benjamin Boyle, Roger Berdella, Thomas Rath, the "Zodiac," and many others.

Confronted with certain death, a victim has nothing to lose.

Surviving relatives of random murder victims suffer both from the traumatic loss of one they love and from the aftermath of a collision with a brutal stranger. In the case of "normal" homicides, where motives, means, and suspects are apparent from the start, there is at least a sense of comprehension and finality. The tragic act is over, done with in a moment, and survivors can begin to cope with grief as they adjust to the reality of sudden death. In cases where a total stranger is responsible — especially where the victim may be missing and the murderer is still at large — survivors are effectively prohibited from moving on, compelled to face a myriad of questions. Where? Who? Why?

Each friend or member of a murder victim's family copes with grief in different ways. Some compensate by taking part in efforts to locate the missing victim or identify the killer, joining with authorities or taking private steps within the law. Once apprehension of the suspect is accomplished, some survivors mitigate their grief by tracking progress through the courts, devoting years or decades to petition efforts that will bar the killer from a subsequent parole. Increasingly, there is a trend toward counseling and other forms of professional help for traumatized survivors, including establishment of various support groups. Some of the organizations recently established to help crime victims and their survivors include:

Citizens for Justice and Crime Victims United
PO Box 19480
Portland, OR 97219

National Association for Crime Victims' Rights
PO Box 16161
Portland, OR 97216-0161

National Organization for Victims' Assistance
717 D Street NW, 2nd Floor
Washington, DC 20004

National Victims' Center
307 West Seventh Street, Suite 1001
Ft. Worth, TX 76102

Parents of Murdered Children
100 East Eighth Street, B-41
Cincinnati, OH 45202

The Stephanie Roper Committee and Foundation, Inc.
14804 Pratt Street, #1
Upper Marlboro, MD 20772

Victims of Crime and Leniency
Box 4449
Montgomery, AL 36103

Victims for Victims
1800 South Robertson Blvd, Suite 400
Los Angeles, CA 90036

The death or disappearance of a child is especially traumatic for all involved. Organizations created to cope with the problem of murdered, missing, or exploited children include:

Adam Walsh Child Resource Center
3111 South Dixie Highway, Suite 244
West Palm Beach, FL 33405

Child Find of America
PO Box 277
New Paltz, NY 12561

Children's Rights of America
12551 Indian Rocks Road, Suite 9
Largo, FL 34644

Find the Children
11811 West Olympic Blvd
Los Angeles, CA 90064

The Kevin Collins Foundation
  for Missing Children
PO Box 590473
San Francisco, CA 94159

Missing Children Clearinghouse
State Office Building, 100 North Senate
Indianapolis, IN 46204

National Center for Missing and Exploited Children
2101 Wilson Blvd, Suite 550
Arlington, VA 22201

The Roberta Jo Society
Box 916
Circleville, OH 43113

Society for Young Victims
Spooner Building, 54 Broadway
Newport, RI 02840

Sun Bay Recovery — International
  Missing Children's Division
PO Box 704
Largo, FL 34649

Vanished Children's Alliance
PO Box 909
Los Gatos, CA 95030

The random killer, too, has needs that blossom in the wake of murder, and for some the reaping of another victim may not be enough to satisfy. The deadly game is still afoot, and there are rules to follow, private rituals to be observed. For ego's sake, some killers must remain at center stage, while others slip away and hide their tracks. In each case, there are patterns of behavior that authorities can use, with luck, to run the stalker down.

But first, they must observe and recognize the signs.

Chapter 6

Post Mortem

For random murderers, the act of killing is a powerful, addictive drug. Some take it as a stimulant, to amplify their morbid fantasies, while others find a sedative in human suffering. Like all narcotic substances, however, homicide has side effects beyond the killer's ultimate control.

And it does not wear off the moment blood is spilled.

As each compulsive killer acts from motives that are private and unique, so each responds uniquely in the wake of murder. Some experience euphoria, a sweet relief from tension not unlike the aftermath of sex. (In fact, as we have seen, for many human predators the act of murder is a kind of sexual release.) In other cases, homicide — however cunningly conceived and executed — fails to do the trick. Instead of pouring oil on troubled waters, it exacerbates the very agitation and anxiety the killer seeks to hold at bay. A third class of compulsive killer lapses into black depression once the dirty work is done. Between crimes, he — or she — falls back on alcohol and drugs, sometimes pursuing help without success, occasionally contemplating or attempting suicide.

"I love my work," wrote gunman David Berkowitz, while he was busy terrorizing New York City. "Now the void has been filled."[1] For Berkowitz and others who derive a transient satisfaction from the act of murder, filling up their private void with corpses, it is helpful if the crime — the fantasy — can be sustained and reenacted, thus prolonging its effect. A case in point is England's Dennis Nilsen, who preserved the bodies of

his prey for weeks or months on end, as "company." In Nilsen's prison journal, he describes a typical encounter with a lifeless "guest."

> A week later I wondered if his body had changed at all or had started to decompose. I disinterred him and pulled the dirt-stained youth up on to the floor. His skin was very dirty. I stripped myself naked and carried him into the bathroom and washed the body. There was practically no discoloration and he was pale white. His limbs were more limp and relaxed than when I put him down. I got him out of the bath and washed myself clean in the water. I carried the still wet youth into the room and laid him on the carpet. Under the orange side-lights his body aroused me sexually. I knelt over him and masturbated on his bare stomach. Before I went to bed I suspended him by the ankles from the high wooden platform. He hung there all night, his fingers just touching the carpet. The next day while he was still hanging there upside down I stood beside him and masturbated again. I wiped him and took him down. I laid him on the kitchen floor and decided to cut him up, but I just couldn't do anything to spoil that marvelous body.[2]

Nor is Nilsen the only serial killer who derived twisted pleasure from keeping his victims nearby. John Gacy, Eugene Butler, Harrison Graham, John Christie, Fritz Honka, and Vera Renczi all lived with the decomposing remains of their victims. In Philadelphia, Graham actually left his women stacked up on the floor of his squalid apartment, while the Hungarian Renczi kept a special chair in her basement, holding court among the zinc caskets of her departed husband, son, and lovers. On opposite sides of the continent, Ed Kemper and Richard Biegenwald planted bodies at the homes of their respective mothers. Jerry Dunbar spent three weeks in a Virginia motel room, his latest female victim tucked away beneath the floorboards. Eddie Cole slept with the body of one female victim three nights running; in a separate crime, he carried a woman's body around in the trunk of his car for two days. In Wisconsin, Ed Gein transformed his farmhouse into a ghoulish museum, decorated with the trophies from a string of homicides and plundered graves.

If whole bodies are too cumbersome, sometimes bits and pieces are sufficient to preserve the fantasy. One prolific "Bluebeard," jailed by Egyptian police in April 1920, kept a collection of 20 women's heads in his home. In Oregon, Jerry Brudos preferred breasts and feet, making paperweights of the former, while the latter were preserved in sexy high-heeled shoes. Henry Lucas once drove from Texas to Arizona with a woman's severed head in the back seat of his car. In Los Angeles, "Sunset Slayer" Douglas Clark decapitated a prostitute and took her head home for purposes of oral sex; Clark's live-in lover, nurse Carol Bundy, further amused herself by painting the lifeless face with makeup. Transient killer Alonzo Robinson also preserved heads on occasion, sometimes satisfying himself with scraps of hair and desiccated flesh. In place of physical remains, killers Robert Berdella, Randy Kraft, and Jerry Brudos took snapshots of their prey, while Leonard Lake and Charles Ng captured their homicides on videotape. Lawrence Bittaker and Roy Norris recorded the screams of their female victims in Los Angeles, while British slayers Ian Brady and Myra Hindley cherished similar sound tracks of torture. Texan Joe Ball amused himself by feeding human flesh to pet alligators on public display, and California's Joe Briggen reaped numerous blue ribbons for the hogs he fattened on a "special feed."

A killer's emotional reaction to murder dictates the frequency and ferocity of attacks. In simple terms, if he or she is satisfied with a particular assassination, weeks or months may pass before the next attack. Conversely, if the homicidal fantasy falls short of expectations, it must be repeated and elaborated, as in Ted Bundy's frenzied assault on the Chi Omega house, in Tallahassee, Florida. Bundy himself discussed the subject of homicidal lag time with journalist Stephen Michaud, carefully couching his revelations in third-person terms, with reference to an anonymous killer "entity."

> Fear of discovery, sure. Fear of a number of things. He was horrified by the recognition that he'd done this, the realization that he had the capacity to do such a thing, or even attempt — that's a better word — this kind of thing. He was fearful, terribly fearful that for one reason or another he might be apprehended.
>
> The sobering effect of that was to... for some time, close up the cracks again. For the first time, he sat back and swore to himself that he wouldn't do something like that again... or even, anything that would lead up to it.
>
> And he did everything he should have done. He stayed away from... he didn't go out at night. And when he was drinking, he stayed with friends. For a period of months, the enormity of what he did stuck with him, and he watched his behavior and reinforced the desire to overcome what he had begun to perceive were some problems that were probably more severe than he would have liked to believe they were.[3]

Severe indeed, with 30 brutal slayings claimed by Bundy on the night before he died. Across the country, homicide investigators still believe that Ted took details of another six or seven murders to his grave.

The lull between successive murders in a series varies, as the federal definition quoted in the introduction notes, from hours to years. Vaughn Greenwood, L.A.'s "Skid Row Slasher," took a decade off between his first two murders. Connecticut's Richard Delage nearly tied Greenwood's record, laying off murder for nine years and four months between his first and second kills. England's Yorkshire Ripper, Peter Sutcliffe, typically claimed victims at three- and four-month intervals, but he allowed thirteen months to pass between his second and third murders. Sexual tension fixed the murder timetable for Gerald and Charlene Gallego, with lapses of nine and ten months between their early homicides; later, as the frenzy mounted, calling for a bigger, quicker "fix," they would dispatch six victims in the space of four months. Where killers remain at large and unidentified, charting a pattern is even more difficult. Italy's elusive "Monster of Florence" was an especially slow starter, committing his first three attacks in 1968, 1974, and 1981 respectively, before hitting his stride with a dependable yearly cycle of murder.

When murder fails to satisfy a killer's need — for sexual release, revenge, whatever — new anxiety may demand a change of scene. For some, like Christopher Wilder and Alton Coleman, suspicion inspires panic, launching high-profile flights to nowhere, with the inevitable climax of capture or death. Alex Mengel fled New York City after the pointless shooting of a traffic patrolman; en route to Canada, he paused long enough to kill and scalp a female victim near Durham, New York, wearing her hair as a flimsy disguise during bungled Toronto abductions. Tired of the game after ten murders, California's Ed Kemper was crossing Colorado when his conscience caught up and urged him to summon police from a roadside telephone booth. Earle Nelson's high-profile murders of elderly landladies kept him forever on the move, crossing the United States from coast to coast before he tried his luck in Canada and wound up stretching rope. Norman Bernard sought to do homeless transients "a favor" by gunning them down and cutting off their genitals, but his first attempt in North Carolina was so traumatic that he fled across country to Los Angeles, where Skid Row killers are seldom in short supply. Female slayers Sharon Kinne and Audrey Hilley each hit the road with murder trials pending. Mere suspicion was enough to put Ken Bianchi on the run, fleeing New York for California, and California for Washington state, when his name was linked to successive homicides. A handful of consummate escape artists — including Belle Gunness, Carl Menarik, and Hungarian Bela Kiss — successfully elude pursuit despite their notoriety, entering criminal legend as "the ones who got away."

An agitated killer frequently engages in erratic or bizarre behavior, thereby calling more attention to himself and risking apprehension in the process. New York's David Berkowitz punctuated his "Son of Sam" murder spree with trash fires, threatening notes to real or imagined enemies, and the shooting of neighborhood dogs. Richard Speck celebrated his Chicago massacre of eight student nurses with a wild night of drinking, fist fights, and attempted suicide. In Cleveland, neo-Nazi gunman Frank Spisak kept his hand in between murders by firing random shots through his apartment windows, thereby prompting neighbors to alert police. South African slayer Gamat Lineveldt had a penchant for indecent exposure, landing in jail on misdemeanor sex charges before police linked his name to a series of local homicides. Ottis Toole compulsively set fire to old, abandoned houses, finally recruiting teenage helpers who would turn state's evidence and earn him 20 years in prison on an arson charge.

Some random killers pass directly from the act of murder into what Joel Norris labels the "depression phase" of homicide.[4] For slayers in this category, murder falls far short of its intended goal as an emotional catharsis. Pattern victims are selected on the basis of resemblance to some actor in the killer's past or private fantasy — a brutal parent figure or unfaithful spouse, for instance — but the chosen victim's death destroys that fragile bond. The murderer, in turn, is faced with yet another failure to erase the painful past, to rewrite history and boost his own self-image in the process.

Psychiatrists described Alton Coleman as a "pansexual, willing to have intercourse with any object." *(Credit: FBI)*

Ted Bundy, Henry Lucas, Joseph Kallinger and other serial killers have reported severe depression in the wake of their various crimes. In many cases, that depression is assuaged with alcohol and drugs. Lucas, for one, reports traveling the country in a state of near-constant intoxication, committing most or all of his murders in a chemical haze. Carlton Gary's reliance on cocaine provided courage in advance of lethal home invasions and a sense of comfort afterward. In California, "Night Stalker" Richard Ramirez used various drugs to intensify his bond with Satan. Massachusetts slayer Antone Costa was far gone on drugs before he began killing; three of his mutilated victims were planted in Costa's rural marijuana garden. Velma Barfield's addiction to prescription drugs increased throughout her murder spree, including four near-fatal overdoses in the 1970s. Eddie Cole, an alcoholic from his adolescent years, drank heavily before and after every homicide, sometimes reporting "blackouts" at the crucial moment of the kill. In some cases, as with New York's quick-trigger Leslie Torres, support for a raging drug habit becomes the motive for murder itself.

It should not be supposed that random killers never try to stop themselves by seeking medical or psychiatric help. The inevitable failure of such self-help efforts hinges primarily on the killer's inability or staunch refusal to "come clean." Eddie Cole repeatedly committed himself to mental hospitals in California and Nevada, confessing his urge to rape and strangle women, always neglecting to mention his first homicide; in each case, he was released as a malingerer, "no danger to society." Florida's Bobby Joe Long once dated a nurse, describing his compulsive sex drive, but stopped short of admitting his serial rapes in progress. Gary Heidnik and Donald Harvey were both frequent tenants of V.A. psychiatric wards. California's Jeffrey Jones was undergoing therapy, reportedly "stabilized" on antipsychotic medication, when he started clubbing men to death in Sacramento. Arthur Goode volunteered for therapy in Maryland, to escape prosecution for child-molesting, but the sessions obviously did not take. Strangler Benjamin Miller spent a month in a Connecticut hospital, before his arrest on five counts of murder. Another Connecticut slayer, Richard Delage, was surprised by police as he signed the paperwork for voluntary self-commitment.

When serial killers lack the courage to seek help directly, some leave a trail of clues for police, as if anxious to hasten their own arrest. Chicago's William Heirens is the classic case, scrawling a lipstick message at the scene of his second murder: "For Heaven's sake catch me before I kill more. I cannot control myself." Ritual killer Robert Liberty left a note emphasizing his M.O. for police — "The candlelight killer strikes again." — and Edmund Kemper likewise penned a message to commemorate his final crime: "Not sloppy and incomplete, gents. Just a 'lack of time.' I got things to do!!!" Donald Dufour, David Bullock, Harry Lanham, Donald Gaskins, and the murderous Penn brothers all boasted of their crimes to friends or total strangers, knowing that the word would get around in time. British child-killer Mary Bell left incriminating graffiti for police in an abandoned school. Johann Hoch and Leonard Lake each ran the deliberate risk of adopting their victims' names as pseudonyms. Germany's Fritz Haarmann visited one victim's family, naming his accomplice as the boy's killer. Another Fritz — North Carolina's Fritz Klenner — recruited a gullible friend to assist in one of his multiple murders, posing as a CIA assassin. Repeat killers Joseph Kallinger, Vaughn Greenwood, Gordon Cummins, and Ed Gein all dropped distinctive items —

including one driver's license — at the scene of their crimes. Sex-slayers Peter Kurten, Edward Leonski, and Bobby Joe Long each allowed victims to live, thus courting arrest. As Long describes his fatal lapse:

> When I started talking to her I knew it was all over. Her own stepfather had raped her and she had to work to support him. She was the first girl that I stopped who didn't come over to me first. I knocked her off her bike. That was a first. I tied her up and brought her back to my apartment, and I knew that if I let her go she would tell the police. I talked to her and asked her not to but she hates me. When they tried me, she was among the people who wanted to see me fried the most.[5]

Spontaneous surrender is rare among serial killers, but it happens on occasion. Austrian immigrant Carl Menarik — alias "Frederick Mors" — stunned New York police in February 1915, with his confession to eight recent murders at the German Odd Fellows Home. Neal Long approached Dayton, Ohio, authorities in 1966, relating the details of a 20-year-old stabbing, but he was released when detectives failed to turn up a victim. California scored two unexpected confessions in 1970, with child-killer Mack Edwards and cannibal-slayer Stanley Baker. Three years later, Edmund Kemper tired of mutilating co-eds around Santa Cruz and turned himself in to police. On the East Coast, paroled killer Joseph Fischer confessed to the murder of his wife in 1979, an admission that paved the way for details of numerous other homicides. And in Texas, Henry Lucas was awaiting trial on misdemeanor weapons charges when he confided to a jailer, "Joe Don, I done some bad things."

At the nadir of depression, random slayers sometimes turn upon themselves. Donald Harvey and Gary Heidnik were both hospitalized after failed suicide attempts, while Velma Barfield dismissed her repeated drug overdoses as "accidents." New Jersey's Richard Biegenwald once set himself on fire. Successful suicides include Mississippi hermit Randal Rolle and New York's Carmello DeJesus, who left behind a well-thumbed Bible and a list of victims for police.

When not programmed for flight or self-destruction, serial killers typically cherish a sense of continued involvement with their crimes, the furor they inspire. Revisiting the murder scene — a tactic overworked in fiction to the point of being dubbed cliche — is one means of preserving the connection. Twenty-seven percent of the FBI's prison correspondents admitted returning to crime scenes, but their stated motives varied widely.[6] One in four came back specifically to relive their crimes and thus prolong the fantasy — Henry Lucas returning for one-sided conversations with a dismembered girlfriend in Texas; Charles Manson dropping by the Tate-Polanski residence to view "his children's" handiwork — but simple visits to the murder site may not provide sufficient thrills. In England, Mary Bell came calling at a victim's house and asked to see the dead boy in his coffin. Closer to home, Michigan's John Norman Collins turned up at an Ypsilanti funeral parlor, begging permission to photograph his first victim's corpse.

For 19% of the FBI's test sample, repeat visits to a crime scene were motivated by interest in the police investigation.[7] For some, it is a simple follow-up procedure, checking to determine if their latest homicide has been discovered. Other predators turn paranoid and double back to cover up their tracks, like Henry Lucas in the case of victim Katherine Rich. Believing that her corpse might be recovered from the Texas highway culvert where he first concealed it, Lucas went back for the body, cut it into pieces, and tried to cremate the remains in his wood-burning stove. A different class of stalker may deliberately return to taunt authorities, as when Seattle's Green River killer came back to his favorite King County burial grounds, ignoring the risk of police surveillance. In Michigan, John Collins goaded authorities by dropping cut flowers and articles of female clothing at one murder site, days after police had swept the area for evidence.

Another motive for revisiting the crime scene, claimed by 8% of the FBI's sampling, is the perpetration of another murder at a favored site.[8] Stationary killers fall into this category by definition, but they are not alone. Vaughn Greenwood claimed his first two victims on the same spot in Los Angeles, their murders separated by a decade. Near San Jose, California, Karl Warner slaughtered three young women at the same picnic site in two separate attacks, the crimes separated by a span of 21 months. New Jersey gunman Clarence Hill did most of his hunting on Duck Island, a dreary landfill on the Delaware River where lovers came to park in peace. Ted Bundy snatched two victims from Washington's Lake Sammamish on the same afternoon in 1974; he also planted the bodies in clusters, returning time and again to specific forest "graveyards." Similar cluster dumps were employed by Oregon's Jerry Brudos, Indiana's Larry Eyler, South Carolina's Donald Gaskins, and numerous others.

The most bizarre reported motive for returning to a crime scene is the killer's urge to further mutilate or sexually assault a decomposing corpse. Six percent of the FBI's sampling confessed such repeated assaults, though their motives were not always clear.[9] Some, like Florida's Bernard Giles and Californian Ed Kemper, are sexually incompetent with living partners. Others, like England's Peter Sutcliffe, apparently lose patience when their crimes are not immediately publicized. Revisiting the body of victim Jean Jordan after it had lain hidden for a week, Sutcliffe inflicted new stab wounds and repositioned the corpse, making it more obvious to passers-by.

Observing or participating in discovery of remains is yet another means by which some random killers manage to elaborate their lethal fantasies. For some, it is enough to simply loiter at the scene and mingle with the crowd as homicide detectives go about their business. Henry Lucas, for example, has admitted "hanging out" around the site of random homicides, including one that ultimately led to the conviction of a blameless suspect. Other slayers crave the added stimulation of participating in a crime's discovery. Ex-G-man Robert Ressler, in his book *Sexual Homicide*, describes the case of an anonymous ambulance driver who murdered women and dumped the bodies along his own route, knowing that he would be called to pick up the remains.[10] Charles Yukl "found" the body of his first known victim, a neighbor in his New York apartment house, and promptly summoned the police. New Mexico's David Dowler repeatedly telephoned friends and relatives of his victims, recounting "premonitions" of danger, urging them to "check and see if everything's all right." In England, Mary Bell directed searchers to the body of her second victim, claiming she had "seen him playing" at the site where he was killed and mutilated. Anonymous notes and phone calls from killer Rickey Brogsdale steered police to one of his female victims in Washington, D.C. Missouri's Sharon Kinne professed amazement when the bullet-riddled woman she discovered on a rural highway proved to be her current lover's missing wife.

Some random killers — one in five of the FBI's test sample[11] — extend their lethal fantasies by following or taking part in the police investigation of their crimes. Vicarious participation is enough for 46% of those, pursuing details of the manhunt in the media, sometimes filling scrapbooks with newspaper clippings or filling diaries with the details of their homicides. Long-distance pursuit of the case allows killers to relive the published details of their crimes, while simultaneously gloating over their ability to baffle the police. New York's David

Berkowitz kept a written log of some 300 arson fires he set between performances as the night-stalking "Son of Sam." Virginia's "Sex Beast," Melvin Rees, attached newspaper photos of his victims to graphic descriptions of their final moments: "Caught on a lonely road... Drove to a select area and killed husband and baby. Now the mother and daughter were all mine." In Florida, Bobby Joe Long maintained a detailed clipping file on his assorted rapes and murders. Transient slayer Randy Kraft, linked to the deaths of 67 young men, recorded his conquests in a coded journal. Gerard Schaefer's detailed instructions for sexual abuse and hanging of female victims, complete with diagrams, were introduced as evidence at his Florida murder trial, prosecutors (and jurors) rejecting his claim that the writings were simply "imaginative fiction." In Germany, butcher Georg Grossmann maintained a diary listing his female victims by name and weight, detailing the sexual indignities they suffered before he dressed their bodies out for sale as ersatz "beef" or "pork."

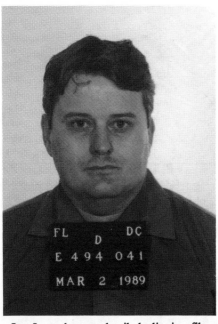

Bobby Joe Long kept a detailed clipping file on the crime spree that left 10 women dead and 50 others raped in Florida. *(Credit: Florida Dept. of Corrections)*

When simply following the progress of their case is not enough, some predators are moved to correspond with journalists or the police. The classic case, from 1888, is London's Jack the Ripper, who addressed his gloating notes "From Hell." (Unfortunately for the Ripper's legend, author Martin Fido makes a telling case against accepting any of Jack's notes as genuine.[12]) Similar gloating letters may — or may not have — been penned by the New Orleans Ax Man, Cleveland's Mad Butcher of Kingsbury Run, and New York's own child-slashing version of Jack the Ripper. Another New York slayer, the anonymous "3X" gunman of 1930, bombarded police and the press with elaborate descriptions of his service in a super-secret society, "The Red Diamond of Russia." California's Zodiac killer had a similar fondness for cryptograms, including ballistics information and bloody swatches of a victim's shirt to certify his authenticity.

Some killers target friends or relatives of chosen victims with their correspondence, tapping into grief and anger for their own emotional rewards. Cannibal-slayer Albert Fish was a compulsive author of lewd correspondence, punishing the parents of one victim with a graphic description of the child's final moments, finally assuring them "she died a virgin." (Fish used a pseudonym, but his selection of distinctive stationery led detectives to his doorstep and eventually landed him in the electric chair.) In Washington, D.C., Rickey Brogsdale left a taunting note at the home of one victim's friend: "I raped and killed your friend, Angela Shaw. You can find her on the bike path behind Marbury Plaza." In England, child-killer Horace Carter was more repentant, promising one victim's parents that he planned to commit suicide after his next murder.

More often, when serial killers take pen in hand, they are inclined to taunt authorities. In Wichita, Kansas, the BTK strangler chastised police and newsmen for suppressing details of his crimes: "How many do I have to kill," he whined, "before I get my name in the paper or some national attention?" David Berkowitz mailed letters to columnist Jimmy Breslin and dropped others at murder scenes, deliberately raising the panic quotient in New York.

I am deeply hurt by your calling me a weman-hater [sic].

I am not. But I am a monster. I am the Son of Sam... I love to hunt. Prowling the streets looking for fair game — tasty meat. The weman [sic] of Queens are the prettyest [sic] of all...

Poland's Lucian Staniak earned his media nickname, the "Red Spider," from his cramped handwriting and preference for crimson ink: "I picked a juicy flower in Olsztyn and I shall do it again somewhere else, for there is no holiday without a funeral." In Columbus, Georgia,

William Hance — a black man — sought to divert police suspicion from himself by posing as the leader of a militant white racist group, signing his letters as the self-styled "Chairman of the Forces of Evil." William Sarmento's anonymous note from Rhode Island was more plaintive: "I hope you will kill me, cops, because I don't know why I killed the children." Berlin's Paul Minow, on the other hand, was staunchly unrepentant when he wrote: "Away, away; in five minutes there will be a corpse. There is a child murderer in the neighborhood." The Italian "Monster of Florence" is less articulate, but his rare correspondence is easily recognized by the inclusion of distinctive pistol cartridges and mutilated female genitalia.

For some, peripheral involvement in the manhunt does not generate sufficient thrills, and these audacious predators are moved to seek more active roles, pursuing themselves as it were, in a bizarre parody of confession once removed. Some killers are ideally suited for the task by virtue of their occupations. In America, policemen Manny Pardo, Steven Smith, Jack Scully, and David Rogers have all been unmasked as serial slayers, while detective Norbert Poehlke carried the tradition to Germany. Gennadiy Mikhasevich, credited with strangling 33 women in the USSR, served as an auxiliary policeman when he was not busy on the factory assembly line. In Stockholm, Dr. Teet Harm served as the city's top forensic pathologist, glibly misleading detectives while he mutilated and cannibalized a series of prostitutes in 1987 and '88. Nor is legitimate involvement in the case an absolute necessity; in Germany, homosexual vampire-slayer Fritz Haarmann enjoyed playing detective, visiting survivors to discuss the fate of his respective victims.

Barring a legitimate connection to the case, some killers still inject themselves in other ways. A few, like Edmund Kemper and Kenneth Bianchi, are satisfied to fraternize with the police, discussing open cases over drinks or signing on for community ride-along programs. Others feel compelled to take a more direct and risky role, most often couched in terms of "clearing their names" and absolving themselves of suspicion. Arizona's Charles Schmid drove to California in a vain attempt to prove his several victims simply "ran away from home," a trip that climaxed in exposure of his crimes and Schmid's arrest for impersonating an FBI agent. Antone Costa likewise insisted that two of his female victims had "hitchhiked to Canada," offering to track them down if the police were so inclined. In Arkansas, James Hall manufactured a bogus letter from

his wife and had it mailed from California back to Little Rock. Confronted with suspicion in his last two murders, Henry Lucas struck off on an aimless tour of the Southwest, seeking to prove that the victims — an 80-year-old woman and a 15-year-old girl — had "run off with a long-haul trucker."

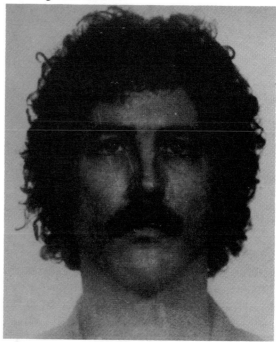

Strangler Kenneth Bianchi dazzled psychiatric experts with his sham performance as a victim of multiple personality disorder. *(Credit: Los Angeles County Sheriff's Dept.)*

A more peculiar — and potentially disastrous — form of self-involvement is displayed by random killers who insist on playing "witness" to their own sadistic crimes. John Brooks, described by homicide investigators as "the largest one-man crime wave in New Orleans history," came forward as the sole eyewitness in a double murder which authorities, in retrospect, believe he probably committed on his own. Paula Sims strained police credulity with her description of the masked strangers who abducted and murdered two of her infant children, three years apart. An intervening decade failed to dazzle homicide investigators when Jane Quinn reported the identical murders of two successive husbands by masked "home invaders." Sharon Kinne took a leaf from the same book, blaming a two-year-old child as the shooter in a 1960 "accident" that claimed her husband's life. In Redding, California, Robert Maury tried to mix business with pleasure, pocketing cash rewards when he phoned the location of corpses to a local Secret Witness hotline.

Most bizarre of all are the handful of killers who pose as *victims* in their own series of crimes. Whether based on some unique guilt complex or a simple over-estimation of their own persuasiveness, such efforts have inevitably backfired on the perpetrator. Hungary's Sylvestre Matushke dynamited several trains without arousing suspicion — until he filed a bogus lawsuit seeking damages for injuries allegedly sustained as a passenger on a train that was blasted with a loss of 22 lives. Closer to home, Florida death nurse Bobbie Sue Terrell stabbed herself in the course of a staged hospital robbery by "persons unknown." And in New Jersey, sex-slayer James Koedatich was free and clear until he filed reports of an unprovoked ambush and stabbing in Morris Township. Police examined the "victim's" car as a matter of course, and instantly matched his distinctive tires to the tracks found at nearby murder scenes.

The random killer's interaction with society is not a one-sided relationship. Serial murder, almost by definition, is a sensational crime, but public reaction is determined by various factors, including media reports, geography, and the societal priority assigned to chosen victims. While some predators inspire instant panic, others toil unnoticed for months or years on end, sometimes until the very climax of their murder spree. Chicago's John Wayne Gacy was the very cornerstone of local charity and politics before he left a clumsy trail of clues with victim number 33. Dean Corll was a nonentity outside his Houston neighborhood, until an argument with his accomplice led to gunfire and detectives went to work unearthing 27 graves. It took three years and 15 murdered prostitutes before Miami homicide investigators finally acknowledged that they had a serial killer on their hands; the victim tally stands at 31 today, with no suspects in sight.

The media is unpredictable where coverage of random killers is concerned. Some outlets seize upon a local case and wring it dry in tabloid style, injecting florid speculation when the facts wear thin. Others take the journalistic "high ground," stubbornly ignoring crime reports until the body count is registered in double digits. (Ironically, the same high-minded journalists are prone to cast their squeamishness aside when suspects have been booked and charged: a classic case in point would be Seattle's latest feeding frenzy with an innocent suspect in the Green River murders; around the same time, Los Angeles papers were quick to list the "evi-dence" against an equally guiltless suspect in the unsolved Southside slayings.) On occasion, the police and media appear as adversaries, racing toward their separate solutions of the case, intent on "scooping" one another in the search for witnesses and evidence.

As noted in another chapter, our society is not above prioritizing murder victims on the basis of their occupation, race, or sexual proclivity. When residents of Lake Elsinore, California, describe their local prostitute-killer as "cleaning up the trash downtown," they reveal a fundamental prejudice that ultimately helps the murderer remain at large. In Yorkshire, England, during Peter Sutcliffe's six-year reign of terror, drunken soccer hooligans regaled visiting teams with a chant of "This is Ripper country!" Around Los Angeles, "Skid Row" killers are distressingly common, drawing serious attention only when they strike in front of witnesses or when, as in the case of slasher Vaughn Greenwood, they shift their hunting ground to more affluent neighbor-hoods. Lacking an organized gay-rights movement, homosexuals are also ranked as low-priority victims in many American communities, as illustrated by a late-breaking case from Indianapolis. There, it required eleven murders in a decade to create a special homicide investigation task force, which is still not fully up to speed.

By contrast, high-profile cases frequently result in widespread panic, public demonstrations, even funda-mental changes in the ways that people go about their daily lives. In March 1919, a purported open letter from the Ax Man of New Orleans urged potential victims to avoid the killer's wrath on St. Joseph's night by playing jazz records at home; the citywide response included numerous performances of a song composed especially for the occasion: "The Mysterious Axman's Jazz." A generation later, Texarkana's "Moonlight Murderer" prompted residents to flee the town or barricade their homes and fire on nocturnal delivery boys. Los Angeles was terrorized in 1977 by the Hillside Stranglers, cousins who began their rampage with the murder of a prostitute and quickly branched out to include wait-resses, honor students, and aspiring actresses on their list of victims. Around the same time, long-haired brunettes were crowding New York beauty parlors in an effort to outwit the trigger-happy "Son of Sam." Another predator from the same era, Michigan's unidentified "Babysitter," panicked Detroit's suburbs with the ritualistic murders of four young children. In Columbus, Georgia, the rape and murder of elderly white women by a black home-invader combined natural fear and knee-jerk racism in the heart of Klan country. And no case in modern times has inspired such widespread publicity as the so-called Atlanta "child murders." So intense was the Atlanta panic, so chaotic the investigation, that no official voice was raised in protest when a local Conference on Children's Safety listed William Sherman, a 56-year-old robbery victim, as one of Atlanta's "missing and murdered children."[13]

Community reactions to the menace of a random murderer at large have historically ranged from passive acceptance to armed vigilante response. Atlanta police were content to speculate about the identity of a "ripper" who disemboweled black prostitutes in 1911 and 1912, but Southern blacks accused of killing whites faced more imminent danger. Multiple slayer Will Lockett narrowly escaped lynching in 1920, en route to his execution at Kentucky's state prison; two years later, an innocent suspect was shot and burned by a mob at Waco, Texas. Angry mobs pursued serial murder suspects in New York and New Orleans, during 1915 and 1918 respectively, and residents of Los Angeles actually captured "Nightstalker" Richard Ramirez in 1985 (dishing out a few lumps in the process). On the less militant side, volunteers often turn out en masse to search for missing victims, especially where children are concerned. Unofficial peace-keepers like the Guardian Angels have mounted neighborhood patrols in some target areas, notably Montreal, Canada, in 1982 and around the Wisconsin Dells five years later. Members of Stamford, Connecticut's black community provided escorts for working prostitutes in the late 1960s, when "Bra Strangler" Benjamin Miller was still at large. Elsewhere, women's groups — including some organized specifically for streetwalkers — have staged public demonstrations aimed at "taking back the night" from sexual predators.

Unfortunately, any panic ultimately spawns a crop of profiteers, and serial murder is no exception. The most obvious are yellow journalists who hype a story with outrageous speculation in the hope of scoring record sales or ratings points, but there are others who deserve a second look despite their noble-sounding motives.

Religious broadcaster James Dobson may be totally sincere in his crusade against pornography, but the fact remains that his California-based organization, Focus on the Family, earned a cool $1 million in 1989 by selling 40,000 tape recordings of Ted Bundy's eleventh-hour confessions at $25 per copy.[14] Between 1979 and 1981, panic-stricken Atlanta became a high-pressure testing ground for bogus psychics (one of whom informed reporters that she had provided homicide detectives with "the killer's name") and pitchmen from the ranks of Hollywood who specialize in instant "benefit" performances. A single concert in Atlanta, graced by the presence of Frank Sinatra and Sammy Davis, Jr., raised $250,000 for the grieving families of murdered children, and the estimates of total donations received generally quote figures in the millions. None are precise, for the simple reason that no one in charge of the massive "relief" effort kept accurate records; documented expenditures included funeral costs and a $900 "tummy-tuck" operation for one victim's mother, but most of the free-flowing cash remains missing today.[15]

Between a gloating killer and his population of prospective victims stands the "thin blue line" of law enforcement, working overtime to close the books on yet another case. Unable to determine who will kill before it happens, the police are left to clean up afterward and track the perpetrator using evidence that may be vague and contradictory, sometimes elusive to the point of nonexistence. It is a deadly contest where the odds seem weighted in the stalker's favor, helping him — or her — evade arrest and kill repeatedly, upon a whim.

In retrospect, it seems almost miraculous that any random killers land in prison for their crimes. But the police are making headway in their search for answers, taking full advantage of psychology and modern science to outwit their lethal adversaries.

Times have changed for homicide investigation, as for homicide itself, but evidence suggests that there is still much work to do, before we turn the corner on our deadly murder epidemic.

Part III

Wheels of Justice

"I'm sorry I killed five people, okay?"

Gary Alan Walker

"I have now a guilt and punishment complex. I am convinced that I deserve everything that a court can throw at me."

Dennis Nilsen

"You'll never get me. I'll kill again. Then you'll have another long trial. Then I'll do it again."

Henry Brisbon

Chapter 7

Blood Spoor

The official search for a killer begins at the moment a body is found — or even sooner, if a victim disappears under suspicious circumstances. In the classic fictional examples, government is mobilized from top to bottom, utilizing every resource to identify and apprehend the murderer, complete with high-speed chases, blazing gunfights, and dramatic trials. The good guys nearly always bag their man — or woman — in the end.

Unfortunately, when it comes to the pursuit of random killers, fact and fiction rarely coincide. The national solution rate for homicides in general has been plummeting since World War II, and serial killers are especially elusive. Nearly one in five escape completely, and are never brought to justice for their crimes.

More often than we care to think about, the bad guys win.

Before police can launch a manhunt, they must first determine that a killer is at large. It seems an elementary concept, but authorities are often slow to recognize the fact of murder, much less make connections in a series of related deaths.

And far too often, the stumbling blocks are self-imposed.

A case in point involves the plight of missing persons, whether children or adults. The 1980s panic over vanished children has apparently resolved itself with law enforcement "experts" branding most of those at large as runaways. In most localities, the faces have been stripped from billboards and milk cartons, relegating the

lost to an occasional mention on programs like "America's Most Wanted" or "Unsolved Mysteries." And, as previously mentioned, no one even tries to count the thousands of adults who disappear each year.

The "runaway" refrain has a familiar ring in Houston, Texas, where police spent two years stubbornly refusing to investigate the fate of 27 boys; it took the murder of a locally respected businessman, Dean Corll, and the surprise confession of his killer to unearth a murder ring that held the nation's record for the next five years. In Illinois, a similar blindness gave John Gacy a free hand with drifters and street hustlers from 1972 through 1978, at a cost of 33 lives. Texan Joe Ball victimized young waitresses during the Great Depression, and another 1930s killer, Cleveland's unidentified Mad Butcher of Kingsbury Run, specialized in victims who were never reported as missing. Juan Corona, Joseph Briggen, and the Missouri Copelands targeted migrant farm workers, trusting their victims to fall through the cracks in a system already overburdened with "throwaways." For Arkansas' James Hall, the story of a younger, straying wife was adequate to squelch police suspicion of a crime. In lily-white Georgia, detectives managed to overlook the racist murders of John Williams and sons for a decade.

Another problem may arise with the discovery of corpses where identity or cause of death remains unknown. Advanced decomposition may prevent a positive finding of murder, but even fresh bodies are not always conclusive. In the notorious Atlanta "child murders," five of 30 "official" victims were listed without definite cause of death, and two more were initially cited as accidents. Asphyxiation is sometimes assumed in the absence of other visible causes, as in three of Michigan's unsolved "Babysitter" homicides, despite a lack of concrete evidence. Indiana killer David Roberts stands convicted in the murder of a child who died from exposure to harsh weather. One of Albert De-Salvo's 13 murders was dismissed as a simple heart attack until he confessed the crime. "Angels of mercy" like Anna Hahn, Dorothy Matajke, and Velma Barfield seek to cover their tracks by preying on elderly victims, staging deaths to look like accidents or illness. A Swedish murderer, still unidentified, pushed four victims to their deaths from speeding trains in 1948; a fifth victim survived the plunge to warn police, but he could not describe the railroad stalker. In England, George Smith drowned two wives in the bathtub before detectives grew suspicious over number three.

Unidentified corpses present a different problem, depriving police of their best chance to link victims to their killer, or to one another. Lacking obvious suspects to work with, the authorities are left to speculate on motives, personal relationships, potential enemies. In Ohio, only three of the Mad Butcher's 16 victims were ever identified, but those three — all petty criminals — suggested that he chose his prey deliberately from those least likely to be missed. Several of the victims linked to Henry Lucas remain unidentified, including a female hitchhiker dubbed "Orange Socks," for the only piece of clothing left to her in death. Ted Bundy, Larry Eyler, Juan Corona, Dean Corll, John Gacy, Wayne Nance, Dennis Nilsen and other infamous killers all numbered nameless victims in their final body counts. In many cases, as with the casual, boozy pickups that were Eddie Cole's stock in trade, a killer may only learn his victim's name from media reports, after the fact... where he knows it at all. (In fact, nearly half of Cole's victims remain anonymous today, with five of the bodies still missing.) In April 1985, FBI agents flew to Nashville, Tennessee, for a meeting with detectives from five states. Their quarry, a still-unidentified strangler with a taste for redheads, had claimed at least six victims in as many months, with *none* of them identified. In such a case, without specific leads, the search for suspects is almost guaranteed to fail.

While some random killers are careless — even deliberately provocative — in the disposal of their victims, many others take pains to cover up their crimes. Disposal of remains is the most obvious approach to hiding any homicide, and serial killers run the full gamut of ingenuity in their attempts to hide the *corpus delicti*. Home burial was preferred by Dorothea Puente, Billy Mansfield, John Gacy, Dennis Nilsen, John Christie, Richard Biegenwald, Ed Kemper, Vera Renczi, and others. In Germany, Fritz Honka left dead hookers stacked in his apartment, trusting cheap cologne to mask the stench of rotting flesh. Dean Corll, Randal Rolle, and Eugene Butler were more adept at private burials, their crimes discovered posthumously. Harry Powers, Marcel Petiot, and Henri Landru fed their victims into private crematoria, while John Haigh preferred an industrial-strength acid bath. Mack Edwards took advantage of his job as a heavy equipment operator, planting three of his victims under southern California freeways. California's Joseph Briggen and Texan Joe Ball fed their prey to pigs and pet alligators, respectively. Richard Kuklinski deep-froze his victims for later disposal, seeking to confuse autopsy surgeons in regard to time of death.

Medical murderers are especially proficient in covering their tracks, as witnessed by a string of un-solved hospital murders in Canada, France, and the United States. America's record-holding serial killer, Donald Harvey, plied his trade for nearly two decades in Ohio and Kentucky, snuffing out 87 lives in a span of 17 years. In Philadelphia, Dr. Morris Bolber and company dispatched an estimated 50 victims before the murder ring was cracked. Jeffrey Feltner, Terri Rachals, Mary Robaczynski, and Bobbie Sue Terrell specialized in "mercy" killings, overdosing their charges or disconnecting life-support equipment as the spirit moved them. Detroit's Roland Clark was suspected of killing several patients before he overstepped the line, murder-ing two of his office receptionists without apparent motive. Even hospital administrators, American Amy Gilligan and Norway's Arnfinn Nesset among them, find ways of covering their tracks where multiple murder is concerned.

The worst scenario, from law enforcement's point of view, arises when a cunning killer is assisted by the bumbling — or deliberate — efforts of "innocent" third parties. Nurses at Cincinnati's Drake Hospital repeat-edly voiced their concern over soaring mortality rates during six months prior to the arrest of Donald Harvey. The official response was a stone wall of silence, with one administrator threatening to fire any nurse who publicly aired her suspicions. In the wake of Harvey's arrest and confessions, the administrator in question pled guilty to falsifying death records for some of Harvey's victims.

Another notorious case involves Texas pediatric nurse Genene Jones, convicted of one murder and suspected of dozens more. Indeed, Jones seemed to lead a charmed life at San Antonio's Bexar County Hospital, breezing through a welter of disciplinary infractions that included drinking on duty and negligent errors in medication dosage. In December 1979, supervisor Pat Belko ignored seven serious infractions over fourteen months of service, praising Jones for "meritorious contributions" on the pediatric ward. When fellow nurses and a resident physician voiced their suspicion that Jones was murdering infants by lethal injection, administrators countered with a demand for "judicious silence on the issue." Resigning her position to seek greener pastures in April 1982, Jones was favored with a letter of recommendation praising her as "an asset to the Bexar County Hospital District." In the wake of her arrest on murder charges, hospital administrators professed to be "shocked and stunned," releasing a public statement that "We have not had any evidence of wrongdoing in this institution." Finally, a month after Jones's February 1984 conviction for one murder in neighboring Kerr County, hospital staffers shredded 9,000 pounds of pharmaceutical records, thereby frustrating further investigations in San Antonio.[1]

One major obstruction to any homicide investigation is the official myopia described by criminologist Steven Egger as "linkage blindness." Variously born of distance, inexperience, incompetence or stubborn pride, this failure to observe the links between successive crimes may sabotage a manhunt from the start. Some investigations never recover, and we can only speculate as to the number of serial killers whose work has passed unnoticed in this century.

Nomadic killers specialize in dazzling the police with footwork, traveling from coast to coast — and sometimes internationally — to break the crucial chain of evidence. For drifters like Henry Lucas, Ottis Toole, Charles Hatcher, and William Guatney, compulsive movement is a life style, on a par with their desire to kill. While living in Seattle, sadist Harvey Carignan would often flee his wife and home for all-night drives that carried him as far away as California. On the east coast, Gerald Stano began his 11-year killing spree in New Jersey, detoured through Pennsylvania, and finished in Florida. Randy Kraft, Gary Robbins, Benjamin Boyle and others took advantage of their transient professions to litter the countryside with bodies. Others — including Eddie Cole, Ted Bundy, Coral Watts, Ken Bianchi, Earle Nelson, and Chris-

topher Wilder — killed repeatedly in one locale before the heat sent them in search of a friendlier hunting ground.

Another handy means of defeating investigation is the deliberate variation of *modus operandi* from one crime to the next. Henry Lucas, in his pre-hoax days, confessed to killing victims "in every way known to man." Henry's traveling partner, Ottis Toole, admits dispatching various targets by gunfire, stabbing, beating, strangulation, arson, and running them down with their own automobiles. In California, the elusive Zodiac killer taunted police with a November 1969 threat to change his method of "collecting" victims: "I shall no longer announce to anyone when I commit my murders. They shall look like routine robberies, killings of anger, and a few fake accidents, etc." (At least one student of the case believes the killer did exactly that, continuing to murder with impunity through 1981.[2]) One of the few medical killers to steer clear of drugs, Missouri dentist Glennon Engelman dabbled in dynamite when he tired of shooting his victims. Atlanta's "child-killer" was even more flexible, assuming one person was responsible for all 30 deaths: victims were variously shot, stabbed, strangled, asphyxiated, drowned, and pushed from railroad trestles to their death. Donald Harvey experimented with asphyxiation and various poisons, but he was not above inserting sharp wires through a patient's catheter to puncture the bladder on occasion. According to California police, one unidentified killer was responsible for a year-long series of murders in 1969 and '70, with nine victims drowned, beaten, shot, strangled, and stabbed. In February 1975, another California police report blamed 14 unsolved murders on an assailant who drugged, stabbed, and strangled his prey, breaking one woman's neck for good measure. Sadly, recognition of a link in such cases is the rare exception, rather than the rule.

As previously noted, police blindness in serial murders is sometimes predicated on a callous disregard for "low-priority" victims. Hookers, homosexuals, the homeless, racial minorities — each in turn has been stalked by serial killers within living memory, their deaths soft-pedaled by authorities in various jurisdictions from coast to coast. The deaths of 11 prostitutes seemed inconsequential in Portland, Oregon, during the 1980s, where a homicide lieutenant remarked that murder was simply an occupational hazard for streetwalkers. Portland police chief Penny Harrington was more tactful but equally obtuse when she told the press, "I don't believe a serial killer is here. We're not going to close our eyes if we see a pattern, but we don't see anything."[3] Miami police needed three years and 15 deaths to find the pattern, and Los Angeles detectives were roundly criticized for delaying announcement of their search for the elusive Southside Slayer. In Indiana, newsmen linked a string of homosexual slayings before authorities caught on; Bloomington's medical examiner was recruited to press for a coordinated manhunt, but state police ignored the doctor's call. Sixteen months later, in April 1984, a Chicago vagrant found a severed hand in the trash behind killer Larry Eyler's apartment house. Police were notified, but they dismissed the call as a prank and dispatched no officers; another month would pass before Eyler was finally jailed — after dumping his twenty-third victim in the same garbage bin.[4]

On occasion, politics intervenes in the search for a serial killer. Black officials in Atlanta saw their hopes for re-election fading as the local death toll mounted in the early 1980s, and a few years later the expensive futility of the "Green River" manhunt became a major campaign issue in the Seattle sheriff's race. Mayors and governors walk a political tightrope in high-profile cases, frightened of looking weak if they request help prematurely, damned by the public if they wait too long at the expense of further lives. Even presidents sometimes get into the act, as when Richard Nixon's published statements on the guilt of Manson family members nearly brought a mistrial in the Tate-LaBianca case.

Most often, though, disruptive "linkage blindness" is the product of professional jealousy, one police agency stone-walling another in the interest of prestige. In 1985, detectives from Portland, Oregon, staunchly refused to cooperate with members of Washington's Green River Task Force, withholding the names of two serial murder suspects. Tension between the Los Angeles Police Department and the L.A. County sheriff's office is legendary, infecting all aspects of area law enforcement. When city detectives were investigating the Tate-La Bianca massacre in 1969, sheriff's officers deliberately withheld vital evidence in the related Gary Hinman murder, thereby delaying apprehension of Charles Manson's homicidal "family." Years later, LAPD's hasty arrest of a black sheriff's deputy in the Southside Slayer case embarrassed all concerned, while leaving the "suspect" out of a job. More than 20 different agencies joined the chaotic hunt for Atlanta's "child-killer," and enduring controversy surrounds their final choice of suspects. In Texarkana, a retired deputy sheriff claims to

have identified — and captured — the 1946 "Moonlight Murderer," but Texas Rangers still list the crime spree as one of their great unsolved cases. Detectives from 26 states and two Canadian provinces helped muddy the waters around Henry Lucas and Ottis Toole, first "clearing" some 200 murders, then "reopening" 90 of those after Lucas withdrew his confessions in April 1985; Arkansas was slow off the mark, filing three new murder warrants against Lucas the month after his change of heart.

The search for an UNSUB — "unknown subject" in official parlance — begins in any case with collection of evidence at the crime scene. No clue is too small to be useful, and the outcome of a case may hinge on flecks of paint, stray hairs, a spot of blood or grains of sand. Aside from any corpses, skillful homicide investigators will collect or photograph and diagram all evidence discovered at the site. Tire tracks, footprints and the like may chart the killer's movements and identify his vehicle or shoes. Blood splatters and other signs of a struggle determine the course of events in a crime. Where bullets are fired through glass, the pattern of cracking tells which shot came first. Fingerprints or palm prints, semen and saliva traces, hairs and fibers — all of these and more may help identify a suspect. The amount of blood discovered at the scene determines if a victim died where he or she was found. In short, no single item is too small or insignificant to be preserved.

Beyond the basic sweep for clues, modern authorities rely on forensic pathology — the expert medical and scientific analysis of evidence recovered in a given case. Post-mortem examination of the victim is critical in determining time and cause of death, the type of weapon used, and so forth. Was the victim sexually abused? If so, was the abuse inflicted prior to death, or as an act of necrophilia? Had the victim been drinking or taking drugs prior to death? Were restraints employed by the killer? If so, what kind? Does mutilation signify an act of torture, an attempt to ease disposal of the body, or some kind of ritual that may allow psychologists to pick the unknown subject's brain? Was the killer right- or left-handed? Do stray hairs recovered from the corpse suggest a black or white assailant? If samples of bodily fluids are found, will they give up the killer's blood type... or better yet, a unique "genetic fingerprint"?

The list of vital questions is long and complex. The more answers authorities obtain, the closer they are to arresting their suspect.

Sometimes.

Eyewitnesses are uncommon in serial cases, though not so rare as one might suppose. Neighbors may remember a suspicious stranger on the block. Street-walkers frequently compare notes on "kinky" customers. A passing motorist may recall vehicles, faces, the details of a violent altercation. Anything at all may ultimately help police track down their quarry.

All the same, a witness may be worse than useless in the wrong hands. Interrogators must take stock of the witness's age and mental state, intoxication, credibility, and any trauma suffered in connection with the incident. Leading questions may produce the answers that detectives want to hear, but they are not always reliable. If police seem hostile, sarcastic, or abusive, intimidated witnesses may "turn off" without supplying information vital to the case at hand. Even good interrogations often produce conflicting results, as in New York's "Son of Sam" investigation, where the wide range of suspect descriptions seems to indicate three or four different killers at work.

Beyond the identification of suspects, forensic evidence can help establish patterns which suggest a serial killer at large. Specific bindings, mutilations, modes of torture, sexual assault, and choice of weapons constitute a killer's "signature," allowing trained investigators to connect a string of crimes. Ballistics, measurement of stab wounds, medical examination of the victim's other injuries all play a part in diagnosis of a killer's style. In cases where the cause of death is not apparent, as in the rash of infant deaths at Toronto's prestigious Hospital for Sick Children, assistance may be rendered by the Atlanta-based Center for Disease Control. CDC experts are skilled at determining probabilities, ruling out accidental death with a fair degree of certainty in even the more obscure cases. In Toronto, CDC found 18 of 36 submitted cases frankly "suspicious," with seven listed as probable homicide and ten more "consistent" with deliberate poisoning. At Prince George's Hospital in Maryland, it was found that 65% of all intensive-care fatalities occurred on one nurse's shift; the suspect had witnessed 57 deaths in 15 months, while no other nurse on staff had lost more than five patients in the same period.

A new area of law-enforcement concern, the examination of suspicious infant deaths, requires a special expertise. Vague reports of sudden infant death syndrome (SIDS) may camouflage a multitude of sins, as in the cases of Diane Lumbrera, Martha Woods and Marybeth Tinning, linked with the murders of 22 children. In Lumbrera's case, Texas authorities shrugged off the first six deaths, but a move to Garden City, Kansas — and a seventh murder there — landed the lethal homemaker in prison for life. New York detectives were suspicious of Marybeth Tinning after four deaths, but it took five more to bring indictments. SIDS is so hard to distinguish from murder, in fact, that some medical examiners frankly rely on what San Antonio's Vincent DiMaio calls the Three-Baby Rule. "You wait until they kill the third kid," DiMaio explains, before exhumations and court-ordered autopsies begin.[5] Each year in the United States, SIDS claims about 5,000 healthy-seeming children, ranging from newborn to one year of age. Only ten states routinely autopsy all alleged SIDS victims; an equal number allow from 20% to 50% of their SIDS deaths to pass unchallenged. In the case of infants, easily shaken to death or suffocated by pinching the nostrils, kindly (or negligent) physicians are sometimes deceived by a killer's simulated grief. Florida medical examiner Ronald Reeves speaks for those who believe child-abuse deaths are "grossly underestimated" in America. "It's very easy to kill a child," Reeves explains, "and not leave a whole lot of evidence."[6]

Finally, accumulated evidence is worthless if mishandled by police. A warrantless search in Indiana cost the state vital evidence against Larry Eyler, leaving the killer at large for six months, at the cost of at least one more life. Even Eyler's final arrest in Chicago left much to be desired, with police ignoring fingerprints and other evidence of a suspected accomplice in the murder series. Elsewhere, analysts reported in 1985 that Washington crime labs, working at their present pace, would need 50 years to cover evidence collected in the Green River slayings. Los Angeles police, for their part, have bungled more than one serial case by mishandling the evidence. In 1969, a pistol used in the Manson-Tate massacre was found by civilians and delivered to patrolmen... who promptly smudged the fingerprints and then "misplaced" the weapon for weeks in their property room. Twenty years later, mistaken ballistics tests led to an innocent suspect's arrest as the Southside Slayer, costing one man his job with the sheriff's department and earning city police no end of embarrassment. In Houston, detectives probing Dean Corll's murder spree were so anxious to beat Juan Corona's California body count that they stopped digging for corpses once the record was broken; statements by accomplices of Corll, recounting other murders, were deliberately ignored once homicide investigators satisfied their egos. Authorities in Louisiana's Monroe Parish insist they once possessed fingerprints linking Henry Lucas to a local slaying, but the crucial evidence was "lost" during an acrimonious change of administrations. In San Diego, where police still regard five of Eddie Cole's murders as "natural deaths," suggestions of possible error are met with a terse "No comment."

One means of tracking down an unknown subject is the psychological profile, emphasized in fictional productions like *The Silence of the Lambs*. The FBI's Behavioral Science Unit epitomizes the modern "mind-hunters," though successful — and some not-so-successful — applications date from the mid-1950s, at least. Properly used, the art of criminal profiling can sometimes lead detectives to the very doorstep of their quarry. Bungled off the mark, it can divert attention from the guilty parties and consign promising investigations to the limbo of perpetually "open" files.

In current FBI parlance, the first step in any profile is deciding whether a killer fits the "organized" or "disorganized" category. Organized offenders exercise control over their victims and crime scenes, binding their prey with restraints, bringing selected tools and weapons to the execution site. Victims are normally targeted strangers, bearing pattern similarities in sex, age, race, occupation, or appearance. Forensic evidence often displays a sadistic element, the crime eroticized with torture and protracted death. Aggressive acts like rape and mutilation are reserved for living victims, the killer's prey personalized through compulsive, ritualistic treatment — the Boston Strangler's habitual "bow tie," for example. When his work is done, the killer frequently transports his victim to another site, taking pains to conceal the body and remove incriminating evidence.[7]

Disorganized killers, on the other hand, commit spontaneous, unplanned crimes, employing the "blitz" technique to overpower and kill their victims. Restraints are unnecessary, since victims are usually killed outright, with mutilation or sexual assault taking place after death. A disorganized killer is often unprepared, finding his weapon at the murder scene and leaving it there, along with his victim and copious evidence. Depersonalization of the victim is typified by specific mutilation or, as in the case of William Heirens, a negation of the crime by covering a lifeless victim's wounds. Because the crimes are poorly planned — if planned at all — the killer often operates upon familiar ground, even in his own neighborhood or apartment complex.[8]

As described by Robert Ressler, once a ranking member of the FBI's Behavioral Science Unit, the process of generating psychological profiles ideally proceeds through six phases.[9] They include:

Phase One: Profiling Inputs. Collection of critical data begins at the crime scene, with physical evidence, placement and condition of the body, patterns of evidence linking other crimes, and any weapons found at the site. Victimology is another vital factor, including a thorough search of the victim's background, habits, health, occupation, family structure, and known movements in the final hours of life. Forensic information provides necessary data on cause of death, nature of wounds, evidence of sexual assault, and any other scientific findings. Preliminary police reports include a list of witnesses (if any), professional observations at the scene, plus the general crime rate and socioeconomic status of the area. Finally, photographs — including aerial shots, crime scene photos, and close-ups of the victim — allow profilers to view the scene in its original state, sometimes months after the fact.

Phase Two: Decision process models. In this phase, profilers sort and arrange the mass of raw data into meaningful patterns. First, the mind-hunters decide which type and style of murder they are dealing with — i.e., single, double, triple, "mass," "spree," or "serial." (In a case of mass murder, the experts further delineate between "classic" and "family" massacres.) Next, the killer's primary intent is determined, with possible motives including: (a) criminal enterprise, as in robbery murders or gangland executions; (b) emotional, selfish, or cause-specific motives — including crimes of passion, mercy killings, and the like — or; (c) sexual motives, which include the majority of serial murders. An assessment of "victim risk" considers the age, sex, occupation, life style, and physical condition of each victim to classify the case as low-, moderate-, or high-risk. This finding, in turn, helps experts gauge their unknown subject's state of mind. Victim risk information is then coordinated with "offender risk" data, to calculate the probability of an arrest brought on by daring, high-risk crimes. Information on the killer's escalation is derived from a comparison of linked cases, the interval between crimes, and the degree of violence employed. Analysis of time factors includes consideration of the time required to kill, to perform additional acts with the body, and to dispose of the corpse. (The more time a killer spends with his victims, the more likely he is to be captured at some future crime scene.) Finally, the experts survey location factors — the point of first approach, the crime scene and disposal site, if they are different — to glean more information on the killer's modus operandi.

Phase Three: Crime assessment. In this stage, experts reconstruct the crime from start to finish, using all the evidence at their disposal to chart the killer's movements and decide upon a proper category — "organized," "disorganized," or "mixed." The process of victim selection is surveyed, along with various crime scene dynamics suggestive of pattern behavior. What kind of restraints are used on the victims? Does the killer gain their trust by posing as an invalid or a policeman? Is the killer's anger fueled by drugs or alcohol?

Phase Four: The criminal profile. With their basic work complete, the experts publish what amounts to a description of their quarry, ranging from psychological factors to such physical aspects as sex, race, age, occupation, vehicle preference, habits and vices. Depending on the nature and quantity of evidence on hand, profilers may feel confident enough to focus the search on a particular neighborhood. In most cases, however, the profile remains a more general assessment of the killer or killers at large.

Phase Five: Investigation. New evidence is collected and digested as the manhunt continues, sometimes spanning months or years. These "feedback filters" may confirm the standing profile or demand adjustments, as data collected from new crimes sheds further light on methods and motives. If a new or revised profile is called for, experts start from scratch to make the appropriate changes.

Phase Six: Apprehension. Ideally, the combination of expert detectives and psychological insight leads to apprehension of the guilty parties, without further loss of life. In fact, we know that nearly one in five serial killers escape scot free, regardless of the forces massed against them. The rest wind up in jail through a variety of circumstances that include coincidence and accidents, rare voluntary surrenders, and apprehension by local police with or without the assistance of psychiatric profiles.

For all the scientific jargon, we must understand that each criminal profile is essentially an educated guess, subject to all manner of human error. An actual example, prepared by Agent Robert Ressler in a Nebraska case that earned killer John Joubert a death sentence, is reproduced in the next column.[10]

UNSUB;

Danny Joe Eberle—Victim

Kidnapping—Murder

(OO: OMAHA)

The circumstances of the disappearance and recovery of the victim's body indicate that the abduction and murder of the victim does not seem to be consistent in modus operandi with the mysterious disappearance of Johnny Gosch, which occurred in Des Moines, Iowa, approximately one year earlier. Although the circumstances of the abductions are similar, the fact that the Gosch victim's body was never found and that Eberle's body was found several days after the abduction in a remote area outside of Bellevue in a rather random and hurried manner, differentiates between the types of individuals who might have committed the two crimes.

Facts indicate that the Eberle victim may have been kept alive by the Unknown Subject for a period of time and the lack of abrasions from any rope or other type of ligature would indicate that the victim had been free during most of his period of captivity and only tied up just prior to his demise. This indicates that the killer or killers may have treated him somewhat well for that period of time indicating that he would be freed if he cooperated in possible sexual assault and even in photographing him during sex acts.

The killer of Danny Joe Eberle is undoubtedly a youthful white male in his late teens or early twenties and there is a distinct possibility that this individual may have known Eberle on a casual basis. Although he may not have known Eberle well, it is possible that Eberle may have known him by sight, at least enough to approach the Unknown Subject's vehicle and possibly even enter that vehicle voluntarily. There is a possibility that the Unknown Subject may have been accompanied by one or two other individuals, also white males, in the same age group. A re-creation of events indicates that Eberle, while delivering newspapers on his paper route, encountered one or more Unknown Subjects in a motor vehicle and that he was either enticed or forced into that vehicle, taken to another location where he was held for a period of several days, possibly sexually assaulted, and eventually killed by a knife assault. Visual examination of crime scene and autopsy reports indicates no gross sexual assault, however, based on the personality of the victim, it is a definite possibility that the victim's death may have come as a result of an attempted sexual assault whereby the victim may have fought his assailant to the point of being killed. Further, forensic evidence indicates that the victim was possibly moved several times after death and the abandonment of his body on a remote roadside several miles outside of Bellevue suggests that the killer may have panicked after killing the victim and had dumped the body rather than bury it or dispose of it in a more permanent manner.

The dumping of the body just off a lightly traveled road suggests that the killer may not have possessed sufficient strength to carry the body further into a wooded area. It also indicates his hasty attempt to dispose of a body and poor planning. Pebble indentations in the victim's body and a pebble located in the mouth of the victim indicates that he had been lying in another location after death and then transported to the final scene of disposal as there were no such pebbles at the final dumpsite. It was a possibility that the Unknown Subject was somewhat aware of the location of the dumpsite of the body and may have traveled this area many times previously.

Examination of evidence indicates that the killer (or killers) would be single and not overly educated, certainly not beyond that of the high school level. The employment would range from unemployed to employed in a rather menial and unskilled capacity, possibly blue collar in nature.

The main perpetrator would definitely have had a chronic sexual problem indicating deviance and bizarre sexual experiences throughout his life. He would likely be an avid reader of pornography and may have been involved in experiments of a bizarre nature throughout his adolescence. This experimentation could definitely involve animals and possibly forced sexual acts on younger children, both male and female.

Indications are that the killer would have been involved in recent stressful events in his life which might include breaking up with a girlfriend, losing a job, being dropped from school, or trouble with

his immediate family. Further, the individual may have been absent from his employment, if employed, for several days before and after the disappearance of Eberle.

In summary, the abduction and killing of victim Eberle indicates a poorly planned and rather spontaneous crime which suggests that the subject or subjects had encountered Eberle during the normal course of their travel throughout the city of Bellevue and are possibly local residents. The abduction probably took place without particular motive or planning which might reinforce the theory that more than one individual is involved. The circumstances of this crime are sufficiently different to the Des Moines, Iowa, case involving victim Johnny Gosch to suggest that the perpetrator of the Gosch abduction would be considerably older, possibly in his thirties, and that there is probably no connection between these two cases.

Joubert, arrested four months later, was a 20-year-old high school graduate and former Eagle Scout, recently enlisted in the Air Force. His adolescent fantasies included necrophilia and cannibalism, in the pursuit of which he had assaulted half a dozen children prior to committing his first known murder at age 18.

In Seattle's "Green River" case, the FBI mind-hunters came up with decidedly mixed results, including elements of both organized and disorganized behavior. Impulsiveness was noted in the random selection of prey, coupled with the unpredictable nature of victim availability and the repeated use of victims' clothing as a weapon. On the flip side, the killer displayed "organized" traits by transporting the corpses to a separate dump site and taking substantial time to either bury his victims or weight their bodies down and sink them in a river. The selection of a common fishing stream led G-men to brand their unknown subject as an "outdoors-type person," while the murder of prostitutes suggested "strong feelings" about fidelity and sex-for-hire. With such vague guidelines, it is small wonder that the killer remains at large ten years after his first known murder.

When the mind-hunters score, their results can sometimes be uncanny. Ex-agent Robert Ressler describes the case of an unnamed serial arsonist whose very residence was picked out by profilers, using intricate computer programs.[11] Years before the advent of the FBI's special diagnostic unit, in 1956, forensic psychiatrist James Brussel prepared an amazingly accurate profile of New York's "Mad Bomber," deducing the unknown subject's impotence from the phallic shape of his pipe bombs, generating a sketch that could have passed for the bomber's photograph, even predicting — correctly — that the suspect would be wearing a double-breasted suit (with the coat buttoned!) at his arrest. An open letter from Brussel provoked bomber George Metesky to a written response, which in turn led police to his doorstep. No other profiler has equaled the Brussel bull's-eye, but forensic psychologists still tout the procedure's validity. As a case in point, FBI spokesmen note the close match between convicted killer Wayne Williams and their profile of a young, black UNSUB in the Atlanta "child murders." Sadly, for the Bureau's argument, there is persuasive evidence that Williams may be innocent — including the suppressed testimony of five eyewitnesses who name a white convicted child-molester as the killer of one "pattern" victim.

Indeed, when profilers miss their target, the results are sometimes truly bizarre. In 1963, a panel of psychiatrists — including Dr. Brussel — was convened to stalk the Boston Strangler from afar. The experts concluded that Boston was plagued by *two* killers, one for the older victims and another — believed to be homosexual — for the young. Beyond that divergence, many similarities were postulated, including a suggestion that both men were teachers, living alone and killing on their scheduled holidays from school. Both men were diagnosed as sexually inhibited, the products of traumatic childhoods featuring weak, distant fathers and cruel, seductive mothers. In fact, confessed strangler Albert DeSalvo was a construction worker, living with his wife and two children, insatiably heterosexual. Examination of his background showed a brutal, domineering father, while his mother had been weak and ineffectual. He *was* in his thirties, as projected for the nonexistent teachers, but there the resemblance ended.

An even more dramatic failure came in early 1975, when another "expert panel" was assembled in Los Angeles, to sketch a profile of the Skid Row Slasher. On January 30, the L.A. media broadcast descriptions of a "sexually impotent coward, venting his own feelings of worthlessness on hapless drifters and down-and-outers." The slasher was a friendless loner, probably a homosexual and possibly deformed, "driven by a frenzy to commit these murders as a substitute for normal heterosexual relations." His violence was most likely "spurred by an unresolved rage he feels toward his father, who could have been a brutal alcoholic."

Sketches drawn to fit the profile showed a white male in his late twenties or early thirties, six feet tall, 190 pounds, with shoulder-length, stringy blonde hair framing an angular face. In closing, the experts lapsed from hopeful speculation into melodrama, blasting the killer as "a jackal, an animal who hides in the dark and preys on weaklings and cripples."[12]

If authorities were trying to provoke the slasher, they succeeded too well, drawing the killer out to claim another victim on the very night his profile hit the airwaves. Two days later, shifting territories from Skid Row to Hollywood, the UNSUB botched a break-in at the home of actor Burt Reynolds, conveniently dropping his driver's license at the scene. Vaughn Greenwood, charged with eleven murders and convicted of nine in the slasher case, was a shock to authorities. For starters, he was black, with no apparent physical deformities, and no sadistic, boozing father could be turned up in the Pennsylvania foster home that he abandoned in his early teens. He *was* a loner and a homosexual, but far from impotent if we believe his partners. Rather than obsessive rage against a parent, Greenwood's murders smacked of some occultic ritual, the slasher drinking cups of blood and sprinkling salt around his corpses, leaving victims with their shoes removed and pointed toward their feet.

It is worth noting that even the experts disagree on the value of criminal profiles. Dr. Norman Barr, assigned to stalk the Skid Row Slasher in Los Angeles, belatedly admitted that "I don't think my statements would make any more sense than those of the average housewife."[13] From Boston University, psychologist Russell Boxley declares: "I think the people who do profiles are bastardizing their discipline with a lot of mumbo-jumbo without really knowing what they're doing. You know, it's a mystical thing, and people are very impressed. It's also a media thing." Boxley concludes that forensic psychologists tracking a murderer "can't do any better than a college student could with the same materials in front of him."[14]

One hopeful cure for "linkage blindness" is the special task force, sometimes called the multi-agency investigative team — or MAIT, for short. In exceptional cases, like those of Henry Lucas and Marybeth Tinning, a task force may be organized after the fact, with suspects already in custody, to facilitate widespread collection of evidence. More often, though, the task force is designed to track a killer still at large and end his reign of terror. Either way, success is predicated on adherence to some basic rules and guidelines, any one of which, if overlooked, can sabotage the effort and result in killers slipping through the net.[15]

Advance planning is helpful — if not essential — to the creation of a successful task force. Serial murder probes are rife with jurisdictional problems, frequently straining the budgets and manpower resources of agencies involved in the hunt. Ideally, leaders of the several agencies within a given area should meet in advance of a crisis, outlining specific responsibilities for their several departments. Advance determination of the task force membership includes selection of investigators from the different agencies, along with medical examiners, psychologists, forensic experts, prosecutors, even politicians who control the civic purse strings. Topics of discussion at the planning sessions should include specialized training, sources of funding and personnel, jurisdictional coordination, access to necessary equipment, information management and media relations. Wherever possible, reticent or hostile agencies should be educated in the value of cooperation toward a common goal.

Advance planning pays off when the threat of a serial killer is recognized, signature patterns identified by systematic comparison of evidence from different cases. With a basic command structure already in place, the task force can be mobilized in short order, hopefully trimming the killer's advantage and hastening apprehension. Unprepared agencies, meanwhile, are hamstrung by administrative problems, lack of coordination in case reviews and information management, chaotic field investigations, and adversarial relations with the news media. With pre-need planning, members of the task force know their jobs and recognize an established chain of command, theoretically reducing confusion and waste to a minimum.

Ideally, MAIT personnel should be chosen on the basis of skill, experience, and commitment to teamwork. In practice, many small departments operate year-round without skilled homicide investigators, but the task force compensates for that deficiency by sharing personnel from larger agencies. Continuity and dedication of assignments on the task force also guard against diversion of investigators toward peripheral administrative duties. Key task force positions, as detailed in federal guidelines, include: (1) a MAIT commander, charged with overall administration of the task force, budget preparation, and liaison with various agencies; (2) an operations commander, in charge of actual in-

vestigation; (3) a lead investigator, to direct and coordinate the field activities of detectives, forensic technicians, and special operations staff; (4) the support unit commander, responsible for information processing, analysis of evidence collected in the field, plus general management of task force facilities; and (5) a case review coordinator, who scans all information on suspects, victims, witnesses, and evidence in search of undetected links or leads. Some task forces utilize volunteer help in support capacities, to trim the budget, but caution is required to avoid security leaks — or, worse, the chance of signing on a killer who enjoys participation in the chase.

A major stumbling block for any task force is the dollar sign. Serial murder investigations may drag on for months — even years — and they are never cheap. Official members of the task force draw their salaries each week, regardless of success or failure. Evidence is waiting to be analyzed and stored. Civilian experts may demand consulting fees, and there are bound to be substantial costs for overhead — everything from gassing up patrol cars to the maintenance of task force headquarters. Even the indictment of a suspect does not plug the money leak, since task force staffers may be caught up in the case through trial, conviction, and a lengthy series of appeals. Indeed, the naming of a suspect may produce new evidence — surviving victims, witnesses, or criminal accomplices — that rates investigation by the team. When random murder coincides with an election year, politicians too often muddy the waters, demanding instant, cut-rate justice in an effort to attract more votes. Advance planning, careful management, and fund-sharing among MAIT member agencies can help alleviate such problems, but the specter of financial backlash never truly dissipates.

Information management is the Achilles' heel of any prolonged serial murder investigation, with detectives frequently overwhelmed by the sheer volume of evidence, tips, and potential suspects. The Green River slayings are a classic case in point, with some 12,000 suspect names and descriptions collected in four years' time. Of those, 978 men made the "A" list, consisting of serious suspects. Of that number, 268 were positively cleared, with another 452 rated "inactive" on the basis of "investigator's opinion." The other "inactive" suspects included 84 who passed polygraph tests, 53 who were never found or identified, 36 who died or left the area, 11 who refused to sit for polygraph tests, three who staunchly refused all cooperation, and two yielding "inconclusive" polygraph results. A total of 69 suspects remained in the active files, with 12 of those still unidentified by name.[16]

Indeed, the Green River manhunt was fraught with problems from Day One. Detectives excluded from the task force bitterly denounced the "special treatment" of their privileged colleagues, while inexperienced task force officers bungled various suspect interviews, collecting data that was superficial and inadequate. A power surge wiped out the MAIT computer's memory on one occasion, and independent experts found the hard-copy files in hopeless confusion, making retrieval of specific data difficult or impossible. In one bizarre incident, a missing victim's driver's license was discovered at the local airport, held by police for five months, and then "routinely" destroyed... without ever being checked for fingerprints.

Another example of curious record-keeping from the Green River probe involves suspect Joe Reardon (a pseudonym). In 1985, Reardon — a Washington shipyard worker — penned three letters to condemned serial killer Eddie Cole over the space of two days. The letters were forwarded to me following Cole's execution in Nevada. Reardon made cryptic references to "my work in Seattle," and quizzed Cole as to his motives, methods of evading capture, and the like. On turning over these letters to the task force, I received a swift response: Reardon was unknown to Seattle detectives, had never been named as a Green River suspect, and could not be cleared on the basis of existing information. I was "unofficially" encouraged to correspond with Reardon, drawing him out on the subject of serial murder and whores, but contact was lost. Four years later, when the Green River case was dramatized on national television, with a toll-free line for tips, I called to see if suspect Reardon had been cleared. To the contrary, a new group of detectives were wholly unfamiliar with his name, and they could find "no record" of him in the task force files. I sent new copies of the Reardon letters to Seattle... and again, the rest is silence. Reardon may, in fact, be innocent of any crime, but it does not inspire confidence to see him twice misplaced by a task force charged with solution of 49 murders.

It should not be supposed that Washington detectives are the only ones with problems when it comes to task force operations. Nebraska manhunters were "99% certain" of an innocent suspect's guilt in the murder of Danny Joe Eberle, later charged to serial killer John Joubert; the false report of a pebble found in Eberle's mouth was finally traced to a lab technician who mixed up his victims, placing critical information in the wrong file. Police in two states ignored repeated tips on Ted Bundy, including several phone calls from the girlfriend he tried to strangle during sex. Larry Eyler claimed an estimated 20 victims before a Central Indiana Multi-Agency Investigation Team was organized to track him down, his name heading a list of six possible suspects, but it would literally take a murder in his own back yard before Chicago homicide detectives made the bust. In Los Angeles, one of the Hillside Strangler's victims was a neighbor of Ken Bianchi; task force detectives questioned their man in that case, and dismissed him as harmless. And few cooperative efforts have been more chaotic than the search for Atlanta's "child-killer." Atlanta police were so busy compiling their official list of dead and missing children, arbitrarily selecting some and barring others, that they totally ignored a geographic pattern in the crimes, pointed out — to the embarrassment of all concerned — by ex-policeman Chet Dettlinger. Later, when Dettlinger's criticism of the task force grew more strident, he was briefly jailed as a "potential suspect," thinly-veiled intimidation overriding common sense.

The media can sometimes make or break a manhunt, based on the relationship between police and journalists. Where a spirit of cooperation prevails — as in the California "Zodiac" case — reporters sometimes withhold critical information to assist police, even when a killer writes directly to the press. In other cases, journalists have helped to turn up missing witnesses and bits of evidence that sometimes help indict — or clear — a suspect in the case. (A television crew, for instance, found discarded clothing worn by members of the Manson "family" the night they killed five persons in Los Angeles.) Friendly media sources may also be used to generate public support for a task force — rounding up volunteer searchers, prompting donations to the official war chest, even jogging the memory of forgetful witnesses with capsule recreations of a given crime.

On the flip side, relations between police and the media are frequently strained, detectives resenting the interference of parallel investigations while journalists harp on the public's "right to know" every detail of a case in the making. Leaks of classified material may jeopardize the prospects of arrest and conviction, providing cranks with persuasive filler for bogus confessions, sometimes tipping off a killer that the time is ripe to flee or change his modus operandi. Where details of an UNSUB profile are released, witnesses sometimes unconsciously tailor their memories to fit police expectations, recalling blonde hair on a dark-haired suspect, and so forth. In the worst-case scenario, rank yellow journalism may amount to deliberate sabotage of a manhunt for private gain, trumpeting classified evidence or taunting unstable offenders with inflammatory headlines.

Police occasionally try to "use" the media in their pursuit of random murderers, with mixed results. Laudatory profiles of a specific detective, building the manhunter up as a "supercop" and relentless pursuer, are sometimes employed to break a killer's morale or inspire correspondence with authorities. When a slayer initiates correspondence, psychologists are often tapped to script the official replies, steering their subject toward surrender. In clumsy hands, as demonstrated by the Skid Row Slasher case, provocative media reports may have the adverse reaction of triggering new murders. Another Los Angeles task force, hunting "Night Stalker" Richard Ramirez in 1985, tried to drive their man out of town by airing predictions of a speedy arrest. The tactic worked so well that Ramirez fled to San Francisco, killing one victim and wounding another there, before returning home to pick up his interrupted murder spree around L.A.

Federal intervention in serial murder cases, as depicted in *The Silence of the Lambs*, is a relatively new phenomenon, spurred by record-breaking murder statistics logged in 1980. The following year, U.S Attorney General William French Smith created the Attorney General's Task Force on Violent Crime, requiring each branch of the Justice Department to submit proposals for remedial strategies. The FBI's response was an expansion of the crack Behavioral Science Unit and a push for funding to create VICAP — the Violent Criminal Apprehension Program.

VICAP was the brainchild of retired Los Angeles police commander Pierce Brooks, a veteran of serial murder investigations dating from the late 1950s who recognized the glaring lack of any information network geared to track nomadic killers on the move. In 1980, Brooks was summoned to Atlanta as a consultant on the continuing "child-murders," and there he met Seattle detective Bob Keppel, a victim of similar geographic frustration in his pursuit of Ted Bundy. Retained by the FBI in 1981, Brooks and Keppel began hammering out the VICAP framework, drafting an investigative questionnaire for local officers, but they still had far to go, in terms of winning over the Washington bureau-

cracy. Best-selling author Ann Rule beat the drum for VICAP with a series of editorials in 1982, joining Brooks and others to plead the FBI's case in July 1983 senate hearings. A year later, in June 1984, President Ronald Reagan finally announced the creation of a National Center for Analysis of Violent Crime, charged with the primary goal of tracking repeat killers. The VICAP computer network, based at the FBI Academy in Quantico, Virginia, went on-line in May 1985, accepting reports of murders, missing persons, and discarded corpses from across the nation.

Unlike the heroes in *Silence of the Lambs*, television's short-lived "UNSUB" drama, or the popular series of "VICAP" novels from Dell Books, members of the VICAP team and the Behavioral Science Unit are paid to analyze crimes, rather than conducting active field investigations. With ten full-time agents in 1991, the BSU is not equipped for staging manhunts, crashing into suspect hideaways and gunning down desperate killers. When VICAP agents do visit a crime scene, their function is advisory, reviewing local task force operations and suggesting more efficient means of handling information. The national program's success or failure ultimately hinges on cooperation from local agencies, the very root of that pernicious "linkage blindness" which retards investigations to the present day.

Six months of operation was enough to highlight VICAP's problems in the field. Overworked police considered the federal questionnaire — 44 pages in length — as too cumbersome and time-consuming. If a killer picked off 10 or 15 victims, and the FBI required a separate questionnaire for each, some locals opted to ignore the federal team and spare themselves a case of writer's cramp. The new, improved VICAP forms (Appendix) are two-thirds shorter than their predecessors, but reduced paperwork has not solved all the Bureau's problems in coordinating manhunts. For many local officers, the FBI is still J. Edgar Hoover once removed, a headline-grabbing agency more interested in claiming credit for recovery of stolen cars and the arrest of "Top Ten" fugitives than helping out the average working cop. Some Bureau spokesmen are still too quick to shoot from the lip, as when an agent working the Atlanta beat blamed anonymous black parents for the deaths of several murdered children, and many agencies still view the feds as rank interlopers, their very presence a tacit indictment of local methods.

In fact, the FBI has been pursuing serial killers, albeit in rather disorganized fashion, since June 1961, when

Richard Marquette was added to the "Ten Most Wanted" list. Since then, at least 15 other repeat killers have earned the "most wanted" title, including Hugh Morse, Joseph Bryan, Lloyd Greeson, William Tahl, Hoyt Cobb, Monroe Hickson, Richard Tingler, Gary Krist, Enrique Estrada, Ted Bundy, Christopher Wilder, Alton Coleman, Billy Waldon, David Roberts, and Darren O'Neall. Most were sought by the Bureau on peripheral charges of interstate flight to avoid prosecution, and all but two were ultimately nabbed by local officers. Monroe Hickson died of natural causes *before* he made the Top 10 list, and Joseph Bryan was tackled by off-duty G-men who spotted him leaving a New Orleans mall, his latest child victim in tow.

Another "Top 10" killer, Monroe Hickson escaped from prison and died of natural causes a year before agents tracked him down. *(Credit: FBI)*

Oregon sex-slayer Richard Marquette was the first serial killer ever posted to the FBI's "10 Most Wanted" list. *(Credit: FBI)*

Results under the new regime are still equivocal. As previously noted, federal profilers tout their success in describing Wayne Williams before his arrest, but new disclosures — unearthed from the FBI's own classified files — cast serious doubt on the Atlanta "child-killer's" guilt. Likewise, the mind-hunters sometimes take credit for capturing Florida's Bobby Joe Long, a case broken only when Long allowed one of his victims to live. Elsewhere — in Seattle, Los Angeles, Miami, San Diego, Honolulu, Washington, D.C. — prolific killers remain at large despite the BSU's best efforts.

Within six years, Lloyd Greeson was dishonorably discharged from the Canadian army, the US Army, and the US Marine Corps. *(Credit: FBI)*

A VICAP case where everything worked out as planned hails from Wilmington, Delaware, where five young prostitutes were tortured to death between November 1987 and October 1988. FBI profilers reviewed the case evidence, sketching a portrait of an UNSUB who was white, a local resident employed in a construction trade, age 25-35, fascinated with police work, and preferring a roomy, insulated vehicle for transport and disposal of his victims. Fiber samples narrowed down the range of carpeting inside the car or van, and VICAP agents recommended a decoy operation, to lure the killer with policewomen disguised as hookers. One such decoy managed to obtain some carpet fibers and a license number for a "creepy" trick whose mannerisms set alarm bells ringing in her mind, and surveillance was established on suspect Steven Pennell. A 31-year-old white man, Pennell was a professional electrician, with two semesters of college criminology behind him. His applications to local police departments had all been rejected, but he clearly fit the VICAP profile as a "police buff." Scientific analysis of hairs, fibers, and blood stains from his van persuaded a jury of Pennell's guilt in two murders, earning him a prison term of life without parole.

Apprehension of repeat killers is not a foregone conclusion, by any means. In this century, 18% of all recognized serial slayers have given detectives the slip, including three classic examples — Belle Gunness, Carl Menarik, and Bela Kiss — who eluded police *after* their names and crimes were publicized. At that, an 82% solution rate is well above the national average for murder cases, but it must not be supposed that every identified serial killer stands trial.

Some choose to die, instead.

Since 1900, 2.5% of American serial stalkers — some 26 killers in all — have slipped through death's escape hatch before their day in court. Suicide accounts for the largest group of casualties, with seven offenders — including Joe Ball, Carmelo DeJesus, Fernando Cota, Michael Player, Fritz Klenner, Gary Robbins, and Randal Rolle — taking their own lives prior to arrest; two others, Leonard Lake and Calvin Perry, killed themselves in custody, before charges were filed. Six predators — including Chester Comer, Alex Mengel, Christopher Wilder, Paul Knowles, Steven Smith, and Bertram Greenberg — were killed in the act of resisting arrest or attempted escape from custody. Natural or accidental causes took five killers off the street, including Philip Husereau, Gary Tison, Stella Williamson, Eugene Butler, and Monroe Hickson. Poetic justice was served with the murders of four serial killers: Dean Corll and Sidney Williams were each killed prior to arrest, while "Mau Mau" gunmen Nathaniel Burse and Edward Moran died in jail, awaiting trial. Two more, Wayne Nance and L.L. Thompson, were shot and killed by their intended victims, during the commission of a crime.

The modern justice system waits for those who manage to survive, examining forensic evidence and passing judgment on their sanity, debating guilt or innocence, deciding who should die or spend the next few decades in a cage. As we shall see, it is a system which professes faith in God... and like Him, it sometimes moves in mysterious ways.

Chapter 8

Trial and Error

The arrest of a serial killer — or suspect — evokes widespread relief, but apprehension is only the first step toward justice. Far from closing the books on a case, identification of the presumed offender is merely a starting point for the state's prosecution team. Fresh evidence remains to be collected, analyzed, interpreted. The capture of a suspect may reveal more crimes, propelling searchers in a new direction. Finally, there is the suspect's day in court.

And even that is not the end.

Our legal system guarantees the basic right of every criminal, no matter how sadistic or depraved, to mount a competent defense. In practice, it is only since the 1960s, with the liberal rulings of the Warren Court, that suspect rights have been enforced with any uniformity. Before that era, "third-degree" techniques were commonplace, if not routine, and few investigators quarreled with confessions in a headline murder case. If the police forgot their warrants for a search, appeals courts were inclined to look the other way. Conviction brought stiff sentences, and when the court's decree was death, an execution might be carried out in weeks or months, instead of years.

The "good old days" undoubtedly produced some travesties of justice. An innocent suspect was lynched in Waco, Texas, while stalker Roy Mitchell remained at large. In Cleveland, during the "Mad Butcher's" heyday, suspect Frank Dolezal was beaten — and perhaps murdered — by overzealous sheriff's deputies; Dolezal's jailhouse suicide remains highly suspicious, at best, and

his several confessions have been thoroughly discredited. Three innocent defendants were tried in the New Orleans Ax Man case, two of them falsely convicted, and a fourth suspect was murdered in Los Angeles before police gave up the fruitless search. In England, shortly after World War II, John Christie framed a neighbor for two of his murders and let the man hang.

For all its safeguards, though, the "liberal" approach is not foolproof. In Colorado, Park Estep stands sentenced to life for a murder claimed by serial killer Ottis Toole. Arrested despite his total lack of resemblance to the suspect, convicted by contradictory statements from a traumatized survivor, Estep remains in prison despite Toole's confession, county prosecutors too embarrassed to admit a critical mistake. Missouri mental patient Melvin Reynolds was browbeaten into confessing the 1978 murder of young Eric Christgen, at St. Joseph; he served four years of a life sentence before nomad Charles Hatcher admitted the crime, naming Christgen as one of his 16 victims.

Despite such highly publicized miscarriages of justice, modern guidelines are more likely to result in killers going free. Police mishandling of Larry Eyler's first arrest, in 1983, resulted in suppression of the very evidence required to take him off the street; at least five other victims — and perhaps twice as many — died at Eyler's hand before detectives built a new case in Chicago. Harvey Carignan was sentenced to die for his first known murder, in 1949, but a sheriff's procedural error reversed the sentence two years later; paroled in 1960, Carignan would kill at least five more women before he was finally caged in Minnesota. Maryland nurse Jane Bolding confessed three murders in 1985, and she was suspected of 19 others, but police interrogation methods — grilling her for 33 hours without an attorney—made her confessions inadmissible in court. Even a case like that of John Gacy, found with 28 victims buried under his house, is not airtight. At this writing, Gacy has challenged the police search warrant for his home; if found to be invalid, it would literally wipe out all the evidence connecting Gacy to a six-year string of homicides.

Defending serial killers in court is an arduous, unpopular, and sometimes hazardous occupation. While some defendants waive their right to an attorney, and a few — like Ted Bundy — exercise their egos by defending themselves, most random slayers welcome the advice of counsel. Few are affluent enough to spring for big-name legal talent, though famous attorneys sometimes attach themselves to a high-profile case for publicity's sake. Boston lawyer F. Lee Bailey helped inflate his reputation in the 1960s by defending serial slayers Charles Schmid and Albert DeSalvo, while across the continent, Melvin Belli offered his services to the elusive Zodiac, part of a vain effort to induce the killer's surrender. More often, public defenders or court-appointed lawyers inherit such cases, and a losing verdict is sometimes the least of their problems. Los Angeles attorney Ronald Hughes vanished without a trace in November 1970, shortly after quarreling with client Charles Manson, and speculation continues regarding his possible murder by members of Manson's bizarre "family." In other cases, lawyers defending a serial killer have more to fear from the public at large. New York attorneys Frank Armani and Francis Belge were bound by rules of confidentiality in 1974, when client Robert Garrow — facing trial on one murder count — revealed the location of two other corpses. They kept the information secret, as required by law, and local residents were outraged when the truth came out. Both attorneys were threatened, and Belge was physically assaulted on the street, before Garrow was finally convicted and sentenced to prison on the standing charge.

With or without an attorney's advice, serial killers often confess their crimes in custody, but detectives must know how to handle their subjects. For Henry Lucas and Ottis Toole, it was a simple matter of respect and being treated "like a man." As Toole explained, "If they get rowdy with me, I just freeze up on 'em." Indeed, rapport is the key to any successful interrogation,

achieved when detectives begin to understand their subject's world. Appeals to vanity are sometimes useful, with investigators stressing the importance of their subject's contribution to law enforcement and protection of the public at large. A low-key approach may gain entree to the killer's private fantasy world, eliciting statements that bear on methods and motives. In extreme cases, an oblique third-person approach may induce certain killers to describe their crimes without accepting personal responsibility. Ted Bundy was a case in point, "speculating" at length on the mental workings of an "entity" responsible for murders "similar" to his own. As Bundy described a Washington double murder for journalist Stephen Michaud:

> Well, again, assuming that we know what we're talking about here... that it's the same person we described in the Healy and Ball cases. Then he shows up at Lake Sammamish. So we would have to reflect back on what presently we know about this entity and compare it to what seemed to happen at the lake.
>
> In that light, the Lake Sammamish cases don't fit, you know. Obviously don't fit the Healy or Ball M.O., for example. And it apparently happened in midafternoon, in broad daylight, with a large number of people in close proximity. Beyond that, however, there is not a lot known.
>
> And of course the girls were killed. I guess that's known. Outside of that, very little.
>
> It's clear that the Lake Sammamish incident was either the result of the venting of a great amount of tension or frustration that had accumulated over a long period of time, or it was an attempt to indulge in a different M.O.
>
> Look at it this way. The individual had contemplated that kind of scheme before, realizing its obvious drawbacks. He would not have ordinarily attempted it, but his reluctance to engage in that kind of scheme was erased or otherwise overpowered by the need to seek out another victim.[1]

FBI psychologists report that a majority of random killers freely admit their crimes once they are arrested. Others, like Eddie Cole, deny conscious memory of specific murders but admit their guilt in the face of physical evidence. Yet another group maintains the pose of innocence against all odds, in spite of overwhelming proof and multiple convictions. Ted Bundy played a mental game of hide-and-seek until the night before his execution, when he suddenly confessed to 30 murders (and, in the opinion of investigators, managed to neglect a few). After twelve years on death row, John Gacy still insists that he was framed on 33 murder counts, a victim of drug-dealing conspirators who used his crawlspace — unbeknown to Gacy — as a private graveyard. William Heirens, after serving nearly half a century in Illinois state prisons, doggedly maintains his innocence in three sadistic homicides despite confessions, fingerprints, and positive ballistics evidence.

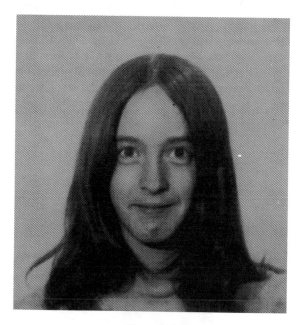

Ex-Satanist Susan Atkins boasted to cellmates of the murders she committed under orders from guru Charles Manson. *(Credit: Los Angeles County Sheriff's Dept.)*

When random murderers confess, another problem enters into play. Some — like Paul Bateson, Susan Atkins, Richard Ramirez, and Joseph Christopher — boast of their crimes to cellmates, providing graphic details to enhance their own prestige. Such conversations may or may not be admissible in court, depending on a judge's whim, and homicide investigators are required to sort out truth from fiction as they try to build a case. When Richard Ramirez declares that "I've killed 20 people; I love all that blood," authorities confront an embarrassing shortage of victims, scrambling to prove — or disprove — the killer's boast.

Official confessions are equally problematic, when suspects claim improbable body counts without supporting evidence. Ecuador's Pedro Lopez, dubbed the "Monster of the Andes," dazzled police with his 1980 confessions to more than 300 murders in three countries.

Most of his victims remain unidentified, but Lopez boosted his own credibility by leading authorities to 53 grave sites around Ambato. As one police spokesman declared, "If someone confesses to 53 you find and hundreds more you don't, you tend to believe what he says." A contrary view prevails in the United States, where several random slayers have confessed to murders by the score or by the hundred, always falling short of final proof. In Idaho, during 1975, Thomas Creech confessed 42 murders, some allegedly committed on the orders of a nationwide Satanic cult; nine slayings were confirmed, spanning six states, but 33 others — and the murderous cult — remain elusive. Charles Hatcher's confession of 16 murders was more modest, but 11 victims remained unidentified at Hatcher's suicide in 1984. Michigan's Richard Clarey was awaiting trial on three murder counts when he confessed to "more than 100 but less than 150" others, dating back to age 15. Called upon to judge the killer's state of mind, Dr. Leonard Donk reported, "I suspect he's killed more people than he's been charged with. How many more, I wouldn't even want to speculate on." Robert Segee, jailed for arson in Connecticut, confessed to a series of slayings in Japan and the United States — including cremation of 169 victims in a deliberate circus fire — but no murder charges were filed, and Segee has since recanted his confessions. In New York, parolee Joseph Fischer confessed his wife's murder in July 1979, escalating from there until he had claimed "about 150" victims in a quarter-century. The claim won Fischer air time on *Geraldo* and *America's Most Wanted,* but detectives have confirmed no more than half a dozen murders in the series.

No case in recent times has spawned more controversy than that of Henry Lucas and Ottis Toole. Arrested in separate states during June 1983, Lucas and Toole soon launched into marathon confessions spanning the next two years, claiming hundreds of victims in the United States and Canada. (As with Thomas Creech, a Satanic cult was implicated but never confirmed.) Detectives from 46 states questioned both men on some 2,000 unsolved cases, with over 200 eventually listed as "cleared." Between them, Lucas and Toole were convicted of 13 slayings in four states, with dozens of charges outstanding... and then, in April 1985, Lucas changed his mind. It was all a hoax, he declared, contrived to embarrass detectives who treated him "like a dog." In fact, he had killed only three victims — or perhaps only one, depending on when he was asked. Police from coast to coast were so intent on clearing ancient cases, Lucas charged, that they provided him with details necessary to substantiate his various confessions. Dallas newsman Hugh Aynesworth published a series of scathing articles on Lucas, claiming private knowledge of the hoax from 1983, but Aynesworth's credibility was damaged by his authorship of articles indicting Lucas as a world-class killer, one of them published as late as February 1985. In Florida, Toole got into the act, shifting daily between pleas of innocence and personal claims of 116 victims.

Overnight, the battle lines were drawn. A Texas judge dismissed murder charges in a case where prosecutors were convinced of Henry's guilt, and 90 of the cases previously cleared were suddenly "reopened." On the other hand, authorities in California, Illinois, and Georgia stood behind their claims that Toole and Lucas were responsible for dozens, maybe scores of murders. Arkansas authorities went further, filing three new murder counts a week *after* Henry's change of heart. At this writing, Lucas and Toole await trial in northern Florida, facing four new counts that could land both men on death row. Lucas, in typical style, first confessed to the homicides and then recanted, while Toole's young nephew is prepared to testify against both men.

The problem, in fact, is not so much Lucas himself, as it is a mistaken perception of fact. Texas Rangers knew from the outset that Lucas would lie, given half a chance. One of his earliest confessions named a victim who was still alive, and some of his tales — delivering poison Kool-Aid to the People's Temple in Guyana or flying to Spain for a political assassination — were patently absurd. On the flip side, he repeatedly sketched floor plans from memory, led police to crime scenes or dismembered remains, and recalled the theft of items missing from police reports that could have given him the facts. On balance, it seems clear that Toole and Lucas are responsible for several dozen deaths, at least, if not the hundreds they originally claimed.

The management of a compulsive killer prior to trial is fraught with built-in risks. Notorious offenders commonly draw threats from cranks in the community, and while the prospects of a lynching are remote — unlike the scene in 1920, when Kentucky national guardsmen were mustered to protect Will Lockett — jailhouse assaults are not unknown. Billy Waldon was severely beaten by cellmates in San Diego, after he ignored their orders to assassinate a fellow prisoner, and two members of De Mau Mau were strangled to death in Illinois' Lake County jail. Suicide is a more common

threat with random slayers in custody, and extraordinary precautions are sometimes required to keep them alive pending trial. Indiana's Calvin Perry and California "Freeway Killer" Vernon Butts were each successful in their jailhouse suicide attempts, while Louise Vermilyea scored a near-miss in Chicago, leaving herself paralyzed and unfit for trial. Henry Lucas, Gary Heidnik, Ottis Toole and many others have attempted suicide in custody by less efficient means. Overseas, cannibal-killers Georg Grossmann and Karl Denke cheated the executioner by hanging themselves in Germany and Poland, respectively, while Robert Succo took his own life in an Italian asylum. It often seems ironic, preserving the life of a killer so that he or she may be sentenced to die, but the strict rules of justice demand nothing less.

"Freeway Killer" Vernon Butts hanged himself in jail, rather than face trial for his crimes. *(Credit: Los Angeles County Sheriff's Dept.)*

A more serious threat, from the public viewpoint, is the risk of a killer's escape. Eleven years and 800 miles apart, Paul Knowles and Alex Mengel were shot dead in the act of disarming their jailers, attempting to flee from custody. Ted Bundy was more successful, twice breaking out of Colorado lockups, claiming three more victims on his dead-end run to Florida. Joseph Franklin followed Bundy's example, striking off for the Sunshine State after he broke jail in Kentucky. Another Colorado killer, Tony Bropst, slipped out of Douglas County's jail and spent a day at large before he was recaptured. In Missouri, Sharon Kinne sat through three murder trials before skipping out on the fourth, running all the way to Mexico and yet another homicide. Alabama's Audrey Hilley was less patient, bailing out in the wake of indictments, eluding pursuers from November 1979 until January 1983. No further victims have been documented in the Hilley case, but the inherent risk of a compulsive poisoner at large and on the run for three full years is obvious.

Secure confinement may insure the public peace of mind, but it does not eliminate the threat of further violence from a random killer. Californian Joseph Morse claimed his third victim in custody, while awaiting trial for the murders of his mother and crippled sister. In Las Vegas, Wayne Horton graduated from rape, robbery, and kidnapping charges with the fatal stabbing of a 19-year-old cellmate. Drifter James French had no explanation for the strangulation of a fellow prisoner in Oklahoma, but the addition of a second murder charge to French's rap sheet guaranteed his execution. In London, slayer Kieron Kelly was spending a night in the drunk tank when he bludgeoned another transient, finishing his victim off with a garrote fashioned from stockings and shoelaces.

Despite the brooding atmosphere of violence that surrounds such inmates, serial killers sometimes exert a hypnotic effect on the opposite sex, attracting "groupies" in a bizarre twist on the celebrity syndrome. Charles Manson is notorious for the lingering devotion of his female "family" members, but other random slayers do quite well on their own, without the benefit of preconditioned disciples. Arizona's Charles Schmid — "The Pied Piper of Tucson" — had his own teenage rooting section at the trial which sentenced him to death. Ted Bundy received numerous love letters from attractive young women, many resembling his pattern victims with their long, brown hair parted in the middle; finally choosing one to be his jailhouse bride, Bundy beat the clock and fathered a child from death row, by means of artificial insemination. In Nevada, Eddie Cole received visits and heart-rending poems of love from a young magazine editor half his age. John Gacy's girlfriend, a twice-divorced mother of eight, wangled a spot for herself on Morton Downey's television talk show, and both Hillside Stranglers — Ken Bianchi and Angelo Buono — have been married since receiving their life prison terms. An old Bianchi paramour, Veronica Compton, drew time of her own for attempted murder,

trying to free her lover by recreating the strangler's technique — complete with a sample of Bianchi's sperm. In prison, long since soured on Bianchi, Compton attached herself to "Sunset Slayer" Douglas Clark. (One letter from Compton to Clark, in a classic case of understatement, declared: "Our humor is unusual. I wonder why others don't see the necrophilic aspects of existence as we do.") On the distaff side, Louise Peete derived immense satisfaction from the suicides of lovers and fiancees traumatized by separation while she cooled her heels in jail.

Female admirers of "Night Stalker" Richard Ramirez include a member of the jury that sentenced him to death for 13 murders. *(Credit: Los Angeles County Sheriff's Dept.)*

Ironically, considering his physical appearance and the nature of his crimes, no modern psychopath has drawn more ardent female groupies than California "Night Stalker" Richard Ramirez. A regular fan club attended his 14-month murder trial in Los Angeles, some of the young women carrying notebooks and couching their interest in terms of a "class project," others frankly admitting their attraction for Ramirez and his outspoken Satanism. One groupie claimed to be Richard's fiancee, but the wedding never came off; another, identified as Bernadette Brazal, told the press: "Do I love him? Yes, in my own childlike way. I feel such compassion for him. When I look at him, I see a real handsome guy who just messed up his life because he never had anyone to guide him."[2] Nor were the Night Stalker's conquests limited to schoolgirls. In the summer of 1991, facing a new murder trial in San Francisco, Ramirez received frequent visits from a female member of the Los Angeles jury that sentenced him to die. Two other groupies, one of them a porno model, circulated revealing photos of themselves around the county jail, one young woman threatening her rival — and the President of the United States — in violent fits of jealousy. So bizarre, in fact, was their behavior that it led to revocation of Ramirez's visiting rights, despite his forlorn plea that "I'm no sex symbol."

In any murder case, the first responsibility of prosecutors and defense attorneys is determination of the suspect's mental state. Our legal system makes allowances for individuals whose aberrant behavior is compelled by mental illness, sparing them from punishment as common criminals. The general public has been outraged, in recent years, by cases like those of mass killer Edward Allaway and would-be presidential assassin John Hinckley, where verdicts of "not guilty by reason of insanity" spared the defendants from prison, instead consigning them to mental institutions for an indefinite term. Surveys of public opinion reveal a consensus that many or most accused felons try to "cop a plea" with bogus insanity schemes, large numbers of them slipping through the cracks and serving "easy time" before they are released once more into society.

In fact, statistics show that only 1% of all American felony suspects plead insanity at trial, and barely one in three of those is finally acquitted.[3] Serial murders, with their bizarre trappings of sadism, necrophilia and the like, seem ideally suited to insanity pleas, but even here the odds against acquittal are extreme. With some 650 American serial killers identified in this century, only 3.6% have been declared incompetent for trial or cleared by reason of insanity.

Unfortunately, there is no firm definition of "insanity" in the United States, beyond the fact that it remains a legal term, divorced from any diagnosis of specific mental illness. Nationwide, the fifty states are free to draft their own peculiar guidelines, chasing abstract terminology around in circles while the individual defendants — and their countless victims — are ignored.

One test of sanity, applied in 16 states, is the M'Naughten rule. Named for a paranoid schizophrenic defendant who murdered the British prime minister's secretary in 1843, this rule is widely favored on the basis of its simple — some would say simplistic — definition of insanity. According to M'Naughten:

> To establish a defense on the ground of insanity, it must be proved that at the time of the committing of the act the party accused was laboring under such a defect of reason from disease of the mind as not to know the nature and quality of the act he was doing; or, if he did know, that he did not know what he was doing was wrong.

A few states chose to supplement M'Naughten with the so-called "irresistible impulse test," established by English courts in 1840 and transplanted to America in 1886. As explained by Justice Somerville of Alabama in an early case: "The disease of insanity can so affect the power of the mind as to subvert the freedom of the will, and thereby destroy the power of the victim to choose between right and wrong, though he perceives it." Prosecutors frequently counter a plea of irresistible impulse with hypothetical arguments of "the policeman at the elbow," seeking admissions that a given defendant could, in fact, restrain himself at chosen times. Today, the question is moot, with a 1984 federal statute abolishing tests for the fabled "irresistible impulse."

In 1954, a judgment from the District of Columbia established the new Durham rule, sometimes called the "products test." In that decision, it was held that "An accused is not criminally responsible if his unlawful act was the product of mental disease or defect." Those terms, in turn, were vague enough to require clarification through a second case in the same jurisdiction, defining "mental disease or defect" as "any abnormal condition which substantially affects mental or emotional processes and substantially affects behavior controls."

Officially unrecognized outside the nation's capital, Durham remained in effect until 1972, when the new Brawner rule — also dubbed the "substantial capacity test" — was inaugurated by the same judge who wrote the Durham decision. Adopted by several states in the interim, as part of a Model Penal Code, the new rule provides that:

> 1. A person is not responsible for criminal conduct if at the time of such conduct as a result of mental disease or defect he lacks substantial capacity either to appreciate the criminality (wrongfulness) of his conduct or to conform his conduct to the requirement of the law.

2. As used in this Article, the terms "mental disease or defect" do not include any abnormality manifested only by repeated criminal or otherwise antisocial conduct.

Another modern guideline for insanity proceedings, pioneered by Michigan in 1975 and since adopted by seven other states, is the verdict of "guilty but mentally ill." Specifics vary, but in most jurisdictions a defendant convicted under this rule is sent directly to a mental institution, there confined until he or she is deemed healthy enough to begin serving the appropriate prison term. Apparently the perfect compromise, this system treats unbalanced offenders to valuable therapy, without letting them "off the hook" for their crimes. Some critics, though, denounce the system as an underhanded abolition of "insanity," exalting public pressure over human rights. The controversy has not been resolved, by any means, and while it rages, antiquated doctrines like M'Naughten will undoubtedly survive.

At that, not every suspect — sane or otherwise — proceeds to trial before a jury of his peers. The rule of law demands that each defendant must be competent to understand the charges and participate effectively in his or her defense. Where such is not the case, incompetent defendants are committed for remedial therapy, working toward the day when they are fit for trial.

In this century, only eight American serial killers — some 1.2% of the total — have been judged incompetent to face a judge and jury. One, Chicago deaf-mute Donald Lang, was physically incapable of taking part in his defense, a handicap that put him on the street despite two murder counts within seven years. Eight other random slayers were deemed incompetent on the basis of mental illness, confined for indefinite periods of treatment. Wisconsin's Ed Gein was a hands-down favorite, preoccupied with severed body parts; recalled for trial in 1968, he was found not guilty by reason of insanity and returned to the hospital where he finished his days. Cincinnati child-killer Charles Bischoff was likewise judged incompetent, while Cleo Green's possession by a "Red Demon" swayed his judge toward commitment in lieu of trial. New York slashers Charles Sears and Erno Soto made their cases with reference to backgrounds of violence, drug abuse, and psychiatric treatment. Another New York killer, Ricardo Caputo, was ruled incompetent for trial in his first known slaying, dispatched to an institution from which he later escaped... with the aid of his therapist. Across the line in Connecticut, 14-year-old Anthony Santo blamed

three murders on a recent illness affecting his mind, and the court agreed. New Orleans authorities found Marcus Hamilton incompetent for trial on two murder counts, in 1986, while his brother was convicted and imprisoned for one of the crimes. Colorado poisoner Gloria Tannenbaum was suspected in two deaths and one disappearance when court-appointed doctors found her mentally unfit for trial.

Considering the stakes involved, it comes as no surprise that random slayers sometimes fake insanity to stump the system. David Berkowitz professed to take his marching orders from an ancient demon, speaking through a neighbor's dog, while Joseph Kallinger was pestered by a floating, disembodied head named Charlie. Peter Sutcliffe heard the voice of God advising him to slaughter British prostitutes, and Satan followed Martha Wise around her small Ohio farm, suggesting targets for a string of arson fires. "Split personality" has been another favorite dodge for killers facing heavy prison time, portrayed in many films and novels, but reality is something else. An estimated 2,500 victims of multiple personality disorder (MPD) have been diagnosed since the disease was officially recognized, after World War II, but *none* have been serial killers. For all that, statistics do not prevent some enterprising slayers from faking MPD symptoms in their own defense. Young William Heirens blamed three murders on alterego "George Murman" — short for "Murder Man" — but now credits police and court-appointed psychiatrists with devising the tale. Another Chicago slayer, John Gacy, briefly conjured up a personality called "Jack," ironically the same name Gacy used while trolling the streets for human prey.

Strangler Ken Bianchi is the undisputed prince of psychiatric hoaxers, famed for his performance as "Steve Walker," a sexist brute who lived to murder "cunts" and "bitches." Primed by viewings of the TV movie *Sybil*, Bianchi duped a panel of psychiatrists — including the eminent Donald Lunde and MPD specialist John Watkins — into swallowing his grandiose performance. The charade inspired a PBS documentary, "The Mind of a Murderer," and author Ted Schwarz published a best-selling book on Bianchi-as-Steve, but no show runs forever. In time, Dr. Martin Orne saw through Bianchi's act, logging instances of inappropriate and contradictory behavior while Bianchi feigned hypnosis. Orne baited a trap, suggesting the likelihood of further personalities, and Bianchi responded on cue, chiming in with the falsetto voice of infantile "Billy" a few moments later. The roof fell in when homicide detectives traced the real Steve Walker, a UCLA graduate whose name and college transcripts had been lifted by Bianchi to obtain a fake psychology diploma at the height of the "Hillside" murder spree. Even then, with Bianchi's scheme dismantled and exposed to public ridicule, Dr. Watkins and others remained convinced of their MPD diagnosis, standing fast on behalf of Bianchi's defense.

Of course, some random killers *are* insane, the fakers notwithstanding. Maryland jurors could find no other explanation for Reginald Oates, after he murdered and cannibalized four children. In San Francisco, William Hanson shot his sister's middle-aged rapist again and again, selecting a different target each time. Wisconsin's Ed Gein spent 11 years in therapy before he was found competent for trial... which resulted in a verdict of not guilty by reason of insanity. Charles Floyd, the "Peeping Tom killer" of Tulsa, Oklahoma, was lost to his hunger for seductive redheads. Massachusetts nurse Jane Toppan convinced a jury of her mental state when she testified: "That is my ambition, to have killed more people — more helpless people — than any man or woman who has ever lived." In Connecticut, policeman Matthew Quintiliano murdered his wife and was found insane, but a second jury was less sympathetic when he repeated the crime, eight years later. California cultist Steven Hurd receives periodic visits from Satan, resplendent in a shiny silver helmet, at the Atascadero state hospital. In Maryland, hallucinations prompted Melissa Norris to kill her mother, sister, and infant son, but a judge found her sane at the moment of trial and released her on the spot.

The case of Albert Fish reveals how psychiatric testimony may be twisted and manipulated to support a preconceived idea. Diagnosed by state psychiatrists as practicing "every known perversion," New York's cannibal-killer was charged with one murder and suspected of at least 14 others when he went to trial in 1935. Insanity was Fish's first — and only — line of defense, perhaps a safe bet for one who admitted torturing himself with needles, whips, and nail-studded paddles, resting on occasion to consume his own excrement with tossed salad. At trial, the state was desperate to win a death penalty, countering Fish's insanity plea with ludicrous psychobabble. Speaking for the state, a battery of doctors testified, straight-faced, that "Coprophagia (eating excrement) is a common sort of thing. We don't call people who do that mentally sick. A man who does that is socially perfectly all right. As far as his social status is concerned, he is supposed to be normal, because the State of New York Mental Hygiene Department approves of that." With Fish's rambling, obscene confessions in hand the jury found him sane and guilty of premeditated murder. He kept his date with the electric chair in January 1936.

Nomadic killers pose a special problem for the system, with their victims scattered over different jurisdictions. Most states cooperate on extradition, but a few remain at odds, notably where philosophical disputes arise over capital punishment. Sentenced to life for one of seven murders around Ann Arbor, Michigan, John Collins was also linked with a similar West Coast slaying in the 1960s. California petitioned for Collins's extradition in 1970, but Michigan governor William Milliken vetoed the request, ruling that no further punishment could — or should — be applied in the case. A similar controversy surrounds the proposed extradition of slayer Charles Ng from Canada, with international treaties forbidding delivery of a suspect facing capital charges. Conversely, some jurisdictions are glad to be rid of a killer, especially when more stringent penalties lie in wait at the other end of the line. Two decades before the arrest of John Collins, Michigan authorities captured "Lonely Hearts killers" Martha Beck and Raymond Fernandez, a more conservative administration happily packing them off to New York and eventual execution. Likewise, Nevada prosecutors realized that Gerald Gallego's California death sentence meant death by old age, rather than lethal gas; financing a new trial by unprecedented public subscription, they tagged Gallego with a second capital sentence, this time in a state which has executed three serial killers since 1985.

The labyrinthine case of Henry Lucas and Ottis Toole provides a classic illustration of how muddled prosecutions for serial murder can be. In Montague County, Texas, Sheriff W.F. Conway was voted "Sheriff of the Year" for bagging Lucas... and then dumped from office by constituents resentful of the cost involved. A convicted murder defendant in Arkansas was freed after Lucas confessed to the crime, but Colorado authorities remain unimpressed by Toole's admission of guilt in the Park Estep case. In West Virginia, more confessions in the death of a police officer overturned a standing verdict of suicide, granting death benefits to the victim's wife and children. Texas Rangers were embarrassed when Lucas withdrew his confessions, and state attorney general Jim Mattox ran for governor — unsuccessfully — on the strength of his role in exposing the "hoax." In Louisiana, two detectives lost their jobs for "misplacing" crucial evidence in a murder charged against Lucas. Prosecutors in Arkansas, Illinois, California, and Georgia remain convinced of Henry's guilt in multiple slayings, but they decline to prosecute for reasons of economy; Florida, meanwhile, forges ahead with proceedings in four new cases. Back in Texas, a prosecutor who trashed three "Lucas cases" won reelection in spite of federal racketeering indictments, and the judge who dismissed a fourth case in El Paso was officially reprimanded, in separate proceedings, for harassing defense lawyers with his "explosive temperament and vindictive attitude." Meanwhile, appeals courts have affirmed Lucas's conviction in one capital case, despite journalistic "evidence" placing him hundreds of miles from the crime scene.

As a practical matter, few serial killers are punished for all of their crimes. Some, like John Gacy and Juan Corona, plant their victims in close proximity, facilitating multiple convictions, but most are less considerate of the authorities. Where evidence is weak or nonexistent — as in many of the crimes attributed to Ted Bundy, Nathaniel Code, John Collins, Posteal Laskey, and others — prosecutors play their strongest hand, settling for one or two murder convictions in lieu of 15 or 20. Some jurisdictions stubbornly deny a killer's guilt for reasons best known to themselves, as typified by San Diego's willful blindness in the case of Eddie Cole. In other cases, politics and economics override the quest for justice, prosecutors ever mindful of the fact that trials cost money and taxpayers vote. Public opinion may demand indictment in a sensational case, but if the trial runs over budget — or the suspect is acquitted — every D.A. understands the risk of backlash at the ballot box.

Prosecution, like politics, makes for strange bedfellows. Negotiation is part of the game, and a shortage of physical evidence sometimes mandates unsavory bargains for testimony. Child-slayer Clifford Olson holds the record for audacity, persuading the Royal Canadian Mounted Police to pay him $10,000 each for the bodies of ten missing victims, but most such bargains are trade-offs, swapping reduced prison time — or complete immunity — for the testimony of a criminal accomplice. In San Francisco, Anthony Harris faced prosecution on two murder counts when he turned state's evidence against his fellow Death Angels in the notorious "Zebra" case. Charlene Gallego drew a lenient 16-year sentence for helping place her husband on death row, while Linda Kasabian earned total immunity with her testimony in the Manson murder trial. Rape-slayer Roy Norris was no prize for Los

Angeles prosecutors, but they bargained a sentence of 45 years to life for his lethal testimony against Lawrence ("Pliers") Bittaker. "Freeway" killers Greg Miley and James Munro were quick to testify against ringleader William Bonin, thereby sparing themselves a trip to the death house. Kenneth Bianchi struck a similar bargain in the Hillside Strangler case, but his clumsy efforts to manipulate the system backfired, leaving Bianchi confined in Washington for life without parole.

Charged with two of California's "freeway murders," Greg Miley testified against ringleader William Bonin to save himself. *(Credit: Los Angeles County Sheriff's Dept.)*

Dramatic trials make headlines, but 90% of American felony cases are settled with negotiated plea bargains, and serial murders are no exception. For some killers — like Mack Edwards, Michael Tenneson, and Eddie Cole — a guilty plea is the settling of overdue accounts, inspired by conscience, a secret death wish, or simple fatigue. A few, like David Berkowitz, apparently plead guilty in a bid to shield unknown accomplices. Others, including the likes of William Heirens, John Wille, Leroy Snyder, Donald Harvey, and David Young, strike bargains to rescue themselves from a capital sentence. Florida's Gerald Stano was pleased to trade corpses for mercy, logging eight life sentences in 24 slayings, but the public was disgusted by the time his body count reached 41, and Stano's ninth trial sent him to death row.

Few citizens complain when murderers are jailed for life, but cries of outrage are routine when a negotiated plea reduces or eliminates a murder charge, sometimes returning a compulsive killer to the street. In Florida, James Pough's first homicide was booked as manslaughter and bargained down to aggravated assault, earning Pough five years probation; at the end of that term, his criminal record was expunged, allowing Pough to legally purchase the firearms with which he killed eight other victims. Nurse Mary Robaczynski admitted the slaying of four Maryland patients, but prosecutors threw in the towel after a mistrial, dropping all charges in return for the surrender of Robaczynski's nursing license. In Boston, attorney F. Lee Bailey negotiated a classic plea bargain for strangler Albert DeSalvo, 13 counts of murder lost in the shuffle as DeSalvo accepted a life term on rape and burglary charges. Coral Watts struck a similar, equally controversial deal in Texas, swapping 12 murder confessions for a 60-year burglary sentence... and dismissal of all pending murder counts. Under the terms of his agreement, Watts will be eligible for parole at age 50, in the year 2002 A.D.

Sensational publicity, routine in cases of serial murder, creates no end of problems for the prosecution. Some notorious defendants, like Philadelphia's Gary Heidnik and California "Trailside Killer" David Carpenter, require a change of venue to escape the headlines and secure impartial juries. Even so, our age of electronic media renders some cases literally inescapable. Weeks or months may be lost in the process of jury selection, with hundreds of prospects dismissed before both sides agree on 12 who make the cut. With the trial in progress, even with jurors sequestered, publicity remains a problem, as when Charles Manson smuggled newspapers into a Los Angeles courtroom and members of Juan Corona's defense team met jurors outside the courthouse, brandishing pejorative headlines in hopes of winning their client a mistrial.

Serial murder trials are often long and costly, particularly in Los Angeles, where lawyers pride themselves on billing by the hour and moving with glacial speed. Charles Manson's first trial, for the Tate-LaBianca murders required a month of jury selection and eight months of testimony to land four defendants on death row. In the case of "Night Stalker" Richard Ramirez, jury selection alone took six months, with nearly 3,000 interviews, while another nine months were consumed by the trial. Randy Kraft's Orange County murder trial lasted 13 months, costing the tax payers more than $10 million. These cases pale,

however, in comparison to the L.A. trial of strangler Angelo Buono, with its 10-month preliminary hearing and two full years of testimony, dragging on from November 1981 through November 1983. By contrast, the Atlanta trial of Wayne Williams, with all its bizarre machinations, took a mere two months from start to finish.

The prosecution's task in any trial, though hypothetically concerned with finding out the truth, comes down to presentation of incriminating evidence and witnesses against the accused. Efficient serial killers leave no witnesses alive, but many are careless, allowing stray victims to slip through their hands and survive. In other cases, neighbors may recall a license number or a stranger loitering around the crime scene, but the bulk of evidence in serial murder trials remains circumstantial. Police and prosecutors spin a web of fingerprints and tire tracks, hairs and fibers, bite marks and ballistics data, bloodstains and semen traces, paint chips and shreds of flesh recovered from beneath a lifeless victim's fingernails. Some jurisdictions — like Atlanta, in the muddled Williams trial — permit the introduction of uncharged "pattern" cases to suggest a defendant's guilt. Other courts limit pattern evidence to the penalty phase, as when California prosecutors convicted Randy Kraft of 16 murders, then aired details of 21 more to convince the jury Kraft should die for his crimes.

From time to time, unfortunately, overzealous prosecutors step across the line dividing courtroom showmanship from actions that are both unethical and frankly criminal. From simple presentation of the evidence and witnesses, the D.A.'s office lapses into subornation of perjury and suppression of critical evidence, pursuing conviction at the expense of justice, vindication in the place of truth.

No case in recent memory so illustrates this point as the trial of Wayne Williams in Atlanta's notorious "child murders." Lacking sufficient evidence to charge Williams in 20-odd slayings, prosecutors filed two murder counts and then persuaded the court to admit "pattern" evidence from ten other crimes, thereby establishing a presumption of guilt across the board. In one "pattern" case, the death of 12-year-old Clifford Jones, prosecutors deliberately suppressed the testimony of five eyewitnesses who named another suspect, convicted child-molester Jamie Brooks, as Jones's killer. Darrell Davis, a witness who *was* called to testify, described himself as working at a carpet store when he saw "pattern" victim Lubie Geter thumb a ride with Williams. The D.A. managed to bury a statement from Davis's boss, revealing that Davis failed to report for work on the day in question. The most damning evidence filed against Williams involved carpet fibers from two cars — a 1979 Ford and a 1970 Chevrolet — which reportedly matched fibers found on the bodies of six "pattern" victims, but even here prosecutors managed to manipulate, distort, and twist the facts. Unknown to jurors, the Ford was dropped off at a shop for repairs at 9 A.M. on July 30, 1980, five hours before the abduction of "pattern" victim Earl Terrell that afternoon. Terrell was long dead before Williams retrieved the car on August 7, and it was returned to the shop with persistent starter problems on August 8. The new bill was so expensive that Williams refused to pay, leaving the junker with his mechanic and purchasing the Chevrolet on October 21. Meanwhile, two more "pattern" victims were murdered on August 20 and October 9, respectively, both bodies bearing carpet fibers from cars that suspect Williams didn't even own! Aside from the forensic sleight-of-hand, Atlanta's D.A. also buried records of an FBI investigation into the local Ku Klux Klan, alleging that Klansmen Charles and Terry Sanders were killing black children as part of a plot to foment racial unrest. One reported target, specifically threatened by Charles Sanders after a personal altercation, was "pattern" victim Lubie Geter.

While the prosecution spins its web, defense attorneys try to clip each strand in turn, attacking witnesses and circumstantial evidence with all the skill and legal tricks at their disposal. Where police are ignorant or careless, as with Larry Eyler's first arrest, a case may be destroyed with the exclusion of vital evidence. Eyewitnesses to a traumatic crime are often hazy in their recollection of events, and skillful cross-examination may persuade a jury they are lying — or, at least, mistaken — when they finger the defendant as a calculating murderer. Inevitably, some questions remain unanswered, as in Ted Bundy's Florida trial for double murder at the Chi Omega sorority house. Forensic evidence in that case labeled the Chi O rape-slayer a "non-secretor" — that is, one whose blood type cannot be determined from semen or saliva traces — but Ted Bundy was a proven "secretor." Jurors were relieved from coping with an evident impossibility, however, when the trademark Bundy overbite was matched to wounds on one young woman's body. Bundy finally resolved the mystery himself in January 1989, confessing both murders — and 28 more — the night before his execution.

If a case seems hopeless from the outset, certain of conviction, the defense may seek to cut its losses, mitigating charges with the presentation of extenuating evidence. The work of random killers rarely lends itself to pleas of self-defense, though Dayton Rogers raised the issue in one of his Oregon murder trials, but several slayers — Eddie Cole among them — have avoided prosecution for their early crimes by blaming suspect deaths on accidents. More commonly, defense counsel argues a lack of premeditation, hoping at least to spare the defendant's life with a verdict of manslaughter or second-degree murder, which carries no capital sentence.

As previously noted, few serial killers fit the legal guidelines of insanity, but the peculiar — often ghastly — nature of their crimes encourages defense attorneys to gamble on the insanity defense. If nothing else, there is the hope that claims of mental illness may persuade a jury to convict on lesser charges, or at least reject the death penalty, but Albert Fish is a hard act to follow. Michigan's Richard Clarey tried an insanity defense in his first murder trial, shifting to a plea of guilty but mentally ill in subsequent proceedings, when jurors failed to buy the argument. In North Carolina, attorneys for Velma Barfield cited their client's long-term drug addiction as a factor in her crimes, but she wound up on death row regardless. Harvey Carignan recalled celestial voices, urging him to rape and bludgeon teenage hitchhikers, but Minnesota jurors were tuned in to a different wavelength when they convicted him of two murders, one attempted murder, and a count of aggravated assault. Eddie Cole claimed blackouts, loss of memory, and sporadic bouts of cannibalism in his trial for three Dallas murders, but a jury found him sane and guilty, paving the way for a sentence of life imprisonment.

Outright acquittals in cases of serial murder are rare, but not unknown. Boston attorneys scored a surprise victory for defendant Mary Kelliher in 1908, persuading jurors that six of her close relatives had absorbed lethal doses of arsenic from a "contaminated mattress" over a three-year period. In New Jersey, Dr. Mario Jascalevich was acquitted of using curare to poison six patients, but adverse publicity surrounding the 12-year investigation drove him back to his native Argentina, where he died of a cerebral hemorrhage in September 1984. Los Angeles jurors acquitted Vaughn Greenwood of two murder counts in 1976, but conviction in nine other cases sent him to prison for life without parole. Eight years later, in another "skid row" case, Bobby Maxwell was convicted of two deaths and acquitted of three more, while a hung jury left five counts unresolved. In Georgia, nurse Terri Rachals confessed three murders and was charged with six, but her precarious mental state prompted jurors to vote for a compromise verdict of guilty but mentally ill on one count of aggravated assault.

With 50 states and countless local jurisdictions trying murder cases every day, it is perhaps too much to hope for any semblance of consistency in sentencing. Since 1900, 68% of America's convicted serial killers have been sentenced to varying prison terms, with some 10% of those dying in custody. Another 25% have been sentenced to death for their crimes, and 40% of those condemned have actually been executed. The final 7% have been sentenced to prison *and* death, with contradictory sentences arising from separate trials. Henry Lucas, for example, faces one death sentence, six life terms, two 75-year sentences, and one 60-year term, with further trials pending as this is written.

Sadly, even multiple convictions and redundant sentences do not insure a solution to serial murder. Our legal system provides for a seemingly infinite course of appeals on felony convictions, dragging on for years or decades, with any number of courts empowered to commute sentences, overturn verdicts, and remand defendants for new, expensive trials. Such safeguards are the cornerstone of liberty, but there are times when they defeat the ends of justice and allow sadistic killers to remain at large. In 1977, two Filipino nurses were convicted of murdering patients at a Michigan veteran's hospital, but the verdicts were overturned on appeal, and the case remains unsolved today. David Carpenter's conviction on five counts of murder and two counts of rape was reversed on appeal because the jury foreman knew of Carpenter's previous death sentence. New York's Joseph Christopher saw a triple murder conviction reversed on grounds that his trial judge improperly barred testimony pointing toward mental illness. Police incompetence overturned Allen Anderson's Florida murder conviction and set Alaska's Harvey Carignan free to kill again. Juan Corona won a new trial on 25 counts of murder because his attorney had negotiated a private publishing contract. Houston's Elmer Henley got a similar break on grounds of excessive pretrial publicity. Dr. John MacGregor was pardoned by Michigan's governor, then hired to treat convicts at the same prison where he was earlier locked up for life.

More often, appeals result in reduction of sentences while leaving convicted defendants confined. Richard Biegenwald's New Jersey murder convictions were affirmed on appeal, but his death sentence was commuted on the basis of procedural error. Herman Billik, a Chicago slayer of five, had his capital sentence commuted to life after six stays of execution. In Texas, Kenneth Granviel waited five years — one for each of his known victims — to see his death sentence reduced by a federal appeals court. Florida's Ottis Toole was twice sentenced to die, both verdicts commuted on grounds that jurors had not considered his "extreme emotional disturbance" as a mitigating factor in the crimes. Frederick Edel was paroled and deported to Germany following commutation of his Connecticut death sentence. Another slayer from the Nutmeg State, Amy Gilligan, served 13 years of a life sentence before she was found insane and removed to a mental institution. Nor should we forget the nefarious "Class of '72," spared from execution by the U.S. Supreme Court's rejection of capital punishment, thereby granting a new lease on life to repeat killers like Richard Speck, George Putt, Winston Moseley, Charles Schmid, Dennis Whitney, the Charles Manson "family," and a host of others.

Critics of the system charge that many — even most — appeals are frivolous, unnecessary, and a costly waste of time. Ted Bundy is a classic case in point, stalling execution for nine years and six months with a string of appeals to state and federal courts. His last-ditch effort was a fine, ironic farce: Bundy, having fought long and hard for the right to serve as his own defense counsel in Florida, sought reversal of his conviction on grounds that his lawyer — that is, himself — had been drunk during parts of the trial! This case, and others like it, have encouraged federal legislators to consider statutory limits on appeals, a move opposed by civil libertarians as the first step toward a fascist police state.

In point of fact, while many random killers love to play the legal game, wasting thousands of hours and millions of dollars on fruitless appeals, only a handful succeed in returning themselves to the street by court order. Appeals are not the only avenue to freedom, though, and it is grossly premature to label any captured predator as "safe."

As we shall see, compulsive killers caged are still compulsive killers, driven by a deep, abiding taste for blood.

Chapter 9

Walls

Society tends to forget about criminals once they are tried, convicted, and sentenced to prison. Each new day brings banner headlines of a fresh atrocity, another bogeyman to conjure waking nightmares. Last year's monster is a fading memory, except for his or her surviving victims, grisly details dusted off for special anniversaries and sporadic parole hearings. Who, aside from crime buffs and a handful of detectives, can recall the name of L.A.'s "Skid Row Stabber?" San Diego's "Candlelight Killer?" Montreal's "Vampire Rapist?" Wisconsin's "Mad Biter?" The "Peeping Tom" gunman of Washington, D.C.?

Unfortunately, the relief engendered by conviction of a ruthless predator is often premature. In far too many cases, disposition through a prison sentence — even life without parole — is anything but final. Random killers have a way of coming back to haunt society at large, beyond the scope of retrospective articles and special broadcasts of *Geraldo*.

All too often, they come back against all odds... to kill again.

Serial killers, like "normal" felons, respond to confinement in various ways. As natural chameleons, skilled from childhood in the art of covering their tracks, some become model prisoners, following every rule to the letter, working overtime to counsel and encourage fellow inmates. Chicago's William Heirens maintained a spotless record over four decades inside, earning transfer to a minimum-security prison where he works in the chaplain's office. Velma Barfield experienced a

death row conversion in North Carolina, helping younger female inmates set their feet upon the straight and narrow path. Other "born-again" killers of note include Susan Atkins, Henry Lucas, Ottis Toole, and Charles "Tex" Watson — a Manson "family" alumnus, now the pastor of his own long-distance ministry, receiving regular donations from his flock.

Once a programmed killer for the Manson "family," Charles Watson is now a "born-again" jailhouse minister. *(Credit: Los Angeles County Sheriff's Dept.)*

It may be argued, and persuasively, that random killers mind the rules or "find the Lord" with self-serving motives in mind, striving to please their captors and influence future parole boards. Joel Norris, on the other hand, describes compliance with authority as a serial killer's natural reflex, induced by imposition of an orderly environment and the removal of those stimuli — drugs, alcohol, pornography, even junk food — which contribute to erratic, aberrant behavior. In the Norris scenario, serial killers conform in prison for the same reason some confess dozens of crimes they did not commit: They simply want to belong.

Whichever theory finally wins out, the fact remains that many random killers never adapt to life in a cage — including 2% who wriggle out of custody by means of suicide. Colorado's Gloria Tannenbaum was an old hand with cyanide, confined to an asylum for her part in two deaths and one disappearance, but institutional safeguards failed to prevent her from getting her hands on the poison she used to kill herself in 1971. Richard Hatcher asked Missouri jurors for a death penalty in 1983, hanging himself in prison when they rejected his plea. In California, Mack Edwards received the death sentence he asked for, but justice moves slowly in the Sunshine State — when it moves at all — and Edwards used a noose to circumvent mandatory appeals. Accumulated prison time exceeding 430 years prompted Richard Macek to hang himself in 1987. In Massachusetts, occult reading matter could not compensate for Antone Costa's lifelong separation from his favorite drugs, leaving suicide as the only viable escape hatch. New York's Charles Yukl had a knack for plea bargains, but 15 years imprisonment for his second murder seemed an unbearable torment, driving Yukl to take his own life. Less efficient prison suicides, like Ottis Toole, Joe Kallinger, and Gary Heidnik, emphasize that random killers caged may turn their pent-up wrath upon themselves.

At that, compulsive slayers may not be their own worst enemies in prison. Sex offenders and child abusers rank with stool pigeons as prime targets of inmate violence the world over, while other repeat killers draw flack on the basis of their "celebrity" status. After his confession to the murder of six-year-old Adam Walsh, Ottis Toole was harassed by prisoners who urinated on him through the bars of his cell. Oregon's Jerry Brudos has suffered a series of prison "accidents," including one that left him with fractured cervical vertebrae in 1971. David ("Son of Sam") Berkowitz had his throat slashed in a near-fatal ambush, soon after he began discussing his alleged involvement with a nationwide Satanic cult. In California, Charles Manson was doused with flammable liquid and set afire by a convict seeking to "earn a name" for himself. Even death row was not safe for John Gacy, assaulted and stabbed in February 1983 by psycho-killer Henry Brisbon.

Within the past two decades, at least four serial killers have been murdered by fellow convicts in American prisons. Lee Roy Martin, strangler of four women around Gaffney, South Carolina, was stabbed to death in May 1972. Eighteen months later, another shiv claimed the life of strangler Albert DeSalvo, in Massachusetts. Tucson's "Pied Piper," Charles Schmid, was stabbed 20 times by prison "friends" in March 1975; he lasted ten days before succumbing to his wounds. In Tennessee, during July 1985, three-time killer Laron Williams was mobbed and beaten to death in the prison exercise yard. (A fifth suspicious death, that of Michigan's Dr. Roland Clark in 1972, was officially blamed on an "accidental fall.")

For all that, convicted serial killers are more often perpetrators than targets of prison violence. Subway killer Willie Bosket has earned national recognition as "New York's most dangerous inmate," for his attacks on fellow cons. In Massachusetts, nurse Jane Toppan urged attendants at the state asylum to provide her with lethal drugs for the murder of other patients. "Get some morphine, dearie, and we'll go out in the ward," she pleaded. "You and I will have a lot of fun seeing them die." Satanist Stanley Baker posed no end of problems for prison guards in Montana; relieved of homemade weapons on 11 separate occasions, Baker threatened correctional officers, recruited inmates for a new Satanic coven on the cellblock, and howled like a wolf at the full moon. Illinois authorities designed a special door for Henry Brisbon's death row cell, to prevent his striking or hurling cups of heated urine at guards and visitors. Pennsylvania's Joseph Kallinger assaulted a fellow inmate and set fire to his cellblock in April 1977; 11 months later, he slashed another prisoner's throat with razor blades, but the inmate managed to survive.

Other victims are less fortunate, statistics revealing that some 2% of America's serial slayers continue to kill behind bars. Illinois cannibal Lester Harrison was serving time for armed robbery when he beat another prisoner to death and was deemed incompetent for trial. Henry Brisbon botched his murder attempt on John Gacy, but he succeeded in killing inmate Ronald Morgan without apparent motive, earning himself a seat on death row. Carl Panzram entered Leavenworth prison in 1928, with a promise to murder the first man who "crossed" him; his chosen target, selected and bludgeoned to death without apparent cause, was a civilian laundry foreman. Gerald Smith was convicted of beating a woman to death in 1980, but it took the slaying of another prisoner to place him in Missouri's electric chair ten years later. Missouri prison officials blamed repeat killer Charles Hatcher for the murder of inmate Jerry Tharrington, but in the absence of conclusive evidence they let Hatcher off with a five-month term of solitary confinement. South Carolina's Donald ("Pee Wee") Gaskins could not resist a prison murder contract, even though it sent him to the death house. In California, hobo-slasher Joseph Danks strangled an elderly cellmate to relieve the boredom of confinement. Lemuel Smith was serving time for double murder and kidnapping in New York, when he beat and strangled to death a female correctional officer. Joseph Bowen, sentenced for killing a policeman, murdered the prison warden and his deputy in 1975; six years later, he led rioting inmates who captured 38 hostages during their rampage.

Alcoholic killer Hoyt Cobb was serving life on a murder conviction when he escaped from prison to kill again. *(Credit: FBI)*

It may be argued that convicted felons are expendable and prison guards are paid to risk their lives, but lofty walls, barbed wire, and tempered bars cannot contain the ongoing threat of violence from identified serial killers. Some escape from custody, while others are paroled. Psychiatrists pronounce some random killers "cured" and return them to society. In all, 13% of those imprisoned or confined to mental institutions make their way back to the streets and kill again.

While some compulsive slayers thrive in captivity, others are consummate escape artists, fleeing dozens of lockups from coast to coast. Nationwide, some 5% of convicted serial killers have jailbreaks on their records, and 71% of those commit one or more murders before they are run to ground. Henry Lucas began his 10-year career as an amateur Houdini at age 15, slipping away from a juvenile detention home in Virginia. Hacksaw blades were once found in Ted Bundy's Florida prison cell, and Richard Clarey crashed a truck through the fence at a Michigan state prison. New York's Joseph Baldi walked away from the Creedmore State Hospital, in Queens, to murder four women. Another vanishing psychopath, Gary Taylor, was a year late for therapy when Michigan authorities finally logged him as missing... too late for the victims he claimed in at least three states. Carlton Gary was a fugitive from New York's prison system when he surfaced as the "Stocking Strangler" in Columbus, Georgia. Another Georgia predator, Hoyt Cobb, was serving life for the beating death of a robbery victim when he escaped to kill again, earning himself a spot on the FBI's "Most Wanted" list. Charles Schmid fled an Arizona prison with mass murderer Raymond Hudgens, holding four hostages near Tempe before the pair split up and both men were recaptured. In another Arizona case, killers Randy Greenawalt and Gary Tison escaped from prison with the help of Tison's sons, killing six innocent persons before a posse ran them down. Laron Williams was confined for killing a Tennessee prostitute when he broke out of prison, rolling on to murder a priest and a policeman. Repeat slayer Robert Garrow was shot and killed while fleeing from a prison in New York. Indiana's David Roberts was between lockups when he slipped away from his guards, at a rest stop. In Alabama, Audrey Hilley never returned from a three-day prison furlough; she was dying of natural causes when searchers finally found her, a week later. Lyda Ambrose was more successful in Idaho, remaining at large for a year after her flight from state prison. Julian Kennedy's nine victims included a female hostage, killed in a Georgia jailbreak. Bob Harper fled a Michigan prison and killed two persons while still at large; returned to custody, he promptly murdered the warden and a deputy. Henry Jarrette was serving time for two Georgia murders when he broke out, fatally stabbing his third victim during a car theft. Carl Richardson was a juvenile fugitive during his murder spree in Maryland and Washington, D.C. Bruce Davis, Earl Durrand, and Gerald Gallego, Sr., all murdered guards or policemen during their separate escapes. William Day, conversely, persuaded a veteran guard to smuggle him out of Michigan's state prison. In Missouri, a psychiatric nurse helped killer Winford Stokes escape from a locked mental ward.

Four-time killer and escapee David Roberts was recaptured on a tip from television viewers of "America's Most Wanted." *(Credit: FBI)*

With an estimated half-million parolees at large in America on any given day, most murderers will ultimately be released without the need of risking life and limb on anything so hazardous as an escape. Nationwide, convicted felons serve an average 35% of their assigned prison time, while inmates in Texas — one of America's five worst states for serial murders — slip by with an average 20% of time served. More to the point, 7% of the nation's serial stalkers kill one or more victims while free on parole from a previous homicide. Their ranks include:

James Koedatich — convicted of killing his Florida roommate in 1971, paroled to New Jersey in 1982, where he murdered at least two women by year's end.

George Adorno — confessed slayer of three at age 15, imprisoned on a lesser charge of robbery and paroled after serving half of his three-year sentence, Adorno killed again within 19 days of his release.

Frederick Wood — paroled after serving 17 years on conviction for second-degree murder, he killed again after less than a month on the street; in custody, Wood confessed four more slayings unknown to police.

Henry Lucas — convicted of killing his mother in 1960, Lucas drew a sentence of 20 to 40 years and was released in ten; a kidnapping conviction kept him behind bars until 1975, when he was freed to launch an eight-year murder spree.

Howard Allen — released in 1985, after serving 11 years for the beating death of an elderly woman, Allen claimed two more victims in 1987.

Richard Biegenwald — slayer of a New Jersey prosecutor in 1958, paroled after 17 years, Biegenwald killed seven more persons before his 1983 arrest.

Harvey Carignan — sentenced to die for a murder in Alaska, reprieved on legal technicalities and later paroled, Carignan slaughtered at least five more women between Seattle and Minneapolis.

Donald Lang — a Chicago deaf-mute, deemed incompetent for trial in a 1965 murder and confined to a mental institution, Lang was released by court order in 1971 and claimed his second victim the following year.

Thomas Viser — paroled in 1985 after serving time for the murder of his second wife, he married — and murdered — again a year later.

Louise Peete — sentenced to life on a 1921 murder conviction, Peete served 18 years before winning parole; at least two more victims died before her next arrest in 1944.

Richard Marquette — convicted of murder and sentenced to life in Washington state, Marquette served 12 years before he was paroled to kill two more victims.

Robert Harris — released after serving 29 months for the beating death of his first known victim, he was free six months before gunning down two teenage boys.

Jimmy Gray — convicted of killing his high school girlfriend, Gray was paroled in time to rape and suffocate a three-year-old girl, leading to his execution in 1984.

Robert Nicolaus — sentenced to death for killing his three children in 1964, Nicolaus won commutation of his penalty on appeal and was paroled in 1977; seven years later, he murdered his ex-wife and was returned to prison.

Joseph Taborsky — spared execution when the chief witness in his 1951 murder trial was ruled insane, Taborsky hit the streets in 1956 and claimed six more victims by February 1957.

Daniel Hittle — sentenced to 30 years for killing his adoptive parents in Minnesota, paroled after serving one-third of his sentence, Hittle moved to Texas and killed five more persons, including a policeman and a four-year-old girl.

M.C. Mayberry — jailed for life in the murder of a girlfriend and released after nine years, he murdered a second lover in 1988.

Richard Jackson — released to a half-way house after serving 23 months of a ten-year sentence for the murder of his infant stepson, Jackson was later convicted of killing an elderly woman in 1977.

Lester Harrison — serving time for armed robbery when he committed his first known murder in prison, Harrison was found incompetent for trial on that charge and soon released to the street; between 1970 and 1973, he killed and cannibalized at least four women in Chicago's Grant Park.

Philip Jablonski — paroled after serving 12 years for second-degree murder and two counts of attempted murder, including the botched strangulation of his mother on a prison visit, Jablonski killed four more women within a year of his release.

Raymond Brown — imprisoned for hacking three relatives to death at age 14, Brown was paroled after serving 13 years, later killing a mother and daughter in identical fashion.

David Young — paroled after serving three years for the murder of his girlfriend, Young was soon married and beat his wife to death a year later; in custody, he confessed the murders of victims in three other states.

Robert Daniels — convicted of manslaughter by an Oregon jury in 1970, Daniels served 11 years before he was released to claim five more victims in three states.

Samuel Walls — sentenced to 20 years for the beating death of a salesman, he served 15 before winning parole; his second victim, a woman, was strangled and left beneath the bed in a New Jersey motel room.

John Miller — locked up for the murder of an infant neighbor, Miller served 17 years before he was paroled... and killed his parents two months later.

Arthur Shawcross — arrested for the murder of an eight-year-old girl, Shawcross confessed the slaying of a second child and was sentenced to 25 years in prison; released after 15 years, he graduated to adult victims with the murders of 16 prostitutes.

Joseph Fischer — served 24 years for the 1954 murder of a New Jersey schoolboy before his 1978 parole, killing his wife a year later; in custody, Fischer confessed a string of murders spanning the United States.

Clarence Wheat — sentenced to five years for the shooting death of a Mississippi policeman and pardoned eight months later on grounds of poor health, Wheat murdered his wife and son before turning the gun on himself.

Gary Rardon — paroled after serving four years on an Indiana manslaughter conviction, Rardon moved to Chicago and killed three more victims in random attacks.

Allen Washington — suspected in the death of one infant daughter and sentenced to ten years when a second was "accidentally" beaten to death, Washington was paroled after serving 30 months; he subsequently beat his three-year-old son to death and was sentenced to serve 40 years.

Parole boards have no monopoly on bad calls, where serial murder is concerned. Some of America's most brutally prolific killers have been studied, diagnosed, and treated by psychiatrists... who set them free to kill again. From coast to coast, time after time, the story is identical: sadistic rapists, child-molesters, and killers released to the streets with a clean bill of health from the "experts." In fact, the system fails so frequently, at such a cost in human lives, that failure almost seems to be the rule.

Cannibal-slayer Albert Fish provides a classic case in point. A veteran killer by the time psychiatrists had their first crack at him, in 1930, Fish was released after two months of observation, the official diagnosis reading: "Not insane; psychopathic personality; sexual type." A year later, found with torture instruments when police nabbed him on a charge of mailing obscene letters, Fish spent a mere two weeks under psychiatric scrutiny before he was discharged. Finally, when the depths of his depravity were fully exposed in 1935, New York psychiatrists closed ranks to help the prosecution make its case, explaining to jurors that Fish's compulsive coprophagia (eating excrement) was "socially perfectly all right."

Eddie Cole first surrendered himself for psychiatric treatment in 1960, at age 22, confessing his desire to rape and strangle women. He spent the next three years in California institutions, playing mind games with his analyst, before he was released as an "anti-social personality" who posed no threat to others. Psychiatrists in Dallas, treating Cole in the wake of a 1963 suicide attempt, ignored his record of violent crime and handled him as a casual out-patient. In 1970, he surrendered to authorities once more, this time in Reno, Nevada, but the learned doctors wrote him off as a malingerer and set him free, on the condition that he leave the state. Cole's file contains the telling evidence of psychiatric failure: "Prognosis: Poor. Condition on release: Same as on admittance. Treatment: Express bus ticket to San Diego, California." Cole took the ticket, and within the next six months he killed at least three San Diego women in a bid to prove the doctors wrong.

James Lockhart was marking time in a Georgia mental institution when his temper got the best of him and he murdered a fellow patient. State psychiatrists helped Lockhart out at the trial, calling him "a severe schizophrene with a very poor prognosis for marked improvement," and a jury found him innocent by reason of insanity. Four years later, the same doctors approved Lockhart's release from custody... and no one, presumably, was more surprised when he soon committed yet another homicide.

It was December 1973 when Richard Chase entered a Sacramento, California, hospital, complaining that someone had stolen his pulmonary artery, leaving him short of breath. On top of that, he said, his head was changing shape. Staff psychiatrists examined Chase, labeling him a chronic paranoid schizophrenic, but they grudgingly released him at the insistence of their patient's "highly aggressive, hostile, and provocative" mother. By April 1976, Chase was killing wild animals and drinking their blood, sometimes injecting it into his veins. Committed by his parents this time, Chase explained that he was "falling apart," a condition alleviated only by shedding — and consuming — blood. Released with a "guarded" prognosis in September

1977, Chase was at large barely four months when police picked him up for killing six persons and drinking their blood.

Philadelphia's Gary Heidnik spent a year in the army before he was discharged on psychiatric grounds, his mental state sufficiently bizarre to earn him a 100% disability rating. Over the next quarter-century, he was repeatedly committed to Pennsylvania mental hospitals, sometimes remaining for months at a time, but none of the experts picked up on his morbid obsession with collecting female "sex slaves." Convicted of kidnapping and molesting a retarded woman, Heidnik served four years and four months in prison — with three side trips to mental institutions following repetitive suicide attempts. By 1986, when he began collecting slaves in earnest, killing those who failed to please, the state and its psychiatrists had seemingly forgotten Heidnik, letting him fall through the cracks.

Another military reject on psychiatric grounds was Donald Harvey, twice committed in Kentucky after suicide attempts, the recipient of 21 electroshock-therapy treatments which failed to reverse his grim preoccupation with death. Poor legislation, inadequate records, and negligent staff allowed Harvey to cover his tracks, obtaining responsible jobs — and killing 87 helpless patients — at hospitals in two states.

No one in California tried to hide Ed Kemper's background. Locked up for butchering his grandparents at age 15, Kemper spent six years in therapy before he was discharged, over his own strenuous objections, to the custody of his carping, shrewish mother. Back in the same old environment, subject to his mother's whims and acid tongue, Kemper gave free rein to the necrophilic passions that had driven him from early childhood. Over a year's time, Kemper killed six college co-eds, dragging their bodies home for bouts of posthumous sex. On one occasion, Kemper drove to visit his psychiatrist with a severed head in the trunk of his car. Finally, tiring of the game, he killed his mother and her best friend, dismembering their remains before he surrendered to police.

Erno Soto's disintegrating marriage, spurred by the birth of an illegitimate black child to Soto's Hispanic wife, produced erratic behavior that led to his commitment during 1969 and 1970. Soto's out-patient treatment continued sporadically over the next three years, but he derived his main relief from the murder and mutilation of young, dark-skinned boys. Three were killed and a fourth maimed by New York's "Charlie

Chop-off," before Soto was captured... and returned to the asylum.

Joseph Bryan first ran afoul of the law at age 19, when he abducted two small boys, tied them to a tree, and sexually abused them. Committed to a New Jersey mental hospital, Bryan was diagnosed as schizophrenic, warning doctors that he liked to see young boys "tied up and screaming." It was strong stuff, but not strong enough to keep Bryan inside. Upon his release, he joined the navy, but was soon discharged after service psychiatrists saw through his mask of sanity. A term in state prison for burglary and auto theft left him hungry for action, killing three boys and abducting a fourth within three months of his parole.

James Ruzicka was facing a ten-year sentence on conviction for a double rape, when the court offered him an escape hatch. Checking into a sex-offender rehabilitation program in Tacoma, Washington, Ruzicka worked his way up to trusty status in record time, telling therapists and nurses everything they longed to hear. Hospital administrators thought enough of Ruzicka to grant him a 48-hour furlough, from which he never returned. In four weeks at large, the "new, improved" Ruzicka murdered two teenage girls in Seattle and brutally raped another in Oregon.

Joseph Kallinger's first brush with psychiatry came in 1957, when he was hospitalized with a "psychopathological nervous disorder" stemming from the breakup of his marriage. Two years later, he was committed to a state hospital following a suicide attempt. In 1972, a conviction on child abuse charges earned him four years probation, with a provision for mandatory psychiatric treatment. Kallinger kept his appointments, but therapists failed to pick up on his conversations with a disembodied head named "Charlie," which directed him to kill and mutilate his son, moving on from there to brutalize other victims in their homes. At this writing, Kallinger stands by his desire to kill every person on earth, at which point he plans to commit suicide and "become God."

Sacramento native Jeffrey Jones was attending college in Arizona when he "began to exhibit abnormal behavior" and counselors sent him home for treatment. Anti-psychotic medication was prescribed after doctors diagnosed Jones as a chronic paranoid schizophrenic, but drugs had little affect. Charged with robbing a disabled victim in May 1984, Jones got off without jail time. A November probation report found him "stabilized," noting that "the probability of threat to others is not significant at this time." It became significant two months later, when Jones launched a one-man crime wave in the neighborhood, killing three men and critically wounding a fourth with his trusty claw hammer.

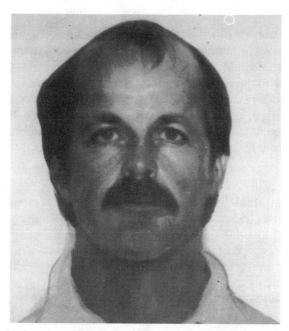

Christopher Wilder had a history of sexual violence and futile psychiatric treatment dating from age 17. *(Credit: FBI)*

Christopher Wilder's psychiatric problems surfaced at age 17, when he was jailed for his role in an Australian gang rape. The court-assigned term of one year's probation included group therapy and electroshock treatments, but all in vain. Similar sex charges dogged Wilder across the Atlantic, earning repeated terms of probation with mandatory counseling. On one occasion, he confessed a sexual assault to his therapist, but the confidential statement was inadmissible at trial, and Wilder was acquitted on the charge. He was still on probation in Florida, and a fugitive from pending sex charges in Australia, when he launched his final murder spree across America in early 1984. His several therapists, from all appearances, were taken absolutely by surprise.

New Yorker George Fitzsimmons never denied the murder of his parents, but a jury found him innocent by reason of insanity. Four years later, state psychiatrists declared that Fitzsimmons posed no further hazard to society, releasing him to the care of an aunt and uncle whom Fitzsimmons claimed to love "like his own mother and father." The analogy was apt enough, as demonstrated when Fitzsimmons stabbed the aging couple to death in their Pennsylvania home. Detectives later found that Fitzsimmons had named himself as beneficiary to the life insurance of all four victims.

Robert Liberty was serving time in a California mental institution when he struck up a relationship with fellow inmate Marcela Landis. On release, he strangled her to death and was declared insane, packed off to another state hospital for treatment. After three years of therapy, a panel of six psychiatrists pronounced Liberty "cured," and he was released to southern California... where he killed another victim six months later.

Gary Rardon served four years on an Indiana manslaughter conviction before a prison psychiatrist deemed him rehabilitated, declaring that "the likelihood of further violence would be unusual." It took eight years to prove the doctor wrong, but Rardon did so with a vengeance, gunning down three Chicago victims in November 1974. Arrested two months later with one victim's credit card, Rardon drew a sentence of 40 to 100 years in prison on conviction for multiple murder.

In Washington state, Westley Dodd traced his sexual feelings for children to age 12, attracting police attention and dropping out of two voluntary counseling programs by age 14. His first arrest for soliciting a minor was logged in 1980, and he continued the habit through two years of naval service, climaxed by a dishonorable discharge linked to accusations of child-molesting. Sporadic counseling sessions, some of them court-ordered, failed to prevent Dodd from murdering three boys in 1990, around Vancouver. Arrested that November, after trying to drag a six-year-old boy from a movie theater, Dodd confessed his murders and was sentenced to die.

California psychiatrists first diagnosed Lawrence Bittaker as a "borderline psychotic" in 1961, expanding their judgment a year later to note Bittaker's "poor control of his impulsive behavior." By 1969, Bittaker was receiving antipsychotic medication, but it failed to keep him out of trouble or out of prison. While serving time, in 1978, Bittaker met rapist Roy Norris, earlier discharged from the navy for "psychological problems" linked to a "severe schizoid personality." Norris was also a veteran of Atascadero state hospital, where he spent five years as a mentally disordered sex offender before doctors released him as "no further danger to others." Bittaker recognized a soul-mate on sight, and

the pair became inseparable, hatching a grisly plot to kidnap, rape, and murder teenage girls "for fun," as soon as they were freed. At least five victims took the oneway ride in Bittaker's van, nicknamed "Murder Mack," their screams recorded for posterity, before a survivor identified the predators in November 1979.

The haunting question lingers: If we cannot trust our prisons to hold compulsive killers, if psychotherapy is useless with sociopaths and serial slayers released on parole invariably kill again... how, then, can our society protect itself? How can we stem the rising tide of violence which, unchecked, threatens to produce a record crop of some 300 new serial killers by the turn of the century?

One answer, written into law by several states since the late 1970s, mandates execution for killers with multiple victims or those who commit murder with "special circumstances" — including torture, sexual assault, or mutilation. At least a dozen serial killers have been put to death in America since 1977, with many times that number sentenced to die, but "liberal" courts and long-winded appeals guarantee that most of the condemned — outside the rural South, at least — will die from old age or disease before they ever see the inside of an execution chamber.

And the controversy rages on.

Opponents of capital punishment stress the intrinsic value of every human life, no matter how sadistic or depraved, but even the American Civil Liberties Union now stops short of suggesting that serial killers can be "cured" or rehabilitated, somehow molded into useful members of society. Instead, we're told, they should be housed securely and humanely for eternity, perpetual objects of study whose motives and crimes may enlighten us all.

Or can they?

Is our present state of scholarship on random murder so deficient that we need a breeding colony of psychopathic guinea pigs to fill out endless questionnaires, examine ink blots, and play word-association games with state psychiatrists? Is the redundant study of convicted slayers *really* worth the time and cost involved... much less the yearly toll of death and human misery?

Accused serial killers are routinely examined by multiple analysts prior to trial, the results of those examinations readily available to law enforcement, social service workers, and the courts. More often than not, those convicted of murder will be analyzed again before their sentence in pronounced. Meanwhile, the media dissects their lives from birth to prison in meticulous detail, unearthing relatives and former classmates, friends and enemies, surviving victims, publicizing every detail of the killer's wasted days on earth.

Nor are we limited to tabloid media accounts of how and why a random stalker kills. Since 1971, at least 11 full-length books about the Manson "family" have been released in the United States, including Charles Manson's first-person autobiography. Seven books were written about Ted Bundy before his death, and an equal number have been published dealing with the British killer team of Ian Brady and Myra Hindley. David Berkowitz fills the pages of five volumes to date. John Gacy, Peter Sutcliffe, and Adolfo Constanzo are the subjects of four books each. Charles Starkweather, Albert DeSalvo, Juan Corona, Henry Lucas, William Heirens, and Albert Fish have been dissected and analyzed in three volumes apiece. Gerald Gallego, Dean Corll, Ken Bianchi, Peter Kurten, Charles Sobhraj, Wayne Williams, Ed Gein, Genene Jones, Audrey Hilley, Fritz Klenner, and Edmund Kemper each have double biographies to their credit. At last count, some 46 other serial killers were surveyed in individual biographies, many including personal interviews, excerpts from diaries, and full-scale psychiatric evaluations.

In short, I submit that there *is* no shortage of available data on serial killers, their methods and motivation. Su' jects for study are already plentiful, and new specimens surface at a rate of nearly three per month. A killer taken off the street today will wait at least six months — perhaps a year or more — before he stands for trial, and mandatory appeals of a capital sentence will delay execution for a minimum average of four to six years, barring an inmate's expressed wish to die. If psychoanalysts cannot complete their study of a subject during six or eight years' time, they never will.

For their part, proponents of capital punishment often feel compelled to support their "hard-hearted" position with erroneous arguments. Executing condemned prisoners will *not* reduce the cost of America's prisons to any significant degree, since the bulk of penal expenditures go for salaries and utilities. No clerks or prison guards are laid off when an inmate dies; the cost of food and medicine, electric power and the like does not go down. Indeed, the cost of housing any single prisoner among the thousands caged at any given time is miniscule.

Likewise, there is absolutely nothing to suggest that executing a convicted psychopath today will stop another, more sadistic predator from claiming other lives tomorrow. Third-party deterrence is a dated, thoroughly discredited argument for capital punishment, deserving of no credence whatsoever.

There *is* deterrence in the act of execution, though. A random killer put to death this afternoon will not escape from jail or be paroled to kill again tomorrow. He — or she — will not assault or murder fellow inmates, menace visitors, or threaten prison personnel. Psychiatrists will not mistakenly pronounce him "cured," when they know full well that no such cure is possible.

The buck stops here.

Capital punishment is not — has never been — about economy, revenge, or the prevention of some unknown killer's future crimes. In fact, execution has little to do with "punishment," per se.

It is a matter of disposal, perfectly analogous to the removal of malignant tumors from a healthy organism or the burial of toxic waste. In all of human history, there is no documented record of a random killer who was rehabilitated and emerged from prison as a peaceable, productive citizen. Repentance and reform have no more meaning to the psychopath than to a hungry shark.

Survival of the human herd demands that predators be weeded out.

As for the generation yet unborn...

Conclusion

Here and Now

As I begin this conclusion, the news is dominated by late-breaking reports from Milwaukee, where a 31-year-old subject has confessed the serial murders of 17 young men and boys. From coast to coast, the networks, local papers, *USA Today*, and *People* magazine are in pursuit of every microscopic detail from the killer's past. One editorial describes him as "a poster boy for the death penalty," while others blast police for failing to prevent his grisly crimes.

Officially, the case began near midnight on July 23, 1991, when Milwaukee patrolmen were flagged down by a frightened young man, handcuffs dangling from one wrist, blurting a tale of attempted murder. The officers followed their witness back to the Oxford Apartments, picking up the smell of rotting flesh as they approached apartment 213. The tenant let them in without a fuss... and none of those involved will ever be the same again.

Inside the reeking flat, police found human body parts stuffed into plastic bags and cardboard boxes. Photographs of mutilated corpses littered the apartment, many of them mounted on the walls. A plastic drum of acid held more skeletal remains. In the refrigerator, human lungs and other organs had been packed away, as the arrestee explained, "to eat later."

Neighbors described suspect Jeffrey Dahmer as "a quiet guy who kept to himself" — the typical refrain — but there had been no lack of warning signs in Dahmer's past. At age 16, while living in Ohio, he dismembered dogs and soaked their bones in acid to remove the flesh,

mounting one stray's head on a stake, beside an enigmatic wooden cross. A college dropout, Dahmer had enlisted in the army and was stationed overseas, but his excessive drinking brought an early discharge. Settling in Milwaukee, he logged his first arrest for lewd and lascivious conduct in 1986, after exposing himself to a group of children. Two years later, convicted of fondling a Laotian boy and asking him to pose for pornographic photos, Dahmer spent ten months in jail.

By that time, based upon his own admissions, Dahmer had been killing for the best part of a decade. To date, he has admitted 17 murders, beginning with an Ohio man killed the week after Dahmer's high school graduation. The remains from his apartment add up to 11 bodies, and detectives feel there may be other victims unaccounted for. In Germany, five homicides remain unsolved around the area where Dahmer served his military time. Police in California are concerned about a severed foot, discovered near the Fresno home of Dahmer's mother... and the search goes on.

For all of the sensational exposure given to our latest horror, no one should have been surprised by Dahmer's crimes. Milwaukee lies within an hour's drive from Plainfield, where Ed Gein once fashioned masks and lamp shades out of human skin. "Mad Biter" Richard Macek prowled suburban Wauwatosa, and Larry Eyler dismembered one of his teenage victims near Kenosha, 20 miles due south. Geography aside, Dahmer's death spree closely parallels the crimes of other well-known predators. His storage of remains around the house mimicked Gein, Harrison Graham, Dennis Nilsen, Fritz

Honka, and numerous others. Dahmer's downfall, at the hands of an escaping victim, mirrored the fate of Robert Hansen, Gary Heidnik, and Robert Berdella. Neighbors complained of the noxious stench from his flat as others griped at Joe Ball, Gary Heidnik, and John Gacy; Dahmer even used Gacy's pet excuse — bad plumbing — to dismiss their concern. A homosexual who hated other gays, Dahmer followed the lead of Gacy, Michael Lupo, Dean Corll and others, punishing his own "sins" through the violated flesh of innocent victims.

There is even a familiar echo of police incompetence in Dahmer's case, reminding us of others through the years. In May, two months before the hacker took his fall, neighbors summoned the law with reports of Dahmer chasing a naked boy in the street. A trio of patrolmen met the victim, a Laotian, bruised and bleeding, but they swallowed Dahmer's story of a "lovers' quarrel" between adults. Perusing Dahmer's flat before they left him with his 14-year-old victim, officers missed gory snapshots scattered in plain sight, a fresh corpse lying in the bedroom. Five more men would die before a second victim managed to escape and finger Dahmer for police. Meanwhile, recorded "jokes" and comments from the Milwaukee P.D. radio log display pervasive contempt for low-priority victims found in the minority and homosexual community.

Dahmer's sudden notoriety dominated headlines and airwaves through the end of July, but he was not the only game in town. Lost in the furor from Milwaukee, a Taiwanese firing squad executed Lin Lai-fu, convicted of murdering 24 victims in five years. The following day, 27-year-old Robert Cloutier pled guilty to his second murder count in Illinois, drawing a sentence of life (plus 146 years on collateral counts of rape and robbery). Two days later, authorities in New Bedford, Massachusetts, dismissed outstanding charges against suspect Kenneth Ponte, returning the serial murders of nine local prostitutes to the "unsolved" column. And in Florida, the same afternoon, jury selection was stalled in the case of Oscar Bolin, facing trial in the second of four murder cases, suspected in dozens more across the country.

And the beat goes on.

Clearly, serial murder is a morbid "growth industry" for the 1990s. If new cases continue to surface at their present rate, the final decade of this century will break all records for random slaughter, both in number of killers and victims. America leads the pack by a three-to-one margin, despite some late stirrings in Europe and developing Third World nations. That said, three vital questions still remain:

Why now?

Why here?

And how can we reverse the deadly killing trend?

The first two questions obviously travel hand in hand. Solve one, and we have answered both, thus moving toward solutions for the third, more pressing riddle. Sadly, no conclusive answers are available from "experts" in the field, where chaos and dissension reign supreme. For all that, there are trends and patterns in our recent history that may combine to point the way, for those with eyes to see.

The stage sets for our murder epidemic were erected with construction of the modern freeway system in the 1950s, branching out from southern California like a giant spider web. The labor pains of World War II produced a restless, rootless generation, with mobility promoted from a personal convenience to a life style. There is dark, delicious irony in the employment of killer Mack Edwards to build those early freeways, piloting heavy equipment by day, returning after dark to plant his victims underneath the very superhighways that would later serve as happy hunting grounds for Randy Kraft, Ken Bianchi and Angelo Buono, William Bonin, Lawrence Bittaker and Roy Norris, Patrick Kearney, and a host of other predators. Literally founded on violent death, the freeway network has continued to deliver — from Los Angeles and San Diego, north to Oakland, San Francisco and Seattle, spreading through the great Midwest and Dixie, covering the eastern seaboard with a net of concrete arteries that pump fresh blood into the headlines, day by day.

Reporter Charles Kuralt once labeled 1966 "the year the world went mad," prophetic words as we reflect upon a quarter-century of random killers run amok. That year, God died on the cover of *Time* magazine and the Church of Satan opened its doors in San Francisco; the sexual revolution and hippie-drug subculture burst into headlines; the Vietnam war entered American living rooms through a television tube and brought thousands of protestors into the streets. It was the year of Richard Speck, Michael Herrington, Posteal Laskey, Ralph Nuss, the Penn brothers, plus unsolved serial murders in Ohio and New Jersey. In more general terms, the mid-1960s were a time when Camelot's gilt-edged optimism degenerated into a brutal "climate of violence," marked by public assassinations, lethal race riots, and urban terrorism. Traditional values were challenged, seemingly overnight, by "free love" and legalized abortion, violent entertainment long on "splatter," and pervasive disrespect for all authority.

The rapid escalation of our murder epidemic through the 1970s and '80s may be due, in part, to what authors Jack Levin and James Fox describe as society's "war on guilt."[1] In 1975, around the same time that experts christened serial killers as a breed apart, Dr. Manuel Smith published his best-seller on assertiveness training, *When I Say No, I Feel Guilty.* Among its provisions was a new "Bill of Assertive Rights," including "the right to offer no reasons or excuses for justifying your behavior," "the right to say 'I don't care'," and "the right to judge your own behavior, thoughts, and emotions." Another self-help guidebook, Julian Miller's *Breaking Through*, denounced guilt as a "disease of incapacitation," while Dr. David Reuben's *Everything You Always Wanted to Know About Sex* blamed "fear of doing wrong" for a presumed American orgasm deficit. As Fox and Levin emphasize, the trend toward greater freedom benefitted millions of Americans — at least, before the spread of AIDS — but there are always those who take a good thing to extremes. For an increasing number of potential predators, the trendy motto — "If it feels good, do it" — suddenly acquired a dark new twist.

If Dr. Ken Magid and Carole McKelvey are correct in their assessment of American society, we have been mass-producing psychopaths for over 30 years. The breakdown of cohesive families — with corresponding damage to the bonding process — may be seen in the divorce rate, single-parent families, and the rising incidence of child abuse. In 1990, more than 25% of American children under the age of 18 were in step-families, many others making due with one parent who worked full-time.[2] Day care is frequently inadequate — or downright hazardous — and foster homes are worse. Teen pregnancies account for more than half a million births in the United States each year, with all the risks accruing from parental immaturity.

And yet...

The plain fact is that no one has a lock on why one child, abused or otherwise, grows up to kill, while thousands of contemporaries lead a relatively normal life. Analysis of roots and origins may keep committees working overtime, but so far it has not defused the threat from walking time-bombs on the street.

Reversal of the random murder epidemic is a two-step process, neither phase effective or complete without the other. First, to guarantee our safety while we search for long-term answers, we must move decisively against the killers in our midst. Education of law enforcement and correctional personnel is a step toward elimination of pernicious "linkage blindness," which allows some killers to remain at large for years on end. Uniform participation in the FBI's computer network would, at least in theory, place detectives on the track of random killers early on, before the list of victims entered double digits. Mandatory autopsies should be required for any case of Sudden Infant Death Syndrome or other suspicious cases. Standardized penalties are unfeasible, working in the "states' rights" morass, but recent calls for federal legislation streamlining trials and appeals are a step in the right direction. Ideally, law enforcement should be adequately staffed and funded, totally divorced from politics at every level, but we have to operate within the confines of reality. If nothing else, perhaps we can begin dismantling the ego barriers that still prevent too many agencies from working in a common cause.

Long-term preventive measures are essential, if we hope to stem the tide of random murder in America. The U.S. Surgeon General has referred to violence as a disease, requiring forceful intervention, but the call to arms has been no more effective than the other federal warnings on tobacco, alcohol, and drugs. We *know* that adequate prenatal care is vital to an infant's physical and mental health, but economics and the rule of privacy short-circuit intervention during pregnancy. In scattered cases, pregnant mothers have been charged with child abuse when they were found ingesting drugs, but civil libertarians resist such moves, in favor of a vague and costly "education program" that is years away, at best. Likewise, intervention in abusive families is fraught with peril, groups like VOCAL — the "Victims of Child Abuse Laws" — filing multimillion-dollar suits against officials who attempt to rescue children from chaotic, violent homes. When children are removed, the legal system aggravates their trauma by subjecting them to foster care or institutions, often heaping new abuse atop the old.

In their treatise on psychopathic children, *High Risk*, Magid and McKelvey list nine prescriptions for reversal of the current "bonding crisis" in America. The proposed solutions include:

1. Uniform adoption of positive parenting techniques.

2. Special training for teachers, to encourage bonding with "unattached" children.

3. Reduction of teen pregnancies by adopting the Scandinavian approach to teaching sex and contraception.

4. Institution of a national leave policy for all working parents, to provide time at home without loss of jobs or other penalties.

5. Provision of well-run, affordable day-care centers for preschool children nationwide.

6. Unspecified reforms to reduce delays in the adoption process and eliminate problems in foster care.

7. Direct intervention and counseling to break the cycle of child abuse.

8. Critical analysis of personal relationships to avoid potentially disastrous marriages or business deals with adult sociopaths.

9. "Reeducating the experts" — medical, legal, and religious — to recognize early warning signs and respond effectively, before a troubled child or teen begins to kill.[3]

All things considered — from the budget deficit to endless arguments about the family and "immorality" of birth control — the authors' last prescription is the only one that seems to offer realistic prospects for success before another decade slips away... and there are problems, even so. Aside from the resistance of abusive or neglectful parents, there are major risks inherent in the act of labeling a suspect child as "murder-prone," attempting to manipulate an individual or family because a sterile checklist of potential symptoms indicates a crime *may* happen, sometime in the future. Overemphasis on spotting would-be killers in the larval stage may stigmatize a child, condemning him or her to years of "special" treatment — even drugs and psychotherapy — that are entirely inappropriate.

That said, there must be *some* dividing line between the "normal" child who sometimes plays with matches, steps on ants, or wets his bed and one who burns the house down, tortures animals for sport, or brutalizes siblings. Logically, it should not be beyond the grasp of a physician, educator, guidance counselor, or clergyman to recognize the difference and to intervene, before sadistic childhood quirks turn into homicide.

There are no easy answers to the questions scrawled in blood across our daily headlines, splattered on the television screen. Security does not come cheap, in Eastern Europe or at home. Somehow, we must eliminate the monsters in our midst and find a way to salvage generations yet unborn. If egos suffer in the process, if established "experts" are discredited and pushed aside, so be it.

We are standing at a cross-roads, facing toward the year 2000, but we still have far to go. Without decisive action to eradicate the plague of random homicide, our next millennium may be a new Dark Ages, shaped and molded by the hands of those who strive to make their nightmares real.

Appendix

VICAP Crime Analysis Report

FD-676 (Rev. 3-11-86)
OMB No. 1110-0011

U.S. Department of Justice
Federal Bureau of Investigation

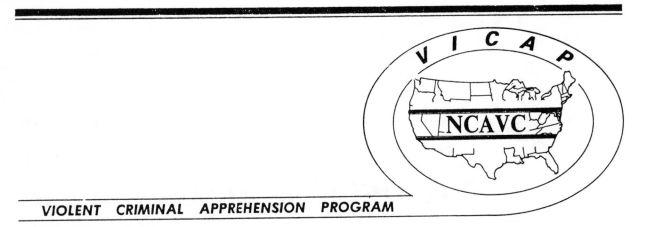

VIOLENT CRIMINAL APPREHENSION PROGRAM

VICAP

Crime Analysis Report

VICAP   NCAVC   FBI ACADEMY   Quantico, VA 22135   (703) 640-6131

NATIONAL   CENTER   FOR   THE   ANALYSIS   OF   VIOLENT   CRIME

HOW TO COMPLETE THE VICAP CRIME ANALYSIS REPORT FORM

VICAP SUBMISSION CRITERIA

The VICAP Crime Analysis Report form has been designed to collect information regarding the following types of crimes whether or not the offender has been arrested or identified:

(1) Solved or unsolved homicides or attempts, especially those that involve an abduction; are apparently random, motiveless, or sexually oriented; or are known or suspected to be part of a series.

(2) Missing person, where the circumstances indicate a strong possibility of foul play and the victim is still missing.

(3) Unidentified dead bodies, where the manner of death is known or suspected to be homicide.

Cases where the offender has been arrested or identified should be submitted so unsolved cases in the VICAP system can be linked to known offenders.

INSTRUCTIONS

- Use black ink or pencil. Legibly print all written responses.

- Unless stated otherwise, check as many boxes as apply for each item.

- If in doubt about how to respond to a given item, be guided by your experience and good judgment. Proof beyond a reasonable doubt is not required, but do not guess either.

- If there are details of the case that you feel are important but that do not fit well into the items provided in the VICAP Crime Analysis Report, describe them in the narrative.

- If you wish to supplement or correct information previously reported to VICAP, submit a new VICAP Crime Analysis Report but complete only Items 1 through 18, 27 and 36 plus the Item(s) you wish to supplement or correct. You need not resubmit unchanged items.

- For advice or assistance regarding this report or its completion, call VICAP at **(703) 640-6131.**

- If you are submitting this VICAP Crime Analysis Report in conjunction with a request for a criminal personality profile evaluation, you **must** contact the **CRIMINAL PROFILE COORDINATOR** assigned to the FBI Field Division in your area. The **CRIMINAL PROFILE COORDINATOR** is charged with the responsibility of assisting you with your request for a criminal personality profile and will advise you of additional materials that must be submitted in order to evaluate your case properly. He/she will review the materials and will submit the entire profile package to the National Center for the Analysis of Violent Crime on your behalf. *Do not submit Criminal Personality Profiling case materials directly to VICAP.* Only the VICAP Crime Analysis Report should be submitted directly to VICAP.

- *Multiple victims & multiple offenders*

    If your incident has **MULTIPLE VICTIMS,** you must complete a separate VICAP Crime Analysis Report form for each victim. Offender information need not be duplicated.

    If your incident has **MULTIPLE OFFENDERS,** submit only one complete VICAP Crime Analysis Report per victim; xerox and attach additional offender page(s) (Items 55 through 84) to each Report as needed.

Examples:

1) For two (2) victims and one (1) offender, you must complete two (2) VICAP Crime Analysis Report forms (one for each victim). Do not duplicate the Offender information (Items 55 through 84) in the second Report.

2) For two (2) victims and two (2) offenders, you must complete two (2) VICAP Crime Analysis Report forms. Victim #1 and offender #1 would go on the first Report form and victim #2 and offender #2 would go on the second Report form.

3) For one (1) victim and two (2) offenders, you must complete one (1) VICAP Crime Analysis Report form. The victim and offender #1 would be reported in the body of the VICAP Crime Analysis Report form, and offender #2 would be reported by copying an additional offender page (Items 55 through 84), completing it, and attaching it to the VICAP Crime Analysis Report.

- Before submitting the VICAP Crime Analysis Report, make a copy for your records.

- Mail all VICAP Crime Analysis Reports, Supplements, and/or Corrections to:
  VICAP
  National Center for the Analysis of Violent Crime
  FBI Academy
  Quantico, VA 22135.

- Enclosing Crime Scene Photographs with the VICAP Crime Analysis Report will assist the VICAP staff in the evaluation of the case.

- A VICAP Case Number will be assigned to your case when it is processed and will be provided to you as soon as possible. The VICAP Case Number should be referenced in any subsequent correspondence or telephone communications with VICAP regarding the case.

- The Narrative Summary is intended to provide VICAP Analysts with a general overview of the case. Minute details of the investigation need not be provided here; the VICAP Crime Analysis Report will capture most of the detail necessary to complete the analysis. A person unfamiliar with your case, however, should have at least a general idea of what happened after reading your brief narrative.

Examples:

1) The partially decomposed body of an adult female was discovered in a wooded area of a state park, one-quarter mile from a major state highway. There are indications of sexual assault. Victim died of gunshot wounds. It appears that the victim was not killed at the body recovery site. The victim's whereabouts prior to her death have not been established.

2) Female juvenile was last seen at school. Investigation indicates that she was possibly abducted at or near the school while en route home. The victim has not returned nor has her body been recovered. Investigation indicates that it is unlikely that the victim is a runaway or that she disappeared of her own accord. This case is strikingly similar to one that occurred approximately 8 months ago in the same vicinity.

3) The reported offender entered a locked single-family residence occupied by a man, his wife, and 2 infant children. While the offender was gathering property in the residence, the husband confronted the offender. The husband was shot immediately and died. The wife responded after hearing the gunshot and was physically restrained by the offender. The offender hit her repeatedly with his fists, forced her to commit oral sex, and raped her repeatedly. The wife survived the attack. The children were not assaulted. The offender left the residence, and a vehicle was heard to leave the area. Offender arrested during the commission of a burglary in the same neighborhood one week later.

TABLE OF CONTENTS

I. ADMINISTRATION

CASE ADMINISTRATION

FOR VICAP USE ONLY

1. VICAP Case Number: _____ 2. FBI Case Number: _____

3. FBI OO: _____ 4. VICAP Assignment: _____

5. Reporting Agency: _____

6. Address: _____ 7. City: _____

8. County: _____ 9. State: _____ 10. ZIP: _____

11. Reporting Agency's ORI Number: _____

12. Reporting Agency's Case Number: _____

13. NCIC Number If Victim Is 1) Missing or 2) an Unidentified Dead Body: _____

14. Investigator's Name: _____

15. Investigator's Phone Number: _____ _____ _____

16. VICAP Crime Analysis Report Type:

   1 ☐ Original Submission of This Case

   2 ☐ Supplement to Previously Submitted Information

   3 ☐ Correction of Previously Submitted Information

17. Investigating Agency's Case Status:

   1 ☐ Open (active investigation)   4 ☐ Cleared by Arrest

   2 ☐ Suspended (inactive investigation)   5 ☐ Exceptionally Cleared (by UCR definition)

   3 ☐ Open —— Arrest Warrant Issued

CRIME CLASSIFICATION

18. This VICAP Crime Analysis Report Pertains to the Following Type Case (check one only):

   1 ☐ Murder or Attempted Murder —— Victim Identified (go to Item 19)

   2 ☐ Unidentified Dead Body Where Manner of Death Is Known or Suspected to Be Homicide (go to Item 19)

   3 ☐ Kidnapping or Missing Person with Evidence of Foul Play (victim still missing) (go to Item 20)

19. Based on Your Experience and the Results of the Investigation of This Case, Do You Believe This Offender Has Killed Before?

   1 ☐ Yes (explain in Narrative Summary)   99 ☐ Unable to Determine

   2 ☐ No

20. There Is an Indication That This Case Is Related to Organized Drug Trafficking:

   1 ☐ Yes   2 ☐ No   99 ☐ Unable to Determine

DATE AND TIME PARAMETERS

21. Today's Date: _____/_____/_____/
            (mo) (da) (yr)

	Date	Military Time	Exact	Approx-imate
22. Victim Last Seen:	_____/_____/_____/ (mo) (da) (yr)	_____	☐	☐
23. Death or Major Assault:	_____/_____/_____/ (mo) (da) (yr)	_____	☐	☐
24. Victim or Body Found	_____/_____/_____/ (mo) (da) (yr)	_____	☐	☐

II. VICTIM INFORMATION

VICTIM STATUS

25. This Is Victim _____ of _____ Victim(s) in This Incident.
    (number) (total)

26. Status of This Victim:
    1 ☐ Deceased (as result of this incident)
    2 ☐ Survivor of Attack
    3 ☐ Missing

VICTIM IDENTIFICATION

27. Name: _____
    (last, first, middle)

28. Alias(es) (including maiden name and prior married names):
    _____
    _____

29. Resident City: _____ 30. State: _____ 31. ZIP: _____

32. Social Security Number: _____—_____—_____ 33. FBI Number: _____

PHYSICAL DESCRIPTION

34. Sex:
    1 ☐ Male   2 ☐ Female   99 ☐ Unknown

35. Race:
    1 ☐ Black   3 ☐ Hispanic   5 ☐ Other
    2 ☐ Caucasian   4 ☐ Oriental/Asian 99 ☐ Unknown

36. Date of Birth: ___/___/___
    (mo) / (da) / (yr)
    99 ☐ Unknown

37. Age (or best estimate) at Time of Incident: _____
    99 ☐ Unknown   (years)

38. Height (or best estimate): _____ feet _____ inches
    99 ☐ Unknown

39. Approximate Weight: _____ lbs.
    99 ☐ Unknown

40. Build (check one only):
    1 ☐ Small (thin)   3 ☐ Large (stocky)
    2 ☐ Medium (average)   99 ☐ Unknown

41. Hair Length (check one only):
    1 ☐ Bald or Shaved   4 ☐ Shoulder Length
    2 ☐ Shorter Than Collar Length   5 ☐ Longer Than Shoulder Length
    3 ☐ Collar Length   99 ☐ Unknown

42. Hair Shade (check one only):
    1 ☐ Light   3 ☐ Neither 1 or 2 Above
    2 ☐ Dark   99 ☐ Unknown

43. Predominant Hair Color (check one only):
    1 ☐ Gray and/or White   5 ☐ Black
    2 ☐ Blond   6 ☐ Other
    3 ☐ Red   99 ☐ Unknown
    4 ☐ Brown

If your victim is either a missing person or an unidentified dead body, respond to Items 44 through 48. Otherwise, go to Item 49.

44. Abnormalities of Teeth:

   1 ☐ None   5 ☐ Decayed   9 ☐ Other (describe): _____
   2 ☐ Braces   6 ☐ Noticeable Gaps   _____
   3 ☐ Broken or Chipped   7 ☐ Some or All Missing   99 ☐ Unknown
   4 ☐ Crooked   8 ☐ Stained

45. Glasses or Corrective Lenses Normally Worn by or Associated with Victim:

   1 ☐ None   6 ☐ Metal Frame
   2 ☐ Prescription   7 ☐ Rimless
   3 ☐ Contacts   8 ☐ Other (describe): _____
   4 ☐ Bifocals   _____
   5 ☐ Plastic Frame   99 ☐ Unknown

SCARS AND/OR BIRTHMARKS

46. Location of Noticeable Scars or Birthmarks (not tattoos):

   1 ☐ None   4 ☐ Torso   7 ☐ Other (describe): _____
   2 ☐ Face, Head, or Neck   5 ☐ Buttocks   _____
   3 ☐ Arm(s) or Hand(s)   6 ☐ Feet or Leg(s)   99 ☐ Unknown

TATTOOS

47. Tattoo Locations:

   1 ☐ None   4 ☐ Torso   7 ☐ Other (describe): _____
   2 ☐ Face, Head, or Neck   5 ☐ Buttocks   _____
   3 ☐ Arm(s) or Hand(s)   6 ☐ Feet or Leg(s)   99 ☐ Unknown

48. Tattoo Designs:

   1 ☐ Initials or Words   4 ☐ Other (specify): _____
   2 ☐ Number(s)   _____
   3 ☐ Picture(s) or Design(s)   99 ☐ Unknown

OUTSTANDING PHYSICAL FEATURES

49. Did the Victim Have Outstanding Physical Features (crossed eyes, noticeable limp, physical deformity, etc.)? (Do not repeat information reported in Items 44 through 48, above.)

   1 ☐ Yes (describe): _____
   2 ☐ No
   99 ☐ Unknown

CLOTHING OF VICTIM

50. Generally Preferred Clothing Style (this item deals with general style of dress typically preferred by the victim, not a detailed clothing description):

   1 ☐ Business Suit   6 ☐ Work Clothes or
   2 ☐ Casual   Uniform
   3 ☐ Gaudy or Garish   88 ☐ Other (describe): _____
   4 ☐ Sport or Athletic   _____
   5 ☐ Western Wear   99 ☐ Unknown

51. Generally Preferred *Predominant* Color Tone of Clothing (check one only):

   1 ☐ Whites   4 ☐ Blues   7 ☐ Browns/Tans
   2 ☐ Yellows   5 ☐ Purples/Violets   8 ☐ Grays/Blacks
   3 ☑ Greens   6 ☐ Reds/Oranges

52. If This Victim Is a Missing Person or Unidentified Dead, Give a Detailed Description of Clothing:

   _____

   _____

MISCELLANEOUS

53. Victim's Residence (check one only):

   1 ☐ Single-Family Dwelling   4 ☐ Motor Vehicle
   2 ☐ Multi-Family Dwelling   5 ☐ Street
   3 ☐ Temporary or Transient Housing   99 ☐ Unknown

54. Current Occupation(s): 1) _____

   2) _____

III.   OFFENDER INFORMATION

OFFENDER DEFINED. As used in this VICAP Crime Analysis Report, "offender" includes arrestees, perpetrators, or persons the investigator has reasonable cause to believe are responsible for the commission of the crime.

OFFENDER STATUS

55. This Is Offender _____ of _____ Offender(s) in This Incident.
          (number)   (total)

56. The Offender Is (check one only):
    1 ☐ Unknown——Not Seen (go to Item 85)
    2 ☐ Unknown——Seen
    3 ☐ Identified (named)——Not in Custody
    4 ☐ In Custody
    5 ☐ Deceased

OFFENDER IDENTIFICATION

57. Name: _____
             (last, first, middle)

58. Alias(es) (including maiden name and prior married names):

    _____ _____

    _____

59. Resident City: _____ 60. State: _____ 61. ZIP: _____

62. Social Security Number: _____—_____—_____ 63. FBI Number: _____

PHYSICAL DESCRIPTION

64. Sex:
    1 ☐ Male   2 ☐ Female   99 ☐ Unknown

65. Race:
    1 ☐ Black   3 ☐ Hispanic   5 ☐ Other
    2 ☐ Caucasian   4 ☐ Oriental/Asian 99 ☐ Unknown

66. Date of Birth: ____/ ____/ ____
                (mo) / (da) / (yr)
    99 ☐ Unknown

67. Age (or best estimate) at Time of Incident: _____
    99 ☐ Unknown   (years)

68. Height (or best estimate): _____ feet _____ inches (to _____ feet _____ inches)
    99 ☐ Unknown

69. Build (check one only):
    1 ☐ Small (thin)   3 ☐ Large (stocky)
    2 ☐ Medium (average) 99 ☐ Unknown

70. Hair Length (check one only):
    1 ☐ Bald or Shaved   4 ☐ Shoulder Length
    2 ☐ Shorter Than Collar Length 5 ☐ Longer Than Shoulder Length
    3 ☐ Collar Length   99 ☐ Unknown

71. Hair Shade (check one only):
    1 ☐ Light   3 ☐ Neither 1 or 2 Above
    2 ☐ Dark   99 ☐ Unknown

72. Predominant Hair Color (check one only):
    1 ☐ Gray and/or White   5 ☐ Black
    2 ☐ Blond   6 ☐ Other
    3 ☐ Red   99 ☐ Unknown
    4 ☐ Brown

73. Was Wearing Glasses:
    1 ☐ Yes   2 ☐ No   99 ☐ Unknown

74. Facial Hair (check all that apply):
    1 ☐ None   3 ☐ Beard   99 ☐ Unknown
    2 ☐ Mustache   4 ☐ Other

75. Appeared Generally Well Groomed:
    1 ☐ Yes   2 ☐ No   99 ☐ Unknown

76. Offender Wore a Disguise or Mask:
    1 ☐ Yes   2 ☐ No   ·99 ☐ Unknown

SCARS AND/OR BIRTHMARKS

77. Noticeable Scars or Birthmarks (not tattoos):
    1 ☐ Yes   2 ☐ No   99 ☐ Unknown

TATTOOS

78. Noticeable Tattoos:
    1 ☐ Yes   2 ☐ No   99 ☐ Unknown

OUTSTANDING PHYSICAL FEATURES

79. Other Outstanding Physical Features of the Offender Not Reported Above
(crossed eyes, noticeable limp, physical deformity, etc.):

    1 ☐ Yes (describe): _____
    2 ☐ No
   99 ☐ Unknown

IV.   IDENTIFIED OFFENDER INFORMATION

If you have an offender in custody or identified in this case, complete Items 80 through 84. Otherwise, go to Item 85.

OFFENDER BACKGROUND

80. Cities and States of Residence during Last 5 Years (exclude current city of residence):

    1) _____   3) _____
    2) _____   4) _____

81. List the States the Offender Has Visited during Last 5 Years (attach separate sheet if necessary):

    1) _____   3) _____
    2) _____   4) _____

82. Foreign Countries Lived or Traveled in:

    1) _____   3) _____
    2) _____   4) _____

PROPERTY OF OTHERS

83. Offender Was in Possession of Property of Others (check all that apply):
    1 ☐ Body Parts   4 ☐ Jewelry
    2 ☐ Clothing   5 ☐ Photo(s)
    3 ☐ Credit Card(s), Checks, or other   88 ☐ Other (specify): _____
        I.D.   _____

OFFENDER'S ADMISSIONS

84. Offender Admits Other Similar Crime(s) of Violence:
    1 ☐ Yes (attach details)   2 ☐ No

V. VEHICLE DESCRIPTION

VEHICLE USED IN THIS INCIDENT

85. Is a Vehicle Known to Have Been Used in This Incident?
    1 ☐ Yes   2 ☐ No or Unknown (go to Item 96)

    NOTE: Complete vehicle information if 1) a vehicle was used by the offender in this incident; or 2) this is a missing person case *and* the vehicle is missing; or 3) this is an unidentified dead case *and* the vehicle has been connected with the victim; or 4) the vehicle is in any way significantly involved in this incident.

86. Did the Vehicle Belong to, or Was It under the Civil Control of, the Victim?

    1 ☐ Yes   2 ☐ No

87. The Vehicle Would Normally Be Described as Being:
    1 ☐ Exceptionally Well Maintained ("sharp")   3 ☐ Neither 1 or 2 Above
    2 ☐ Not Generally Well Kept ("beat-up")   99 ☐ Unknown

88. The Vehicle Would Normally Be Described as Being:
    1 ☐ Newer/Late Model   3 ☐ Neither 1 or 2 Above
    2 ☐ Older Model   99 ☐ Unknown

89. License Number: _____   90. License State: _____

91. Vehicle Year: _____ 92. Make: _____ 93. Model: _____

94. Body Style:
    1 ☐ Passenger Car   6 ☐ Motorcycle
    2 ☐ Van   88 ☐ Other (specify): _____
    3 ☐ Pick-up Truck   _____
    4 ☐ "Jeep" Type (i.e., Bronco, Blazer, etc.) 99 ☐ Unknown
    5 ☐ Tractor-Trailer

95. Color: _____   _____
              (top)   (bottom)

VI. OFFENSE M. O.

OFFENDER'S APPROACH TO VICTIM AT TIME OF INCIDENT

96. The Victim or a Witness Reported That the Offender's Approach to Victim Was:
    1 ☐ No Living Victim or Person Witnessed the Offender's Approach to Victim
        (go to Item 100)
    2 ☐ By Deception or Con: Openly, with Subterfuge or Ploy (e.g., offers assistance or requests
        direction) (go to Item 97 and then go to Item 100)
    3 ☐ By Surprise: Lay in Wait or Stepped from Concealment
        (go to Item 98 and then go to Item 100)
    4 ☐ By "Blitz": Direct and Immediate Physical Assault (go to Item 99)

97. If the Offender Initiated Contact with the Victim by Means of Deception, Indicate the Type of Deception Below:
    1 ☐ Posed as Authority Figure   7 ☐ Asked for or Offered Assistance
    2 ☐ Posed as Business Person   8 ☐ Caused or Staged Traffic Accident
    3 ☐ Asked Victim to Model or Pose for   9 ☐ Phony Police Traffic Stop
        Photos   10 ☐ Solicitation for Sex
    4 ☐ Offered Job, Money, Treats, or Toys   11 ☐ Offered Ride or Transportation
    5 ☐ Implied Family Emergency or Illness   12 ☐ Other Deception
    6 ☐ Wanted to Show (something)

98. If the Offender Initiated Contact with the Victim by Means of Surprise, Indicate the Type of Surprise Below:
    1 ☐ Lay in Wait——Out of Doors   4 ☐ Victim Sleeping
    2 ☐ Lay in Wait——In Building   5 ☐ Other Surprise
    3 ☐ Lay in Wait——In Vehicle

99. If the Offender Initiated Contact with the Victim by Direct and Immediate Physical Assault,
Indicate the Type of Direct and Immediate Physical Assault Below:

1 ☐ Immediately and Physically Over-
   powered Victim (picked up, carried
   away, etc.)
2 ☐ Hit Victim with Hand, Fist, or
   Clubbing Weapon

3 ☐ Choked Victim
4 ☐ Stabbed Victim
5 ☐ Shot Victim
6 ☐ Other Direct Assault

EXACT GEOGRAPHIC LOCATION

100. Last Known Location of Identified Victim or Location of Unidentified Dead Body Recovery Site:
   a. ☐ City of (if within incorporated city, town, etc.)

   _____

   b. ☐ County of (if not within incorporated city, town, etc.)

   _____

   c. State: _____ d. ZIP: _____

LOCATION OF EVENTS

BODY RECOVERY SITE

101. Description of General Area of the Body Recovery Site (check one only):
   1 ☐ Rural
   2 ☐ Suburban
   3 ☐ Urban
   99 ☐ Unknown

102. The Neighborhood of the Body Recovery Site Is *Predominantly* (check one only):
   1 ☐ Business, Industrial, or Commercial
   2 ☐ Farm or Agricultural
   3 ☐ Residential
   4 ☐ Uninhabited or Wilderness
   99 ☐ Unknown

103. The Body Recovery Site Was (check as many as apply):
   1 ☐ Any Residence
   2 ☐ At or Near a School or Playground
   3 ☐ In a Retail Shopping District
   4 ☐ On a Public Street
   5 ☐ In a Vice Area
   6 ☐ A Densely Wooded Area
   7 ☐ In an Open Field
   8 ☐ In a Vehicle
   9 ☐ On Public Transportation
   88 ☐ Other (specify): _____
   _____
   99 ☐ Unknown

104. The Body Recovery Site Was Victim's Residence:
   1 ☐ Yes   2 ☐ No   99 ☐ Unknown

105. The Body Recovery Site Was Victim's Work Place:
   1 ☐ Yes   2 ☐ No   99 ☐ Unknown

106. Potential Witnesses at the Time the Offender Left the Body at the Body Recovery Site:
   1 ☐ Other People Were Present in the   2 ☐ Area Was Essentially Deserted
      Immediate Area   99 ☐ Unknown

MURDER OR MAJOR ASSAULT SITE

107. Was the Murder or Major Assault Site the Same as the Body Recovery Site?
   1 ☐ Yes (go to Item 113)   2 ☐ No or Unknown

108. Description of General Area of Murder or Major Assault Site (check one only):
   1 ☐ Rural
   2 ☐ Suburban
   3 ☐ Urban
   99 ☐ Unknown

109. The Neighborhood of Murder or Major Assault Site Is *Predominantly* (check one only):
   1 ☐ Business, Industrial, or Commercial
   2 ☐ Farm or Agricultural
   3 ☐ Residential
   4 ☐ Uninhabited or Wilderness
   99 ☐ Unknown

110. The Murder or Major Assault Site Was (check as many as apply):
   1 ☐ Any Residence
   2 ☐ At or Near a School or Playground
   3 ☐ In a Retail Shopping District
   4 ☐ On a Public Street
   5 ☐ In a Vice Area
   6 ☐ A Densely Wooded Area
   7 ☐ In an Open Field
   8 ☐ In a Vehicle
   9 ☐ On Public Transportation
   88 ☐ Other (specify): _____
   _____
   99 ☐ Unknown

VI.   OFFENSE M. O. (cont.)

111. The Murder or Major Assault Site Was Victim's Residence:
  1 ☐ Yes   2 ☐ No   99 ☐ Unknown

112. The Murder or Major Assault Site Was Victim's Work Place:
  1 ☐ Yes   2 ☐ No   99 ☐ Unknown

113. Potential Witnesses at the Time of the Murder or Major Assault:
  1 ☐ Other People Were Present in the   2 ☐ Area Was Essentially Deserted
      Immediate Area   99 ☐ Unknown

SITE OF OFFENDER'S INITIAL CONTACT WITH VICTIM

114. Was the Site of the Offender's Initial Contact with the Victim the Same as the Murder or Major Assault Site?
  1 ☐ Yes (go to Item 120)   2 ☐ No or Unknown

115. Description of General Area of Initial Offender-Victim Contact (check one only):
  1 ☐ Rural   3 ☐ Urban
  2 ☐ Suburban   99 ☐ Unknown

116. The Neighborhood of Initial Offender-Victim Contact Is *Predominantly* (check one only):
  1 ☐ Business, Industrial, or Commercial   4 ☐ Uninhabited or Wilderness
  2 ☐ Farm or Agricultural   99 ☐ Unknown
  3 ☐ Residential

117. The Initial Offender-Victim Contact Was (check as many as apply):
  1 ☐ Any Residence   7 ☐ In an Open Field
  2 ☐ At or Near a School or Playground   8 ☐ In a Vehicle
  3 ☐ In a Retail Shopping District   9 ☐ On Public Transportation
  4 ☐ On a Public Street   88 ☐ Other (specify): _____
  5 ☐ In a Vice Area   _____
  6 ☐ A Densely Wooded Area   99 ☐ Unknown

118. Initial Offender-Victim Contact Was Victim's Residence:
  1 ☐ Yes   2 ☐ No   99 ☐ Unknown

119. Initial Offender-Victim Contact Was Victim's Work Place:
  1 ☐ Yes   2 ☐ No   99 ☐ Unknown

120. Potential Witnesses at the Time of the Initial Offender-Victim Contact:
  1 ☐ Other People Were Present in the   2 ☐ Area Was Essentially Deserted
      Immediate Area   99 ☐ Unknown

VICTIM'S LAST KNOWN LOCATION

121. Was the Site of the Victim's Last Known Location the Same as the Site of the Initial Contact between the Victim and Offender?
  1 ☐ Yes (go to Item 127)   2 ☐ No or Unknown

122. Description of General Area of Victim's Last Known Location (check one only):
  1 ☐ Rural   3 ☐ Urban
  2 ☐ Suburban   99 ☐ Unknown

123. The Neighborhood of Victim's Last Known Location Was *Predominantly* (check one only):
  1 ☐ Business, Industrial, or Commercial   4 ☐ Uninhabited or Wilderness
  2 ☐ Farm or Agricultural   99 ☐ Unknown
  3 ☐ Residential

124. The Victim's Last Known Location Was (check as many as apply):
  1 ☐ Any Residence   7 ☐ In an Open Field
  2 ☐ At or Near a School or Playground   8 ☐ In a Vehicle
  3 ☐ In a Retail Shopping District   9 ☐ On Public Transportation
  4 ☐ On a Public Street   88 ☐ Other (specify): _____
  5 ☐ In a Vice Area   _____
  6 ☐ A Densely Wooded Area   99 ☐ Unknown

125. The Victim's Last Known Location Was Victim's Residence:
    1 ☐ Yes   2 ☐ No   99 ☐ Unknown

126. The Victim's Last Known Location Was Victim's Work Place:
    1 ☐ Yes   2 ☐ No   99 ☐ Unknown

EVENTS AT ASSAULT SITE

127. There Is Evidence That the Offender Disabled the Telephone, Other Utilities, or Security Devices:
    1 ☐ Yes   2 ☐ No   99 ☐ Unknown

128. The Property at the Crime Scene(s) Was Ransacked, Vandalized, or Burned:
    1 ☐ Yes   2 ☐ No   99 ☐ Unknown

129. There Are Indications That the Offender Took Steps to Obliterate or Destroy Evidence at the Scene:
    1 ☐ Yes   2 ☐ No   99 ☐ Unknown

OFFENDER'S WRITING OR CARVING ON BODY OF VICTIM

130. Writing or Carving *on Body:*
    1 ☐ Yes (describe): _____   2 ☐ No

131. Instrument Used to Write or Carve *on Body:*
    1 ☐ Knife or Other Sharp Instrument   4 ☐ Writing Instrument (pen, etc.)
    2 ☐ Blood   88 ☐ Other (specify): _____
    3 ☐ Lipstick   _____

OFFENDER'S WRITING OR DRAWING AT THE CRIME SCENE

132. Writing or Drawing *at Crime Scene(s):*
    1 ☐ Yes (describe): _____   2 ☐ No

133. Instrument Used to Write or Draw *at Crime Scene(s):*
    1 ☐ Knife or Other Sharp Instrument   4 ☐ Writing Instrument (pen, etc.)
    2 ☐ Blood   88 ☐ Other (specify): _____
    3 ☐ Lipstick   _____

SYMBOLIC ARTIFACTS AT CRIME SCENE

134. Was There Evidence to Suggest a Deliberate or Unusual Ritual/Act/Thing Had Been Performed on, with, or near the Victim (such as an orderly formation of rocks, burnt candles, dead animals, defecation, etc.)?
    1 ☐ Yes (describe): _____   2 ☐ No
    _____   99 ☐ Unknown

OFFENDER'S COMMUNICATIONS

Item 135 deals with communications initiated by the offender with respect to the crime. Examples would be: an offender sending a letter or tape recording to the police or media claiming responsibility for the crime; a ransom note; or a suspicious communication received by the victim prior to the crime. (This item does not refer to conversation between the offender and victim during commission of the crime.)

135. Was There Any Communication from the Offender Before or After the Crime?
    1 ☐ Yes (enclose a copy or synopsis   2 ☐ No
       of the communication)   99 ☐ Unknown

VII. CONDITION OF VICTIM WHEN FOUND

BODY DISPOSITION

136. There Is Reason to Believe the Offender Moved the Body from the Area of the Death Site to the Area of the Body Recovery Site:

1 ☐ Yes   2 ☐ No   3 ☐ Unable to Determine

137. Evidence Suggests the Offender Disposed of the Body in the Following Manner:

1 ☐ Openly Displayed or Otherwise Placed to Insure Discovery
2 ☐ Concealed, Hidden, or Otherwise Placed in Order to Prevent Discovery
3 ☐ With an Apparent Lack of Concern as to Whether or Not the Body Was Discovered
99 ☐ Unable to Determine

138. It Appears the Body of the Victim Was *Intentionally* Placed in an Unnatural or Unusual Position *after Death* Had Occurred (e.g., staged or posed):

1 ☐ Yes   2 ☐ No   3 ☐ Unable to Determine

139. Body Was Discovered...

1 ☐ Buried
2 ☐ Covered
3 ☐ In a Body of Water (stream, lake, river, etc.)
4 ☐ In a Building
5 ☐ In a Container (e.g., dumpster, box refrigerator)
6 ☐ In a Vehicle
7 ☐ Scattered (body parts)
8 ☐ None of the Above

140. If the Body Was Discovered in Water, Was It Weighted?

1 ☐ Yes —— With What? _____   2 ☐ No

RESTRAINTS USED ON VICTIM

141. Was the Victim Bound?

1 ☐ Yes   2 ☐ No (go to Item 146)

142. Article(s) Used to Bind or Restrain the Victim or the Body:

1 ☐ An Article of Clothing
2 ☐ Tape
3 ☐ Cordage (e.g., rope, string, twine, wire, leather thong, etc.)
4 ☐ Chain
5 ☐ Handcuffs or Thumbcuffs
88 ☐ Other (specify): _____
_____

143. The Evidence Suggests That the Restraining Device(s) Was (check one only):

1 ☐ Brought to the Scene by the Offender
2 ☐ An Article Found at the Scene by the Offender
3 ☐ Both 1 and 2 Above
99 ☐ Unknown

144. Parts of Body Bound (check as many as apply):

1 ☐ Hands or Arms
2 ☐ Feet, Ankle(s), or Legs
3 ☐ Neck
4 ☐ Arms Bound to Torso
5 ☐ Hands and Ankle(s) Bound Together
88 ☐ Other (specify): _____
_____

145. The Bindings on the Victim Were Excessive (much more than necessary to control victim's movements):

1 ☐ Yes   2 ☐ No   3 ☐ Unable to Determine

146. The Body Was Tied to Another Object:

1 ☐ Yes   2 ☐ No

147. Was a Gag Placed in or on the Victim's Mouth?

1 ☐ Yes (describe):_____
_____
2 ☐ No
99 ☐ Unknown

148. Was a Blindfold Placed on or over the Victim's Eyes?

1 ☐ Yes (describe):_____
_____
2 ☐ No
99 ☐ Unknown

149. Was Victim's Entire Face Covered?

1 ☐ Yes —— With What? _____
_____
2 ☐ No
99 ☐ Unknown

CLOTHING AND PROPERTY OF VICTIM

150. Clothing on Victim When Found:
1 ☐ Fully Dressed   3 ☐ Nude
2 ☐ Partially Undressed   88 ☐ Other (specify): _____

151. There Is Evidence the Victim Was Re-dressed by Offender:
1 ☐ Yes   2 ☐ No   3 ☐ Unable to Determine

152. There Is Evidence to Suggest That Any or All of the Victim's Clothing had been *Ripped* or *Torn*:
1 ☐ Yes   2 ☐ No   3 ☐ Unable to Determine

153. There Is Evidence to Suggest That Any or All of the Victim's Clothing had been *Cut* from the Body:
1 ☐ Yes   2 ☐ No   3 ☐ Unable to Determine

154. Items of the Victim's Clothing Were Missing from the Body Recovery Site:
1 ☐ Yes (identify):_____   2 ☐ No
_____   99 ☐ Unknown

155. Victim's Clothing (not on the body) Recovered at the Body Recovery Site Was:
1 ☐ Piled Neatly   3 ☐ Hidden
2 ☐ Scattered   4 ☐ Not Applicable

156. Based on the Investigation, There Is Evidence to Suggest That the Offender Took Small Personal Items (other than clothing) From the Victim (these items may or may not be valuable, e.g., photos, driver's license, real or costume jewelry, etc.):
1 ☐ Yes (specify):_____   2 ☐ No
_____   99 ☐ Unknown

VIII.   CAUSE OF DEATH AND/OR TRAUMA

CAUSE OF DEATH

If victim is a survivor, go to Item 158.

157. Medical Examiner's or Coroner's Officially Listed Cause of Death:
1 ☐ Gunshot Wound(s)   11 ☐ Burns —— Fire
2 ☐ Stab Wound(s)   12 ☐ Burns —— Chemical
3 ☐ Cutting or Incise Wound(s)   13 ☐ Burns —— Scalding
4 ☐ Blunt Force Injury   14 ☐ Hypothermia or Exposure
5 ☐ Strangulation —— Manual, Ligature,   15 ☐ Malnutrition or Dehydration
    Undetermined (circle one)   16 ☐ Electrocution
6 ☐ Smothering   17 ☐ Crushing Injury
7 ☐ Airway Occlusion —— Internal   18 ☐ Explosive Trauma
8 ☐ Torso Compression   19 ☐ Undetermined
9 ☐ Hanging   88 ☐ Other (specify): _____
10 ☐ Drowning   _____

TRAUMA

158. *Major* Trauma Location(s) (check as many as apply):
1 ☐ Head / Face / Neck   7 ☐ Genitalia
2 ☐ Arm(s) / Hand(s)   8 ☐ Anus
3 ☐ Torso   88 ☐ Other (specify): _____
4 ☐ Leg(s) / Feet   _____
5 ☐ Breast(s)   99 ☐ Unable to Determine
6 ☐ Buttocks

159. Extent of *Blunt Force* Injury:
1 ☐ None
2 ☐ Minimal   (minor bruising only, possibly caused by offender's slapping to control the victim)
3 ☐ Moderate   (injury inflicted which in itself could not have caused death)
4 ☐ Severe   (injury which in itself could have caused death, whether it was the cause of death or not)
5 ☐ Extreme   (injury inflicted beyond that necessary for death. Overkill)

VIII.   CAUSE OF DEATH AND/OR TRAUMA (cont.)

160. Estimated Number of Stab Wounds: _____

161. Estimated Number of Cutting Wounds: _____

162. Number of Entry Gunshot Wounds: _____

163. Range of Gunfire:
 1 ☐ Not Applicable
 2 ☐ Distant (no stippling / tattooing)
 3 ☐ Intermediate (stippling / tattooing)
 4 ☐ Close (powder residue / tattooing)
 5 ☐ Contact

BITE MARKS ON VICTIM

164. Bite Marks Were Identified on the Victim's Body:
 1 ☐ Yes
 2 ☐ No (go to Item 166)

165. Location of Bite Marks:
 1 ☐ Face
 2 ☐ Neck
 3 ☐ Abdomen
 4 ☐ Breast(s)
 5 ☐ Buttocks
 6 ☐ Groin
 7 ☐ Genitalia
 8 ☐ Thigh(s)
 88 ☐ Other (specify): _____

ELEMENTS OF TORTURE OR UNUSUAL ASSAULT

166. There Is Evidence to Suggest That the Offender Disfigured the Body of the Victim in Order to Delay or Hinder Identification of the Victim (burned body; removed and took hands, feet, head; etc.):
 1 ☐ Yes
 2 ☐ No

167. Elements of Unusual or Additional Assault upon Victim:
 1 ☐ None
 2 ☐ Victim Whipped
 3 ☐ Burns on Victim
 4 ☐ Victim Run Over by Vehicle
 5 ☐ Evidence of Cannibalism / Vampirism
 6 ☐ Offender Explored, Probed, or Mutilated Cavities or Wounds of Victim
 88 ☐ Other (specify): _____

168. Body Parts Removed by Offender:
 1 ☐ None (go to Item 170)
 2 ☐ Head
 3 ☐ Scalp
 4 ☐ Face
 5 ☐ Teeth
 6 ☐ Eye(s)
 7 ☐ Ear(s)
 8 ☐ Nose
 9 ☐ Hand(s)
 10 ☐ Arm(s)
 11 ☐ Leg(s)
 12 ☐ Breast(s)
 13 ☐ Nipple(s)
 14 ☐ Anus
 15 ☐ Genitalia
 16 ☐ Internal Organs
 88 ☐ Other (specify): _____

169. Dismemberment Method:
 1 ☐ Bitten Off
 2 ☐ Cut —— Skilled/Surgical
 3 ☐ Cut —— Unskilled/Rough-Cut
 4 ☐ Hacked / Chopped Off
 5 ☐ Sawed Off
 88 ☐ Other (specify): _____

SEXUAL ASSAULT

170. Is There Evidence of an Assault to Any of the Victim's Sexual Organs or Body Cavities?
 1 ☐ Yes   2 ☐ No (go to Item 178)   3 ☐ Unable to Determine

171. Type Sexual Assault, or Attempt (check all that apply):
 1 ☐ Vaginal
 2 ☐ Anal
 3 ☐ Victim Performed Oral Sex on Offender
 4 ☐ Offender Performed Oral Sex on Victim
 88 ☐ Other (describe): _____
 99 ☐ Unable to Determine

172. Semen Identification In a Body Cavity of the Victim:
   1 ☐ No   3 ☐ In Anus   5 ☐ Unable to Determine
   2 ☐ In Vagina   4 ☐ In Mouth

173. Evidence of Other Ejaculation:
   1 ☐ No   3 ☐ Elsewhere at the Scene
   2 ☐ On Body of Victim   4 ☐ Unable to Determine

174. There Is Evidence to Suggest Postmortem Sexual Assault:
   1 ☐ Yes   2 ☐ No   3 ☐ Unable to Determine

175. Is There Evidence of Sexual Insertion of Foreign Object(s) (other than the penis) into the Victim's Body?
   1 ☐ Yes   2 ☐ No (go to Item 178)

176. Evidence of Sexual Insertion of Foreign Object(s) *Still in Body* When First Discovered (e.g., rocks, twigs, knife, clothing):
   (object) (object)
   1 ☐ Vagina _____   4 ☐ Mouth _____
   2 ☐ Penis _____   88 ☐ Other _____
   3 ☐ Anus _____

177. There Is Evidence of Sexual Insertion of Foreign Object(s) into Victim's Body, but the Object Was *Not In The Body* When the Body Was First Discovered:
   1 ☐ Yes —— _____ into _____
   2 ☐ No   (describe object)   (body cavity)
   3 ☐ Unable to Determine

IX.   FORENSIC EVIDENCE

WEAPONS

178. Weapons Used by Offender in This Assault:
   1 ☐ None   5 ☐ Ligature
   2 ☐ Firearm   6 ☐ Hands or Feet
   3 ☐ Stabbing or Cutting Weapon   88 ☐ Other Weapon (describe): _____
   4 ☐ Bludgeon or Club   _____

179. Assault Weapon(s) Used by Offender:
   1 ☐ Weapon of Opportunity (offender finds weapon at or near scene)
   2 ☐ Weapon of Choice (offender preselects weapon and brings to scene)
   3 ☐ Both 1 and 2 Above
   99 ☐ Unknown

180. Recovery of Assault Weapon(s) (check as many as apply):
   1 ☐ Not Recovered   3 ☐ Recovered Elsewhere —— Where? ___
   2 ☐ Recovered At Scene   _____

181. Type Firearm Used:
   1 ☐ Handgun   88 ☐ Other (specify): _____
   2 ☐ Rifle   _____
   3 ☐ Shotgun   99 ☐ Unknown

182. Caliber or Gauge of Firearm(s) Used: _____

183. Number of Grooves and Direction of Twist of Recovered Bullet or Firearm: _____

184. Size of Shotgun Shell Pellets Recovered or Used: _____

BLOOD

185. What Is the Offender's Blood Type?
   1 ☐ A   3 ☐ AB   99 ☐ Unknown
   2 ☐ B   4 ☐ O

186. What Is the Rh Factor of the Offender's Blood?
   1 ☐ Positive   2 ☐ Negative   99 ☐ Unknown

X. REQUEST FOR PROFILE

187. Is This VICAP Crime Analysis Report Being Submitted in Conjunction with a Request for a Criminal Profile Evaluation?

   1 ☐ Yes (see note below)   2 ☐ No

NOTE: If this VICAP Crime Analysis Report is being submitted in conjunction with a request for a Criminal Personality Profile evaluation, you must contact the CRIMINAL PROFILE COOR-DINATOR assigned to the FBI Field Division in your area. The CRIMINAL PROFILE COORDINATOR is charged with the responsibility of assisting you with your request for a criminal personality profile and will advise you of additional materials that must be submitted in order to properly evaluate your case. He/she will review the materials and will submit the entire profile package to the National Center for the Analysis of Violent Crime on your behalf. Do not submit Criminal Profiling case materials directly to VICAP. Only the VICAP Crime Analysis Report should be submitted directly to VICAP.

XI. OTHER RELATED CASES

188. Are You Aware of Any Other Cases Which May Be Related to This One or In Which This Offender May Have Been Involved?

   1 ☐ Yes (provide details below)   2 ☐ No

If Yes, List the Agency Name, State, Case Number, Investigator, and Phone Number of the Investigating Agency:

Agency Name	State	Case No.	Investigator	Phone No.

148

XII.   NARRATIVE SUMMARY

189.   Give a BRIEF Narrative Summary of This Case So the Reader Will Have a General Overview of the Case, the Details, the Most Unusual Characteristics, and the Sequence of Events. Also Include Any Details of This Case You Feel Are Important, But That Have Not Previously Been Addressed (see examples of Narrative Summaries in the Instructions):

_____

_____

_____

_____

_____

_____

_____

_____

_____

_____

_____

_____

_____

_____

_____

_____

_____

_____

_____

_____

_____

_____

_____

_____

_____

_____

_____

_____

Notes

Introduction: Making the Nightmare Real

1. Robert Ressler, Ann Burgess, and John Douglas. *Sexual Homicide*, Lexington, MA: Lexington Books, 1988, p. 139.

2. *Ibid.*, pp. 138-39.

3. *Ibid.*, p. 139.

4. *Ibid.*, p. 140.

5. National Institute of Justice. *Multi-Agency Investigative Team Manual*, Washington, D.C.: NIJ, 1988, p. vii.

6. Except where noted otherwise, statistics cited in the text are drawn from analysis of serial murder cases collected for this work.

7. Eric Van Hoffman. *A Venom In The Blood*, New York: Zebra, 1990, p. 7.

8. James Reinhardt. *The Psychology of Strange Killers,* Springfield, IL: Charles C. Thomas, 1962.

9. Federal Bureau of Investigation. *Crime In the United States: 1966-1989.* Washington, D.C.: U.S. Government Printing Office, 1966-89.

10. Ted Gest and Douglas Lyons. "Behind a nationwide wave of unsolved murders." *US News & World Report*, March 16, 1981, p. 58.

11. "Stateline: 50 cities' crime statistics." *USA Today*, October 22, 1990.

12. Associated Press. "Repeat murderers still stalk streets." *The Bakersfield Californian*, October 27, 1983.

13. Mike Billington. "The mind of the murderers." *Nevadan*, December 16, 1984, p. 15.

14. Brad Darrach and Joel Norris. "An American tragedy." *Life*, August 1984, p. 58.

15. Joel Norris. *Serial Killers: The Growing Menace*, New York: Doubleday, 1988, p. 35.

16. Van Hoffman, p. 7.

17. Sam Meddis and Tracy Walmer. "Multiple killers usually not 'crazy,' experts say." *USA Today*, March 31, 1987.

18. Darrach and Norris, p. 60.

19. Sam Meddis. "Computer clearinghouse draws crime data from across USA." *USA Today,* March 31, 1987.

20. Norris, p. 15.

21. David Gelman and Susan Agrest. "Stolen Children." *Newsweek*, March 19, 1984, p. 78.

22. John Keel. *Strange Creatures From Time And Space,* New York: Fawcett, 1970, p. 274.

23. Carl Sifakis. *The Encyclopedia Of American Crime*, New York: Facts on File, 1982, p. 84.

Chapter 1: Making Monsters

1. Vera Fahlberg. *Attachment And Separation: Putting The Pieces Together*, Michigan Dept. of Social Services, DSS Publication #429, 1979, p. 5.

2. Mary Ainsworth. *Patterns Of Attachment*, Hillsdale, NJ: Lawrence Erlbaum Associates, 1978.

3. Foster Cline. *Understanding And Treating The Severely Disturbed Child*, Evergreen, CO: Evergreen Consultants in Human Behavior, 1979.

4. Selma Fraiberg. *Every Child's Birthright: In Defense Of Mothering*, New York: Basic Books, 1977, pp. 51-54.

5. Ken Magid and Carole McKelvey. *High Risk: Children Without A Conscience*, New York: Bantam, 1987, p. 68.

6. American Psychiatric Association. *Diagnostic And Statistical Manual Of Mental Disorders*, Washington, D.C.: APA, 1980, pp. 317-18.

7. Magid and McKelvey, p. 5.

8. Marvin Wolfgang, Robert M. Figlio, and Thorsten Sellin. *Delinquency In a Birth Cohort*, Chicago: University of Chicago Press, 1972.

9. Claudia Wallis. "Children having children." *Time*, December 9, 1985, pp. 79-90.

10. Norris, p. 236.

11. John Bowlby. *The Making And Breaking Of Affectional Bonds*, London: Tavistock Publications, 1979, p. 73.

12. Glen Hester and B. Nygren. *Child Of Rage*, Nashville: Thomas Nelson, 1981, p. 178.

13. *USA Today*, March 14, 1991.

14. Ressler et al., pp. x-xi.

15. *Ibid.*, pp. 69-71.

16. *Ibid.*, p. 19.

17. Norris, p. 182.

18. Ressler et al., p. 19.

19. Donald Lunde. *Murder And Madness*, San Francisco: San Francisco Book Company, 1976, p. 94.

20. Federal Bureau of Investigation. *Crime In The United States: 1989*, Washington, D.C.: U.S. Government Printing Office, 1989.

21. Ressler et al., pp. 70-72.

22. Jack Levin and James Alan Fox. *Mass Murder: America's Growing Menace*, New York: Plenum, 1985, p. 28.

23. Mortimer Gross. "The Mind of a Murderer." *Medical World News*, November 23, 1973, p. 42.

24. Ressler et al., p. 19.

25. James Q. Wilson and Richard J. Herrstein. *Crime And Human Nature*, New York: Simon & Schuster, 1985, p. 255.

26. Ressler et al., p. 24.

27. *Ibid.*, pp. 72-73.

28. *Ibid.*

29. *Ibid.*, p. 29.

30. *Ibid.*, p. 31.

31. *Ibid.*, p. 29.

32. *Ibid.*

33. *Ibid.*

34. *Ibid.*

35. *Ibid.*

36. "Tapes fight pornography." *USA Today*, January 24, 1990.

37. Ann Rule. *The Stranger Beside Me*, New York: Signet, 1989, p. 495.

38. Ressler et al., p. 29.

39. *Ibid.*

40. Magid and McKelvey, pp. 85-86.

41. Ressler et al., p. 29.

42. *Ibid.*

43. *Ibid.*, pp. 74-75.

44. Levin and Fox, p. 27.

45. Norris, pp. 240-41.

46. *Ibid.*, pp. 177-78.

47. *Ibid.*, pp. 179-81.

48. *Ibid.*, pp. 120-21.

49. *Ibid.*, pp. 184-86.

50. *Ibid.*, pp. 121-22.

51. Conversation with the author, April 2, 1990.

Chapter 2: Silent Rage

1. Magid and McKelvey, pp. 174-75.
2. Hervey Cleckly. *The Mask of Sanity*, St. Louis: Mosby Books, 1982, p. 341.
3. Ressler et al., p. 31.
4. *Ibid.*, p. 66.
5. Magid and McKelvey, p. 273.
6. Ressler et al., p. 29.
7. *Ibid.*
8. *Ibid.*
9. Joyce Egginton. *From Cradle To Grave*, New York: William Morrow, 1989, pp. 200-203.
10. Ressler et al., p. 29.
11. Magid and McKelvey, p. 7.
12. Ressler et al., p. 29.
13. *Ibid.*, p. 24.
14. *Ibid.*, p. 29.
15. *Ibid.*
16. Seattle *Post-Intelligencer*, March 14, 1991; *USA Today*, March 15, 1991; *Indianapolis Star*, March 20, 1991.
17. Ressler et al., p. 29.
18. *Ibid.*
19. *Ibid.*, p. 31.
20. Michael Newton and Judy Ann Newton. *The Ku Klux Klan: An Encyclopedia*, New York: Garland, 1991, pp. 536-37.
21. Anton LaVey. *The Satanic Bible*, New York: Avon, 1969, p. 81.
22. *Ibid.*, p. 22.
23. *Ibid.*, pp. 87-90.

Chapter 3: Voices of Death

1. Execept where noted below, all quotations in this chapter are drawn from *Hunting Humans*, Loompanics, 1990. In several cases, spelling and grammar have been corrected for clarity's sake.

On life...

Lucas: Elliott Leyton. *Compulsive Killers*, New York: New York University Press, 1986, pp. 17-18.

Bundy: *Ibid.*, p. 91.

Berkowitz: *Ibid.*, p. 151.

Starkweather: *Ibid.*, pp. 233-34.

Watson: Reinhardt, p. 151.

DeSalvo: George Rae. *Confessions Of The Boston Strangler*, New York: Pyramid, 1967, p. 47.

Nilsen: Brian Masters. *Killing For Company*, London: Jonathan Cape, 1985, pp. 54-55.

Fish: Harold Schechter. *Deranged*, New York: Pocket Books, 1990, p. 184.

On sex...

Schaefer: Norris, p. 62.

Lucas: *Ibid.*, p. 122.

Heirens: Lucy Freeman. *"Before I Kill More..."*, New York: Crown, 1955, pp. 354-55.

DeSalvo: Rae, pp. 7-8.

Nilsen: Masters, p. 142.

Kemper: Leyton, p. 50.

Fish: Schechter, p. 183.

Judy: Bette Nunn. *Burn, Judy, Burn*, Indianapolis: The Author, 1981, p. 140.

Starkweather: Leyton, pp. 236-37.

Gein: Robert Gollmar. *Edward Gein*, New York: Charles Hallberg, 1981, pp. 42-43.

Carpenter: Robert Graysmith. *The Sleeping Lady*, New York: Dutton, 1990, pp. 250-51.

Long: Norris, pp. 140-41.

Bundy: Stephen Michaud and Hugh Aynesworth. *Ted Bundy: Conversations With A Killer*, New York: New American Library, 1989, p. 251.

On murder...

Long: Norris, p. 144.

Falling: Clifford Linedecker. *Thrill Killers*, New York: Paperjacks, 1987, p. 160.

Hatcher: Terry Ganey. *St. Joseph's Children*, New York: Lyle Stuart, 1989, p. 164.

Gallego: Ray Biondi and Walt Hecox. *All His Father's Sins*, New York: Pocket Books, 1988, p. 163.

Olson: Levin and Fox, p. 167.

Danks: Rob Walters. "Prisoner denies he admitted strangling Tehachapi cellmate." *The Bakersfield Californian*, December 13, 1990.

Heirens: Freeman, p. 344.

DeSalvo: Rae, pp. 122-23.

Kemper: Leyton, p. 43.

Starkweather: Leyton, p. 222.

Nilsen: Masters, p. 277.

Dudley: Reinhardt, p. 70-71.

Brown: *Ibid.*, pp. 134-35.

Mullin: Donald Lunde and Jefferson Morgan. *The Die Song*, New York: W.W. Norton, 1980, p. 185.

Watson: Reinhardt, p. 159.

Fish: Schechter, p. 117-18.

Carpenter: Graysmith, p. 250.

On death...

Lucas: Norris, p. 112.

Starkweather: Leyton, pp. 245, 250.

Nilsen: Masters, p. 273.

Clark: Levin and Fox, p. 199.

Chapter 4: Hunting Humans

1. Thomas Harris. *The Silence Of The Lambs*, New York: St. Martin's Press, 1988, p. 18.

2. Ressler et al., pp. 121-122.

3. *Ibid.*, pp. 122, 130.

4. Federal Bureau of Investigation. *Crime In The United States: 1989*. Washington, D.C.: U.S. Government Printing Office, 1989.

5. *Ibid.*

6. Mary Fischer. "Was Wayne Williams Framed?" *GQ*, April 1991, p. 234.

7. Ike Flores. "Woman charged in 1 of 7 slayings linked to her." *Indianapolis Star*, January 18, 1991.

8. Ressler et al., p. 48.

9. *Ibid.*

10. *Ibid.*, pp. 123, 130.

11. Norris, p. 22-24, 203-4.

12. Ressler et al., pp. 46-47.

13. *Ibid.*, p. 48.

14. *Ibid.*, pp. 122-123, 130.

15. *Ibid.*, pp. 49-50.

16. *Ibid.*, pp. 121-24.

17. *Ibid.*, pp. 123, 131.

18. FBI. *Crime In The United States: 1989*.

19. Ressler et al., p. 54-55.

20. *Ibid.*, p. 64.

21. Norris, pp. 32-33.

22. Ressler et al., p. 65.

23. *Ibid.*, p. 123.

24. *Ibid.*, p. 59.

25. *Ibid.*

26. *Ibid.*

Chapter 5: Targets of Opportunity

1. FBI. *Crime In The United States: 1989*.

2. Testimony before the U.S. Senate, July 12, 1983.

3. FBI. *Crime In The United States: 1989*.

4. Ressler et al., p. 201.

5. *Ibid.*

6. *Ibid.*, pp. 204-206.

Chapter 6: Post Mortem

1. Leyton, p. 183.

2. Masters, p. 113.

3. Michaud and Aynesworth, p. 75.

4. Norris, pp. 33-34.

5. *Ibid.*, p. 145.

6. Ressler et al., p. 62.

7. *Ibid.*, p. 63.

8. *Ibid.*

9. *Ibid.*

10. *Ibid.*

11. *Ibid.*, p. 64.

12. Martin Fido. *The Crimes, Detection And Death Of Jack The Ripper,* London: Weidenfeld and Nicolson, 1987.

13. Chet Dettlinger and Jeff Prugh. *The List*, Atlanta: Philmay Enterprises, 1983, pp. 311-314.

14. "Tapes help fight pornography." *USA Today*, January 24, 1990.

15. Dettlinger and Prugh, pp. 269-275.

Chapter 7: Blood Spoor

1. Peter Elkind. *The Death Shift*, New York: Viking, 1989, pp. 46, 90-91, 107-108, 185-186, 208-209.

2. Robert Graysmith. *Zodiac*, New York: St. Martin's, 1987.

3. Carlton Smith and Tomas Guillen. *The Search For The Green River Killer*, New York: Onyx, 1991, p. 322.

4. Gera-Lind Kolarik. *Freed To Kill*, Chicago: Chicago Review Press, 1990, pp. 11, 256.

5. Rochelle Sharpe and Marjie Lundstrom. "SIDS sometimes used to cover up child-abuse deaths." *USA Today*, December 17, 1990.

6. Marjie Lundstrom and Rochelle Sharpe. "Prevention is aim of more states." *USA Today*, December 17, 1990.

7. Ressler et al., p. 123.

8. *Ibid.*

9. *Ibid.*, p. 137.

10. Mark Pettit. *A Need To Kill*, New York: Ivy Books, 1990, pp. 53-56.

11. Ressler et al., p. 111.

12. Colin Campbell. "Portrait of a Mass Murderer." *Psychology Today*, May 1976.

13. *Ibid.*

14. *Ibid.*

15. Unless otherwise noted, guidelines for MAIT organization and operation are drawn from the U.S. Justice Department's *Multi-Agency Investigative Team Manual*, published in 1988.

16. Smith and Guillen, p. 380.

Chapter 8: Trial and Error

1. Michaud and Aynesworth, pp. 128-129.

2. Clifford Linedecker. *Night Stalker*, New York: St. Martin's, 1991, pp. 202-203.

3. Levin and Fox, p. 178.

Conclusion: Here and Now

1. Levin and Fox, pp. 64-65.

2. Magid and McKelvey, p. 185.

3. *Ibid.*, pp. 243-337.

Bibliography

Abrahamsen, David. *Confessions Of Son Of Sam.* New York: Columbia University Press, 1985.

Adam, H.L. *Trial Of George Chapman.* London: William Hodge, 1930.

Alibrandi, Tom, and Frank Armani. *Privileged Information.* New York: Harper Collins, 1984.

Allen, William. *Starkweather: The Story Of A Mass Murderer.* Boston: Houghton Mifflin, 1967.

Altman, Jack, and Martin Ziporyn. *Born To Raise Hell: The Untold Story Of Richard Speck.* New York: Grove, 1967.

Anderson, Chris, and Sharon McGehee. *Bodies Of Evidence.* New York: Lyle Stuart, 1991.

Angelella, Michael. *Trail Of Blood: A True Story.* New York: New American Library, 1979.

Baden, Michael M. *Unnatural Death.* New York: Ivy Books, 1989.

Bakos, Susan. *Appointment For Murder.* New York: Putnam, 1988.

Berg, Karl. *The Sadist.* London: Heinemann, 1932.

Biondi, Ray, and Walt Hecox. *All His Father's Sins.* New York: Pocket Books, 1988.

Blackburn, Daniel J. *Human Harvest: The Sacramento Murder Story.* Los Angeles: Knightsbridge, 1990.

Bledsoe, Jerry. *Bitter Blood.* New York: E.P. Dutton, 1988.

Bradlee, Ben, Jr., and Dale Van Atta. *Prophet Of Blood: The Untold Story Of Ervil LeBaron And The Lambs Of God.* New York: Putnam, 1981.

Brussel, James A. *Casebook Of A Crime Psychiatrist.* New York: Bernard Geis, 1968.

Bugliosi, Vincent, and Curt Gentry. *Helter Skelter.* New York: Norton, 1974.

Burn, Gordon. *Somebody's Husband, Somebody's Son.* New York: Viking, 1984.

Cahill, Tim. *Buried Dreams.* New York: Bantam, 1985.

Chaney, Margaret. *The Co-Ed Killer.* New York: Walker, 1976.

Chynoweth, Rena, and Dean Shapiro. *The Blood Covenant.* Austin, TX: Diamond Books, 1990.

Clark, Tim, and John Penycate. *Psychopath.* London: Routledge & Kegan Paul, 1976.

Clarke, James W. *Last Rampage.* New York: Houghton Mifflin, 1988.

Cox, Mike. *The Confessions Of Henry Lee Lucas.* New York: Ivy, 1991.

Cox, Robert V. *Deadly Pursuit.* New York: Ballantine, 1977.

Cray, Ed. *Burden Of Proof.* New York: Macmillan, 1973.

Crockett, Art. *Serial Murderers.* New York: Pinnacle, 1990.

—— *Spree Killers*. New York: Pinnacle, 1990.

Cross, Roger. *The Yorkshire Ripper*. London: Granada, 1981.

Damio, Ward. *Urge To Kill*. New York: Pinnacle, 1974.

Damore, Leo. *In His Garden: The Anatomy Of A Murderer*. New York: Arbor House, 1981.

Dettlinger, Chet, and Jeff Prugh. *The List*. Atlanta: Philmay, 1983.

Dickson, Grierson. *Murder By Numbers*. London: Robert Hale, 1958.

Dillman, John. *Blood Warning*. New York: G.P. Putnam's Sons, 1989.

Downs, Thomas. *Murder Man*. New York: Dell, 1984.

Egginton, Joyce. *From Cradle To Grave: The Short Lives And Strange Deaths Of Marybeth Tinning's Nine Children*. New York: William Morrow, 1989.

Elkind, Peter. *The Death Shift*. New York: Viking, 1989.

Emmons, Noel, and Charles Manson. *Manson In His Own Words*. New York: Grove, 1986.

Englade, Ken. *Cellar Of Horror*. New York: St. Martin's, 1988.

Fawkes, Sandy. *Killing Time*. London: Hamlyn, 1978.

Fero, Kelly. *The Zani Murders*. Austin, TX: Texas Monthly Press, 1990.

Frank, Gerold. *The Boston Strangler*. New York: New American Library, 1967.

Freeman, Lucy. *"Before I Kill More..."* New York: Crown, 1955.

Gaddis, Rhomas E., and James O. Long. *Killer: A Journal Of Murder*. New York: Macmillan, 1970.

Ganey, Terry. *St. Joseph's Children: A True Story Of Terror And Justice*. New York: Lyle Stuart, 1989.

Gaute, J.H.H., and Robin Odell. *The New Murderers' Who's Who*. New York: International Polygonics, Ltd., 1989.

Gelb, Barbara. *On The Track Of Murder*. New York: William Morrow, 1975.

Ginsburg, Philip E. *Poisoned Blood*. New York: Warner, 1987.

Gibney, Bruce. *The Beauty Queen Killer*. New York: Pinnacle, 1984.

Godwin, George. *Peter Kurten: A Study In Sadism*. London: Acorn, 1938.

Godwin, John. *Murder USA*. New York: Ballantine, 1978.

Gollmar, Robert H. *Edward Gein*. New York: Charles Hallberg, 1981.

Graysmith, Robert. *The Sleeping Lady: The Trailside Murders Above The Golden Gate*. New York: Dutton, 1990.

—— *Zodiac*. New York: St. Martin's, 1986.

Green, Jonathon. *The Greatest Criminals Of All Time*. New York: Stein & Day, 1982

Grombach, John V. *The Great Liquidator*. New York: Doubleday, 1980.

Gurwell, John K. *Mass Murder In Houston*. Houston: Cordovan Press, 1974.

Harrison, Fred. *Brady & Hindley: Genesis Of The Moors Murders*. London: Ashgrove Press, 1986.

Heimer, Mel. *The Cannibal: The Case Of Albert Fish*. New York: Lyle Stuart, 1971.

Hickey, Eric. *Serial Murderers And Their Victims*. Pacific Grove, CA: Brooks/Cole Publishing Co., 1991.

Holmes, Ronald, and James De Burger. *Serial Murder*. Newbury Park, CA: Sage, 1988.

Howard, Clark. *Zebra*. New York: Berkley, 1980.

Humes, Edward. *Buried Secrets*. New York: Dutton, 1991.

Jeffers, H. Paul. *Who Killed Precious?* New York: Pharos Books, 1991.

Jones, Ann. *Women Who Kill*. New York: Holt, Rinehart and Winston, 1980.

Jouve, Nicole Ward. *"The Street Cleaner": The Yorkshire Ripper Case On Trial*. London: Marion Boyers, 1986.

Kahaner, Larry. *Cults That Kill: Probing The Underworld Of Occult Crime.* New York: Warner, 1988.

Kendall, Elizabeth. *The Phantom Prince: My Life With Ted Bundy.* Seattle: Madrona Publishers, 1981.

Kennedy, Dolores. *William Heirens: His Day In Court.* Chicago: Bonus Books, 1991.

Kennedy, Ludovic. *10 Rillington Place.* London: Gollancz, 1961.

Keppel, Robert D. *Serial Murder: Future Implications For Police Investigations.* Cincinnati: Anderson Publishing Co., 1989.

Keyes, Daniel. *Unveiling Claudia: A True Story Of Serial Murder.* New York: Bantam, 1986.

Keyes, Edward. *The Michigan Murders.* New York: Pocket Books, 1976.

Kidder, Tracy. *The Road To Yuba City.* New York: Doubleday, 1974.

Klausner, Lawrence D. *Son Of Sam.* New York: McGraw-Hill, 1981.

Kolarik, Gera-Lind, and Wayne Klatt. *Freed To Kill: The True Story Of Larry Eyler.* Chicago: Chicago Review Press, 1990.

Kuncl, Tom, and Paul Eisenstein. *Ladies Who Kill.* New York: Pinnacle, 1985.

Langlois, Janet L. *Belle Gunness: The Lady Bluebeard.* Bloomington, IN: Indiana University Press, 1985.

Larsen, Richard W. *Bundy: The Deliberate Stranger.* Englewood Cliffs, NJ: Prentice-Hall, 1980.

Leith, Rod. *The Prostitute Murders: The People vs Richard Cottingham.* New York: Lyle Stuart, 1983.

Levin, Jack, and James Alan Fox. *Mass Murder: America's Growing Menace.* New York: Plenum, 1985.

Leyton, Elliott. *Compulsive Killers.* New York: New York University Press, 1986.

Linedecker, Clifford L. *Hell Ranch: The Nightmare Tale Of Voodoo, Drugs, & Death In Matamoros.* Austin, TX: Diamond Books, 1989.

—— *The Man Who Killed Boys.* New York: St. Martin's, 1980.

—— *Night Stalker.* New York: St. Martin's, 1991.

—— *Serial Thrill Killers.* New York: Knightsbridge, 1990.

—— *Thrill Killers.* New York: Paperjacks, 1987.

——, and William A. Burt. *Nurses Who Kill.* New York: Pinnacle, 1990.

Livsey, Clara. *The Manson Women: A "Family" Portrait.* New York: Marek, 1980.

Lucas, Norman. *The Sex Killers.* London: W.H. Allen, 1974.

——, and Phil Davies. *The Monster Butler.* London: Arthur Barker, 1979.

Lunde, Donald T. *Murder And Madness.* San Francisco: San Francisco Book Company, 1976.

——, and Jefferson Morgan. *The Die Song: A Journey Into The Mind Of A Mass Murderer.* New York: W.W. Norton, 1980.

Magid, Ken, and Carole A. McKelvey. *High Risk: Children Without A Conscience.* New York: Bantam, 1987.

Marchbanks, David. *The Moors Murders.* London: Frewin, 1966.

Markman, Ronald, and Dominick Bosco. *Alone With The Devil: Famous Cases Of A Courtroom Psychiatrist.* New York: Doubleday, 1989.

Master, R.E.L., and Eduard Lea. *Perverse Crimes In History.* New York: Julian, 1963.

Masters, Brian. *Killing For Company.* London: Jonathan Cape, 1985.

McConnell, Brian. *Found Naked And Dead.* London: New English Library, 1974.

——, and Douglas Bence. *The Nilsen File.* London: Futura, 1983.

McDonald, R. Robin. *Black Widow.* New York: St. Martin's, 1986.

McDougal, Dennis. *Angel Of Darkness.* New York: Warner, 1991.

McIntyre, Tommy. *Wolf In Sheep's Clothing: The Search For A Child Killer.* Detroit: Wayne State University Press, 1988.

Meyer, Gerald. *The Memphis Murders.* New York: Seabury, 1974.

Michaud, Stephen, and Hugh Aynesworth. *The Only Living Witness.* New York: Simon and Schuster, 1983.

——, and —— *Ted Bundy: Conversations With A Killer.* New York: New American Library, 1989.

Moore, Kelly, and Dan Reed. *Deadly Medicine*. New York: St. Martin's, 1988.

Moser, Don, and Jerry Cohen. *The Pied Piper Of Tucson*. New York: New American Library, 1967.

Nash, Jay Robert. *Bloodletters And Badmen*. New York: Evans, 1973.

—— *Look For The Woman*. New York: Evans, 1981.

—— *Murder, America*. New York: Simon and Schuster, 1980.

Neville, Richard, and Julie Clark. *The Life And Crimes Of Charles Sobhraj*. London: Jonathan Cape, 1979.

Newton, Michael. *Hunting Humans*. Port Townsend, WA: Loompanics, 1990.

—— *Mass Murder*. New York: Garland, 1988.

Nickel, Steven. *Torso: The Story Of Eliot Ness And The Search For A Psychopathic Killer*. Winston-Salem, NC: J.F. Blair, 1989.

Norris, Joel. *Henry Lee Lucas*. New York: Zebra, 1991.

—— *Serial Killers: The Growing Menace*. New York: Doubleday, 1988.

Nunn, Bette. *Burn, Judy, Burn*. Indianapolis: The Author, 1981.

O'Brien, Darcy. *Two Of A Kind: The Hillside Stranglers*. New York: New American Library, 1985.

Olsen, Gregg. *Abandoned Prayers*. New York: Warner, 1990.

Olsen, Jack. *The Man With The Candy: The Story Of The Houston Mass Murders*. New York: Simon and Schuster, 1974.

Penn, Gareth. *Times 17: The Amazing Story Of The Zodiac Murders In California And Massachusetts*. Foxglove Press, 1987.

Pettit, Mark. *A Need To Kill*. New York: Ivy Books, 1990.

Provost, Gary. *Across The Border: The True Story Of The Satanic Cult Killings*. New York: Pocket Books, 1989.

Rae, George W. *Confessions Of The Boston Strangler*. New York: Pyramid, 1967.

Raschke, Carl A. *Painted Black*. San Francisco: Harper & Row, 1990.

Reinhardt, James M. *The Murderous Trail Of Charles Starkweather*. Springfield, IL: C.C. Thomas, 1960.

—— *The Psychology Of Strange Killers*. Springfield, IL: C.C. Thomas, 1962.

Ressler, Robert K., Ann W. Burgess, and John E. Douglas. *Sexual Homicide: Patterns And Motives*. Lexington, MA: Lexington Books, 1988.

Reynolds, Richard. *Cry For War: The Story Of Suzan And Michael Carson*. San Francisco: Squibob Press, 1987.

Ritchie, Jean. *Myra Hindley: Inside the Mind Of A Murderess*. London: Angus & Robertson, 1988.

Rule, Ann. *The I-5 Killer*. New York: New American Library, 1984.

—— *Lust Killer*. New York: New American Library, 1983.

—— *The Stranger Beside Me*. New York: New American Library, 1980.

—— *The Want-Ad Killer*. New York: New American Library, 1983.

Rumbelow, Donald. *Jack The Ripper: The Complete Casebook*. New York: Berkley, 1988.

Sanders, Ed. *The Family*. New York: Dutton, 1971; New American Library, 1989.

Sasser, Charles W. *Homicide!* New York: Pocket Books, 1990.

Schaefer, G.J. *Killer Fiction: Tales Of An Accused Serial Killer*. Atlanta: Media Queen, 1990.

Schechter, Harold. *Deranged: The Shocking True Story Of America's Most Fiendish Killer*. New York: Pocket Books, 1990.

—— *Deviant: The Shocking True Story Of The Original "Psycho."* New York: Pocket Books, 1989.

Schreiber, Flora R. *The Shoemaker: The Anatomy Of A Psychotic*. New York: Simon and Schuster, 1983.

Schutze, Jim. *Cauldron Of Blood: The Matamoros Cult Killings*. New York: Avon, 1989.

Schwartz, Ted. *The Hillside Strangler: A Murderer's Mind*. New York: Doubleday, 1981.

Sereny, Gitta. *The Case Of Mary Bell*. London: Methuen, 1972.

Sifakis, Carl. *The Encyclopedia Of American Crime*. New York: Facts on File, 1982.

Smith, Carlton, and Tomas Guillen. *The Search For The Green River Killer.* New York: Onyx, 1991.

Spinks, Sarah. *Cardiac Arrest: A True Account Of Stolen Lives.* Toronto: Doubleday, 1985.

Sullivan, Terry, and Peter Maiken. *Killer Clown.* New York: Grosset & Dunlap, 1983.

Tannahill, Ray. *Flesh And Blood: A History Of The Cannibal Complex.* New York: Stein and Day, 1975.

Tannebaum, Robert K., and Peter S. Greenberg. *The Piano Teacher: The True Story Of A Psychotic Killer.* New York: New American Library, 1987.

Terry, Maury. *The Ultimate Evil.* New York: Doubleday, 1987.

Thompson, Thomas. *Serpentine.* New York: Dell, 1979.

Tobias, Ronald. *They Shoot To Kill: A Psycho-Survey Of Criminal Sniping.* Boulder, CO: Paladin Press, 1981.

Trotter, William, and Robert Newsom III. *Deadly Kin.* New York: St. Martin's, 1988.

U.S. Senate Judiciary Committee. *Serial Murders: Hearing On Patterns Of Murders Committed By One Person, In Large Numbers With No Apparent Rhyme, Reason, Or Motivation.* Washington, D.C.: U.S. Government Printing Office, 1984.

Van Hoffman, Eric. *A Venom In The Blood.* New York: Donald I. Fine, 1990.

Villasenor, Victor. *Jury: The People vs Juan Corona.* Boston: Little, Brown, 1977.

Wagner, Margaret S. *The Monster Of Dusseldorf.* London: Faber, 1932.

Waumbaugh, Joseph. *The Blooding.* New York: Perigord Press, 1989.

West, Donald. *Sacrifice Unto Me.* New York: Pyramid, 1974.

Wilcox, Robert K. *The Mysterious Deaths At Ann Arbor.* New York: Popular Library, 1977.

Williams, Emlyn. *Beyond Belief.* New York: Random House, 1967.

Wilson, Colin, and Patricia Putnam. *The Encyclopedia Of Murder.* New York: Putnam, 1961.

——, and Donald Seaman. *The Encyclopedia Of Modern Murder, 1962-1982.* New York: Putnam, 1983.

——, and —— *The Serial Killers.* New York: Carol, 1990.

Wilson, Robert. *Devil's Disciples.* Poole, England: Javelin Books, 1986.

Winn, Steven, and David Merrill. *Ted Bundy: The Killer Next Door.* New York: Bantam, 1980.

Yallop, David. *Deliver Us From Evil.* New York: Coward, McCann, 1982.

Index

YOU WILL ALSO WANT TO READ

☐ **34050 HUNTING HUMANS: An Encyclopedia of Modern Serial Killers,** *by Michael Newton.* More than 500 detailed case histories of serial killers from the 20th Century. This disturbing book describes their lives and their exploits without any varnish or puffery — the chilling details speak for themselves. More than 60% of the killers described here have never been mentioned in a published book before. This huge book is an unforgettable chronicle of the world's most deranged homicidal maniacs. *1990, 8½ x 11, 353 pp, illustrated, hard cover.* **$34.95**

☐ **34056 EXECUTION: Tools & Techniques,** *by Bart Rommel.* A chilling examination of capital punishment, including detailed descriptions of all the techniques used by governments to put people to death: ● Hanging ● Electrocution ● Beheading ● Shooting ● Gassing ● Lethal Injection ● Burning ● Drowning ● Entombment ● Death by Nature ● And many others, including a section on future technology such as microwaves and lasers. WARNING: The explicit writing in this book may be disturbing to some readers. *1990, 5½ x 8½, 119 pp, soft cover.* **$12.95**

☐ **34047 HOMICIDE INVESTIGATION,** *by Burt Rapp.* A detailed police manual on the procedures for investigating a murder. This is a fairly grisly book, not for the weak at heart. Covers ● Arriving on the Scene of a Murder ● Handling Murder Suspects ● Estimating Time of Death ● The Investigators Log ● Sketching a Murder Scene ● Using Psychics and Hypnosis ● What Really Happens at an Autopsy ● And Much More. *1989, 5½ x 8½, 180 pp, illustrated, soft cover.* **$14.95**

☐ **55071 SEX CRIMES INVESTIGATION,** *by Burt Rapp.* All sorts of sex crimes are in the news these days — more than ever before. This book is a police manual for the investigation of sex crimes. A practical guide to investigating rapes, prostitution, pornography, child molestation, snuff films, sex in the mails, computer sex crimes, and much more. No modern police or investigative library is complete without this book. 1988, 5½ x 8½, 198 pp, soft cover. **$14.95**

☐ **40071 THE BIG HOUSE: How American Prisons Work,** *by Tony Lesce.* Our prison system is in a state of crisis. Reforms will cost billions of dollars and touch the lives of thousands. That's why *The Big House* is so important. This book is an incredibly detailed look at exactly how prisons work: the housing, feeding, and controlling of violent, angry people. It examines the prison system from all sides: the inmates, the guards, the politicians, the taxpayers. And it takes a gritty look at issues like capital punishment, psychosurgery, riot control and dealing with the sexual needs of prisoners. *1991, 8½ x 11, 184 pp, illustrated, index, soft cover.* **$19.95**

And much more! We offer the very finest in controversial and unusual books — a complete catalog is sent *FREE* with every book order. Enjoy the best — from *Loompanics Unlimited!*

_____SSLT

LOOMPANICS UNLIMITED
● PO BOX 1197 ●
Port Townsend, WA 98368

"Yes, there are books about the skills of apocalypse — spying, surveillance, fraud, wiretapping, smuggling, self-defense, lockpicking, gunmanship, eavesdropping, car chasing, civil warfare, surviving jail, and dropping out of sight. Apparently writing books is the way mercenaries bring in spare cash between wars. The books are useful, and it's good the information is freely available (and they definitely inspire interesting dreams), but their advice should be taken with a salt shaker or two and all your wits. A few of these volumes are truly scary. Loompanics is the best of the Libertarian suppliers who carry them. Though full of 'you'll-wish-you'd-read-these-when-it's-too-late' rhetoric, their catalog is genuinely informative."

—**THE NEXT WHOLE EARTH CATALOG**

THE BEST BOOK CATALOG IN THE WORLD!!!

We offer hard-to-find books on the world's most unusual subjects. Here are a few of the topics covered IN DEPTH in our exciting new catalog:

- *Hiding/concealment of physical objects! A complete section of the best books ever written on hiding things!*

- *Fake ID/Alternate Identities! The most comprehensive selection of books on this little-known subject ever offered for sale! You have to see it to believe it!*

- *Investigative/Undercover methods and techniques! Professional secrets known only to a few, now revealed to you to use! Actual police manuals on shadowing and surveillance!*

- *And much, much more, including Locks and Locksmithing, Self-Defense, Intelligence Increase, Life Extension, Money-Making Opportunities, and more!*

Our book catalog is 8½ x 11, packed with over 500 of the most controversial and unusual books ever printed! You can order every book listed! Periodic supplements to keep you posted on the LATEST titles available!!! Our catalog is free with the order of any book on the previous page — or is $5.00 if ordered by itself.

Our book catalog is truly THE BEST BOOK CATALOG IN THE WORLD! Order yours today — you will be very pleased, we know.

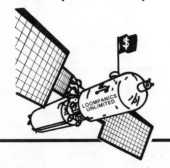

LOOMPANICS UNLIMITED
PO BOX 1197
PORT TOWNSEND, WA 98368
USA